TAROT
and the
TREE *of* LIFE

TAROT
and the
TREE *of* LIFE

Finding Everyday Wisdom in the Minor Arcana

ISABEL *Radow* KLIEGMAN

A publication supported by
THE KERN FOUNDATION

Quest Books
Theosophical Publishing House

Wheaton, Illinois ♦ Madras, India

The Theosophical Publishing House
P.O. Box 270
Wheaton, IL 60189-0270

www.questbooks.net

Library of Congress Cataloging-in-Publication Data
Kliegman, Isabel Radow.
Tarot and the tree of life : finding everyday wisdom in the minor arcana /
Isabel Radow Kliegman. — 1st Quest ed.
p.   cm.
"A publication supported by the Kern Foundation."
"Quest books."
ISBN-13: 978-0-8356-0747-6
ISBN-10: 0-8356-0747-X
1. Minor arcana (Tarot).   2. Tree of Life—Miscellanea.   3. Cabala.
I. Title.
BF1879.T2K55   1997   97-47
133.3'2424—dc21   CIP

Book and cover design by Beth Hansen

8   7   6   5   4   3   *   05   06   07   08   09   10

This book was set in Cheltenham, Castellar, and Savoy.
Printed in the United States of America.

DEDICATION

For Tom Kampe,

magician, alchemist, and increasingly intimate friend

CONTENTS

ACKNOWLEDGMENTS

*M*Y DEEPEST gratitude is to my mother, Rae Radow Kliegman, who was convinced I could do anything and made a point of telling me so, and to my father, Moe Kliegman, who has always expressed his amazement and pride in my accomplishments. Every day convinces me further that I am uniquely blessed. Loving thanks, too, to my daughter, Alisa Tatiana Radow Gilinsky, a highly gifted Tarot card reader and my closest friend, and to Gary Scott Fowler for his enthusiasm, patience, and support.

HEAVY DUTY thanks to Mark Kampe, for his incomprehensible, incalculable generosity of time and effort on the computer. In no way can I adequately express my gratitude for his long and diligent labors.

Heartfelt thanks to my spiritual teachers (who may well disagree with much I have written): Bishop Stephan Hoeller, who first introduced me to Kabbalah and was my first Tarot teacher, and Rabbis Ted Falcon, Mordecai Finlay, Stan Levy, Steve Robbins, and Don Singer. You have restored my soul in ways you will never suspect.

Thanks to Mark Kampe, for his merry nature and lively involvement in our work.

Thanks to Jerry Ziegman, who showed me my first deck of Tarot cards, Tricia Kelly who encouraged me to work with them professionally, and Beverly Hollidy, who helped me when I most needed her.

Thanks to Mark Kampe, whose insights about the cards were uniformly fascinating.

Thanks to Ivan Hoffman, for offering me the benefit of his experience, both as an author and a lawyer, and to Anthony Pearson, who actually got me to smile for the camera!

Thanks to Mark Kampe; his perspective on the book and organizational suggestions were more than helpful.

Much appreciation for Beth Hansen's beautiful cover and the hard work of everyone at Quest: Sharron Dorr, Vija Bremanis, and most of all Brenda Rosen. It has been an education, as well as a pleasure, to work with her. I will always be grateful for her crisp, orderly direction, her fine suggestions, and her respectful attitude toward my preferences. Because of her this is a better book than the one I submitted. Most of all, I am grateful for her transforming me from a writer into an author.

Thanks to Mark Kampe for his interesting ideas regarding both content and style.

And finally, thanks to Mark Kampe for teaching me the difference between "which" and "that," assuming that he has . . . .

FOREWORD
by Stephan A. Hoeller

*I*NTEREST IN the mysterious Tarot is at an all-time high. Only a few short decades ago, one had to send to distant and obscure sources if one wished to procure a deck of these intriguing cards, for they could not be found in local bookstores or even at dealers of antiquities. A choice among several designs was unknown; one was lucky to find even a solitary deck. Today there is a profusion of Tarot decks on the market. One could spend a fortune if one desired even the majority of decks of various designs available.

What then is the Tarot? Ostensibly it is a series of seventy-eight playing cards displaying symbolic designs, many of which claim ancient provenance. Aficionados tell us that after mastering the interpretation of these cards, one gains access to the future and to other mysteries of existence. While such enthusiastic claims may appear exaggerated, admirable and insightful persons over the centuries have expressed views not unlike these. Madame Helena Blavatsky, the redoubtable founder of the Theosophical movement in the late nineteenth century, is said to have carried an old hand-painted Tarot deck in her battered suitcase on her many travels. My neighbor in the Hollywood Hills, Aldous Huxley, a few months prior to his death in 1963, became vitally interested in the Tarot and asked a mutual friend to procure a deck for him. Albert Einstein was known to study the Tarot on certain occasions. Shakespeare refers to Tarot cards (or at least to cartomancy) in *Hamlet* (V.i.) when he writes:

> How absolute the knave is! We must speak
> by the card, or equivocation will undo us.

But perhaps the most impressive tribute came from the French magus and Kabbalist Eliphas Levi (Alphonse Louis Constant) who stated that if one were confined for a long period in a deep dungeon or on a secluded island, one would only need a Tarot deck to keep one informed and inspired.

Tarot cards are the oldest form of playing cards handed down to us. In a more credulous age of esotericism, it was sometimes assumed that they could be traced as far back as the times of fabled Atlantis. It was sometimes assumed that Chaldean or Egyptian initiates received the Tarot from Atlantis and eventually carried it to Europe. At the turn of the last century, the French leading light of esotericism, Papus (Dr. Gerard Encausse), was equally convinced that the Tarot originated in India and that its four suits symbolize the four principal castes: cups standing for priests, swords for warrior-rulers, coins for merchants, and wands for agricultural laborers. The mysterious Gypsies, whose origins might well be in India, then carried the Tarot cards into Europe and from there to America as well. Certainly in my childhood I observed the divinatory activities of many Gypsies who employed Tarot cards as well as a deck that is closely related to the Tarot, called Tarock. Tarot wisdom was often passed on through the oldest wise woman of the tribe. Most Gypsies I encountered believed that they, as well as their divinatory arts, originated in India.

Aside from such informal accounts, the mystery of the origins of these cards remains unsolved. There is virtually no factual information available about the history of the cards and their symbols past the early centuries of this era. We can't even be sure what the word *Tarot* means. Some have suggested that it comes from an Egyptian hybrid word meaning "royal road." This hypothesis is unproven, though very frequently accepted.

The experiences one has using the Tarot deck tend to leave a lasting impression. As a student and practitioner of the Tarot, I can certainly attest to this. Some of my greatest joys and deepest regrets were connected with information I received by way of the cards. One card, which I drew at a particularly critical time of my life, instructed me to await some singularly promising opportunities which were hastening my way. If I managed to take advantage of the opportunity thus arising (or so I discerned from the symbolism of the card that was before me), I would be lifted out of my sorrow and hopelessness and carried to exciting places. The prophecy of the Tarot was fulfilled in three days time! A more tragic incident started with a telephone call from a close friend who had decided to undergo heart surgery. The card I drew from my deck to illuminate the matter turned out to be the Major Arcana card called The Tower, which carries catastrophic implications. Despite my apprehension, I refrained from advising my friend against the surgery, since he was quite enthusiastic about the prospect. As a result of complications arising from surgery, my friend died in great agony some three weeks later. I still feel a good deal of guilt for the sin of omission I committed by not cautioning him more vigorously on the basis of the Tarot prognostication.

As the author of this book tells us, the uses of the Tarot are manifold. In my experience I have found three. First, the Tarot serves as a pictorial textbook of the universal symbolic philosophy and cosmology. Second, the plan and structure of the deck depicts the structure and development of the human psyche, somewhat in the manner envisioned by the analytical psychology of C. G. Jung. The last and most controversial use of the Tarot is, of course, divination, which, as Isabel Kliegman wisely reminds us, is a very different thing from fortune telling.

In ancient times divination was the art whereby one consulted the gods, who were also known as *divinities*. The ancients believed that these divinities are essentially benignly disposed toward humans and thus are likely to offer useful guidance and advice when consulted. While the belief in divinities is not particularly great in our day, the philosophy of divination that developed on the basis of such a belief is still valid. In order to effectively consult an authentic oracle such as the Tarot, we must first of all possess an attitude that is appropriate for the invoking of helpful forces of a superior character. The proper attitude is one that lies somewhere between superstitious awe and frivolousness. If we employ an oracle in idle jest, the results will be appropriate. At the same time, it is good to be reminded that the cards in themselves are not sacred objects worthy of veneration. We need not keep them in precious containers, wrap them in red silk, or approach them in elaborate ceremonies. The magic is not in the cards but in ourselves. What matters is the response the cards evoke from the deeper regions of our psyches; all else is of small importance. The divinities I referred to above may be most profitably envisioned as at least related to psychological archetypes, if indeed they are not themselves the archetypes.

Another important requisite for accurate divination is what has been called "magical imagination." This is the ability to relate meaningfully subjective or psychic reality to the material clues of the cards. A talent for this kind of imagination may be found to some degree in most folk, but with skill, one may foster its growth. The once very prominent Hermetic Order of the Golden Dawn used the Tarot expressly as a tool for developing the magical imagination. These days much publicity is given to the ideas which are directed to what is called "creating one's reality." It is my view that most of these teachings are nothing more than an excessive application of the principle of magical imagination. It is not very likely that we shall ever truly create our own reality, but with the aid of the Tarot, we may discover a reality that is vastly preferable to the humdrum consensus reality in which the majority of our culture lives.

Isabel Kliegman is one of the most truly skilled and sensitive practitioners of the Tarot I know. A number of years ago it was my good fortune to introduce her to this field of study and practice, and the strides she has made since that time impress me deeply. As the following pages reveal, her greatest dedication has been to the so-called Minor Arcana, or the four suits of numbered cards of the Tarot, including their uniquely powerful and revelatory court cards of Kings, Queens, Knights, and Pages. While many of us are justly fascinated by and devoted to the sublime archetypal images embodied in the Major Arcana (Trump Cards), it is obvious that the Minor Arcana, with their symbols of the manifest cosmos, are of immense significance also, although this significance is often overlooked or neglected. This neglect has now been insightfully and eloquently remedied by the author of this book, which may well become the normative text on the Minor Arcana, even as the splendid work of the late Paul Foster Case, *The Tarot: A Key to the Wisdom of the Ages* is still the basic text on the Major Arcana. My much more humble book, *The Royal Road: Kabalistic Meditations on the Tarot,* published by Quest in 1975, may still serve the student of the Tarot who wishes to use the cards of the Major Arcana as visual tools for meditating on the symbolic contents of the cards, but the present work may be said to pick up where mine leaves off. Readers who enjoyed my efforts in *The Royal*

Road will assuredly be delighted when they follow it up with reading *Tarot and the Tree of Life*.

The Tarot is an endless source of wonder and delight to those who enter its inner precincts. Still, its practice and study are somewhat curtailed when not combined with the mystical system of the Kabbalah. Although Eliphas Levi is generally credited with making the connection between Tarot and the Kabbalah available, the most effective advocate of this connection was the Hermetic Order of the Golden Dawn, an organization that in spite of its brief public functioning exerted an immense influence on the Western esoteric tradition. My late friend, Dr. Israel Regardie, one of the last adepts of that Order, always held that without the Kabbalah, the Tarot tends to become a mere plaything. The author of *The Tarot and the Tree of Life* has earned the gratitude of those of us who respect the Golden Dawn and its teachings. Anyone reading this book will never again wish to separate the disciplines of Tarot and Kabbalah.

Often when I contemplate the cards of the Tarot, I perceive a sunlit medieval landscape with small, luminous figures moving like magical toy figurines. The Fool with staff and bundle, the Emperor on rock-hewn throne, the Empress in her flowering garden of delights. Death is reaping his harvest of souls, the Hermit climbs unscaled heights with staff and lamp, and the Hanged Man swings serenely from his gibbet. To these we may now add, as a result of Isabel Kliegman's efforts, the Queen of Cups gazing in rapt attention at her mystical Grail, the Knight of Swords charging into furious battle, the Hand of God holding the Aces of the four suits, and many more. Behind them all looms the Holy Tree of Life, mystical diagram of the Heavenly Human and map of the ascent of the soul to its final home. The ten Sacred Vessels glow with the luminosity of a world in which things are never what they seem but are revealed in their meaning that is ordinarily concealed, while the twenty-two flaming letters pulsate on the branches of the Tree. Perhaps a vision similar to this may arise in the minds of some who read this book. Of one thing, however, we may be certain: Whatever visions and feelings may be stimulated by such reading, boredom and lack of inspiration will not be among them.

INTRODUCTION

Mystery without Mystification

*T*HIS BOOK is intended for use by anyone whose imagination is fired by the Tarot. For the total novice, it offers a system by which fifty-six of the seventy-eight cards can be rescued from chaos, finding their places in a reasonable order without losing their individual timbre. Much of what would be experienced as an overwhelming kaleidoscope of isolated, unrelated images suddenly snaps into a manageable, conceptually consistent pattern.

This order is derived from examining the cards in the context of the Kabbalistic Tree of Life. While distinct in origin and self-contained, Kabbalah and Tarot have long been combined in a search for guidance and truth. Over the last hundred years, the very designs of the cards have been heavily influenced by Kabbalistic symbols. Such giants in the history of Tarot as Eliphas Levi, Papus, Arthur Edward Waite, Aleister Crowley, and Paul Foster Case have drawn on the Kabbalah to illuminate the cards. While Kabbalah, like all great metaphysical systems, is universal in application, its origin is in the Jewish tradition. This rich legacy sheds light and warmth on the Tarot. The *midrashen,* or traditional interpretive stories, are expressions of fundamental perspectives in the Jewish cultural heritage, meant to give authenticity and authority as well as flavor to the interpretations offered.

For the experienced card reader, the advanced student, the serious practitioner, this book offers an opportunity to vary and perhaps improve skills. I am confident that at least some of the material will be entirely new for the simple reason that it is autobiographical. I include it, not in the conviction that my personal experiences are of unique value, but rather as an expression of two of my most deeply held convictions about the Tarot: 1) there's a card for it; and 2) conversely, there's an experience for it!

We learn the meanings of the cards best by relating them to our flesh-and-blood lives. They repay us by clarifying and sometimes even defining our experiences when we seek the card that governs them. A corollary of these convictions is that exhausting the meaning of the Tarot is no more likely than exhausting the mystery of human nature itself. Each of us can continue to bring meaning to—as well as find meaning in—the cards for as long as we interact with them. This book is written for the intelligent reader: reflective, astute, spiritually driven, and open to self-examination. If you share in my conviction that meaning can be derived from the Tarot, what follows is an approach to how that meaning can be discerned and/or created.

The idea for this book was engendered by comments I heard most frequently after my lectures on both Tarot and Kabbalah: "Now I understand!" or, "The way you put things, they made sense for the first time!" and, "I've read a lot of books on the Tarot, but they only confused me more."

The line between reductionistic thinking and the translation of abstract concepts into concrete experience is a thin one. I hope I have not crossed it. If, however, meaning is *experienced* rather than vaguely ideated as a result of explicit example, then the Tarot can come alive in a new way. It is my hope that the cards can have a pulse.

Many works on the Tarot, of which those by Waite are an example, offer brief, formulaic interpretations of the cards that need to be memorized by rote. The reader, consequently, is dependent on the source, and must continually refer to the written word in the course of the reading. The unprofessional nature of working in this way and the lack of expertise it proclaims to a client are the least of its problems. Far more serious is the effect on the consciousness of the reader in trusting an external and, finally, arbitrary authority for absolute, closed-ended definitions of rich images that are designed to be evocative and mysterious. This is a problem for those who memorize the definitions no less than for those who refer to them. (I am particularly amused by such identifications as the Queen of Cups as a blond, blue-eyed woman; thus, there are entire continents for which this card is irrelevant.) It is my hope that in addition to providing the proverbial fish, this book will teach the serious reader "how to fish" from the Tarot.

Much has been written on the Major Arcana; our discussion will be restricted to the less-explored, relatively accessible, and highly evocative Minor Arcana. It is the Minor Arcana that reflect our daily experience; the Minor Arcana are where we live! I have confined my subject to these cards for three reasons.

First, they are the portion of the deck that is usually treated as of secondary importance and in consequence, dealt with summarily. Many books on Tarot exclude the Minor Arcana completely, focusing entirely on the twenty-two powerhouses of archetypal force, the Major Arcana. It is my conviction that the Minor Arcana have received short shrift and are deserving of fuller exploration than I have seen in my studies. The dazzling stature of the Tarot Trumps, or Major Arcana, in no way diminishes and should not blind us to the considerable potential for discovery carried by the "small secrets" of the Minor Arcana.

Second, the relative simplicity of the Minor Arcana imagery makes them, for most of us, more accessible than the Major Arcana. For the novice or those whose interest is tentative, the Minor Arcana prove less formidable, more inviting companions with which to initiate a relationship with the Tarot. While the Major Arcana can be seen as archetypes whose likeness we are never to encounter on this earth, the Minor Arcana, in almost every case, portray people involved in ordinary behavior that we see around us in the course of our own lives. These images have an unremarkable, immediate nature. From homey to frightful, from joyful to painful, what we see is generally simple to identify and easy to identify with.

From this perspective, it is clear that the importance of the Minor Arcana cannot be overemphasized. The key to their usefulness is their availability. If I am caught up in the grief of loss, the Five of Cups reflects my pain. My anxiety, regret, and isolation are mirrored back to me with force and compassion by the Nine of Swords. (The universality and intimacy of these cards are underscored by a simple fact I have observed in my practice: the intentionally androgynous central figures are almost invariably perceived as male by men and as female by women. We each see ourselves in these images.) The Nine of Pentacles shows me fulfillment and peace in a way that is direct; when I am standing my ground under challenge, my experience is revealed to me in the most straightforward way by the Seven of Wands.

Once the initial gut-level recognition occurs, we can learn a great deal from working with the card. We can move from merely identifying with its image to exploring it in detail and depth, thereby learning something new about the experience that led us to it and therefore about ourselves. Does the image of the Five of Cups shift the way we feel—and if so, how? What are we to think about the symbols on the quilt of the Nine of Swords? Is that actually a snail we perceive in the foreground of the Nine of Pentacles? What does its presence tell us? What is our sense of a person who, like the figure in the Seven of Wands, wears one shoe and one boot?

We next can relate the image we see in the card to one of the vessels that make up the Kabbalistic Tree of Life. Each vessel, or *sefirah,* is associated with a numerical value. Thus, for example, we can associate the fives in the Tarot deck with the fifth sefirah of Gevurah. The nines of each suit pair with the ninth sefirah, Yesod, while the sevens belong to the seventh sefirah, Netzach. Since each sefirah is characterized by a distinct quality, we can gain further insight into the card. We can ask in each case how the sefirah supports or expands what we have discovered.

With few if any exceptions, the Major Arcana do not mirror our lives, experiences, or states of mind in this obvious yet provocative way. Only the Minor Arcana offer us the opportunity to see ourselves as we are, without the temptation for self-aggrandizement offered by the Major Arcana.

This brings us to the last of my reasons for devoting my attention exclusively to the Minor Arcana. It seems to me that the way we can best understand the Minor Arcana is substantially different from the way in which we can most profitably approach the Major. The latter, in their geometrically more complex structure and symbolism, require either scholarship or highly evolved meditational practice to release their meanings and, ideally, both. The humble Minor Arcana are content simply to be examined with care and responded to with openness. We are all experts on what it is we perceive and how we respond to what we see.

The purpose of this book is twofold: to provide information about the fifty-six cards of the Minor Arcana (the fish) and to suggest an approach for gleaning information from the cards (a method for catching your own fish). My intention is to offer concepts that may be useful to the reader in exploring the Tarot and deriving meaning from it. It is not my intention to lay down meanings cast in concrete.

If I am right in holding that the Tarot can facilitate our understanding of our lives—and conversely that our life experiences can lead us to a deeper grasp of the Tarot—then this book is offered as a bridge between the two. By use of anecdote, it is my hope that the abstract may become accessible, not just intellectually, but experientially. The meaning of the cards is not an abstruse concept set out by me, but *your* experience of them when provided with down-to-earth, immediate perspectives. My intent is to offer a book that is readable without being reductionist.

If the Tarot is of universal and enduring value, it must be understandable in contemporary terms, amenable to a practical and personal view. In taking this approach, it has been my goal to demystify the cards, which in no way diminishes their mystery! With modern medicine came accurate anatomical charts, invaluable instruments in demystifying the body. We now know that organs belong to various systems, that air moves from nostrils to lungs and not to intestines, that embryos develop in the womb and not the stomach. The mysteries of life—of respiration, of reproduction—remain in pristine majesty, unassailable and remote. The Tree of Life provides the structure that supports seventy-eight images that might otherwise be perceived as random. Within the Kabbalistic system, an order emerges from this visual jumble. The great mysteries of the Tarot cards are only enhanced by our clearing the confusion that shrouds their grandeur and providing a chart by which they can be understood and remembered.

What I wish to impart to the reader through this work is manifold: a context, a system within which to understand the Minor Arcana; an orientation that allows each card a range of meanings that is virtually inexhaustible; a willingness and capacity to work with multiple interpretations of a single card, confident that there is no need to choose among them; and equal confidence that any new idiosyncratic interpretation of a card that can be justified graphically, ideologically, or intuitively has validity.

I hope as well that my readers will find in the Tarot a source of insight, comfort, and spiritual guidance; a source of empowerment, a reference point for processing experience and deepening understanding; a way, even in difficult times, to flip from the perspective of ego consciousness to that of the greater One. These, in addition to belief in ourselves as interpreters of the cards and trust in our own perceptions, responses, ideas, and inklings, will, I hope, generate a lasting excitement about the Tarot. Perhaps for some this book will be a stimulus to creative consciousness in which the Minor Arcana prove a generous facilitator.

While I don't suggest that you lay out the Tarot cards in patterns called *spreads* (or readings) for interpretation without some knowledge and understanding of the Major Arcana, it is possible to use the Tarot cards from the outset of your study. A simple yet valuable procedure can be performed daily; an appropriate attitude is the sole requirement. The cards should be shuffled thoroughly, particularly if the deck is new. Taking care to turn half the deck with each shuffle assures that about fifty percent of the cards are facing in each direction, so that there is roughly an even chance that a card drawn will appear rightside up or upside down.

Once shuffled, the Tarot deck can be kept in a night-table drawer, handbag, or glove compartment, depending on your lifestyle. Each morning or evening or whenever the day affords a quiet moment, the deck can be cut. While it might not seem that much can be learned from looking at the card exposed by that single cut, practice and experience will soon dispel that illusion! If you are prepared to work with the card in a serious way, it will begin to reveal its wealth of usefulness immediately. It is often helpful to have a particular question in mind before cutting the cards and, at first, one that is limited to a specific situation. For example, "What difficulties am I likely to encounter at the work place today?" or "How will the disagreement with my friend over where we vacation resolve itself?" By limiting the question in this way as opposed to "Am I in the right job?"or "Am I with the right mate?", it is possible to avoid repeating questions that the Tarot has answered earlier in this process.

After the question is formulated, it is useful to calm the mind and open yourself to the cards. Cut the deck; the card that emerges at the bottom of the pile can then be observed closely. There are, to my knowledge, no randomly chosen symbols or random designs in the deck. Applying what you perceive, feel, think, or intuit to the question raised can be an exhilarating awakening! (If your daily cut turns up a Major Arcanum and your experience with the cards is limited, you might choose to cut again until you get a Minor Arcanum, with which this book may be of help to you.)

In this context you can already begin to work with the tricky issue of reversed cards. The suggestion that reversal signifies meaning opposite to its interpretation when it is rightside up seems to me both simplistic and foolish. The image is there, present for us to explore. How can its reversal mean the absence of that image? Yet a reversal does change the card's meaning.

We can imagine, in the case of the first hypothetical question, that our focused cut reveals the Five of Wands. Even at first glance, most of us perceive conflict of some sort and degree. When the card is reversed, some spin must be put on that observation, and only experience, heightened intuition, and reflection will reveal what that variation might be. Is it more bitter, harsher, because of the reversal? Is it perhaps subtle, opaque, a current running under the surface that is not overtly exposed or clearly understood? Is it perfectly obvious, but handled with denial so that a patina of politeness covers genuine malice?

In relation to the second question, let us imagine that the single cut reveals the Two of Cups, a couple in harmonious union. The indication here is that in the context of a loving, mutually respectful, growth-promoting relationship, where you vacation will be of little moment in terms of the big picture. If the card is reversed, however, the suggestion might be that the issue could develop into an argument with serious consequences. How the two of you succeed or fail in solving disagreements could determine the course of the relationship. Inability to compromise, to make adjustments, could turn the relationship on its ear.

If your days are hectic and you are pressed for time, this simple experience can transform a long traffic light from a source of irritation to a welcome opportunity. Once the card is released from the deck it can be kept on a desk, in a drawer, or on the passenger seat, and referred to at intervals throughout the day when the moment allows it. Meanwhile, the single image is making multiple impressions on the brain, and the unconscious mind continues its dialogue with the card independent of conscious transactions of a mundane kind. The work has begun.

When your schedule permits, more committed exercises can be performed in relation to the single-card cut. You can cut the card just before going to sleep, making it the last image you feed into your unconscious for the day. You can ask your unconscious for a dream involving the image on the card. You can leave it on your nightstand, assuring that it will be the first image you focus on the following morning. If you were to sleep with it under your pillow, you wouldn't be the first.

Meditation using the card as a mandala can be helpful, as can journaling, using the card as a stimulus. In meditation, apart from simply allowing the image to work on the quieted mind, you can engage in more active imagining. You could, for example, become any or each of the figures pictured, relating to the environment in which you find yourself. Or, still entering the card, you could join the figures pictured and enter into a conversation. With which of the figures in the Five of Wands do you identify? (This alone entails a close and feeling-toned scrutiny of the card.) What would you ask the couple in the Two of Cups if you encountered them in the course of a journey?

Journaling can begin as a record of such meditations, but it can go further. Releasing the unconscious from the need for logical progression or sensible juxtaposition can yield astonishing revelations. For some, automatic writing, usually done with the less dominant hand, facilitates free associations whose connections are more profound and deeply felt than the rational ones of conscious discourse. Is the red of the winged lion in the Two of Cups exciting? Why? Disturbing? What memories are triggered by it, perhaps only partially recalled? What else is red? What does red make you want to do? How about wings? Snakes?

Lest anyone feel that a single card is that and only that and is therefore limited in the amount of information it can impart, let me suggest that the information gleaned is limited, not by the card, but by the question posed, the time, and the depth of thought and feeling that you bring to it. In terms of subtlety and depth, you could ask, "What quality that irritates me in others is a disowned part of myself?" or "What is the secondary gain that accrues to me from my worst fault?" The Knight of Wands, Four of Pentacles, Seven of Swords, and many others offer food for thought ample for weeks of rumination!

Enter into a relationship with the Tarot in the way you would enter into any relationship in which you experience initial excitement and sincere interest. Spend time with the cards. Stay in close touch. Ask questions, express delight, pay attention. The result will be a companionship of which you will never tire and that you can never outgrow.

CHAPTER ONE

Fifty-Six Mirrors: Overlooked Looking Glasses

WELCOME to the great adventure! Together we are about to embark on an exploration of a time-honored facilitator of psychic growth—the Tarot cards. Before our scrupulous, respectful investigation of individual Tarot images, however, I would like to introduce you to the Tarot as I understand it and offer a perspective that will prove essential in the work to follow. Both a clear grasp of what a Tarot deck is and how, from this writer's view, it can be used to greatest profit are necessary orientation for what follows.

Many facets of the Tarot's origins, history, and evolution remain enmeshed in controversy and mystery. However, the briefest of introductions will do for our purposes: a concise context within which we can focus on the interpretations of the cards for inner growth.

Tarot refers to a deck of seventy-eight pictured cards which most people associate with Gypsy fortune tellers. Others, for various reasons, have traced their origins back to the Egyptians. A more scholarly approach would say that Tarot first appeared in thirteenth-century France, in the still-available Marseilles deck. At that time, they were produced on leather and metal, predating both the invention of paper and the arrival from India of the Gypsies.

The seventy-eight cards are of two basically different kinds: the

Major Arcana (Arcana, as in our word *arcane* meaning "secret," "esoteric," or "hidden away"), of which there are twenty-two; and the Minor Arcana, of which there are fifty-six. So we have the "great secrets," the Major Arcana, and the "small secrets," the Minor Arcana.

The Major Arcana relate to the soul's journey. For those of us who believe in reincarnation, they refer to that part of us that outlives the body and returns to the earth plane. For those who do not, they relate to that part of us that continues after the body is gone, the God energy that has become manifest in a vessel that it outlives. Clearly then, to associate them primarily with fortune telling is as erroneous as associating them primarily with Gypsies!

Tarot cards may have been the original deck of playing cards. In fact the Italian word for Tarot is *Tarrochi,* and there are those who believe that the first Tarot deck was designed for the Visconti family by Bonifaccio Bembo for the purpose of gambling. Here we see the emergence of good from evil, or at least trivial, interests.

In fact, the Tarot eventually became associated with the Holy Kabbalah, and in particular, the Kabbalistic Tree of Life. There is the predictable controversy about when and how these two giants of metaphysical thought came together, with theories ranging from biblical times to the nineteenth century. However, it is clear that by the nineteenth century, the two modalities were used in concert, to the great enhancement of the Tarot cards. We will explore Kabbalah in the next chapter; what follows is a brief history of its association with the Tarot.

In 1856, Alphonse Louis Constant, known as Eliphas Levi, published the first book to associate the twenty-two cards of the Major Arcana with the twenty-two letters of the Hebrew alphabet and the four suits of the Minor Arcana with the Tetragrammaton—the four-letter name of God. In 1889, Gerard Encausse, a student of Levi known as Papus, published *The Tarot of the Bohemians,* which asserts that the Tarot was generated by the Tetragrammaton and is to be understood in terms of it. Another student of Levi, Paul Christian, created a system combining Tarot with Kabbalistic astrology. Also in 1889, Oswald Wirth published a deck of Major Arcana whose twenty-two designs incorporated the twenty-two Hebrew letters. Both his teacher, Stanislos De Guaito, and Papus were members of the Kabbalistic Order of the Rose Cross, which has come into modern times as the Rosicrucians.

The connection between Kabbalah and Tarot continued to be recognized in the execution of decks by such proponents as Aleister Crowley, Paul Foster Case, and Manley Palmer Hall. The Rider Waite deck, to which the discussions in this book specifically refer, furthers this tradition. Although the Hebrew letters do not appear in his deck, Arthur Edward Waite, a member of the Hermetic Order of the Golden Dawn, assigned Hebrew letters to the cards in his writings. The Golden Dawn deck, executed by Robert Wang, associates the ten *sefirot*, or vessels, with the ten numbered cards, and the four *olams*, or realms, with the suits of the Minor Arcana. Aleister Crowley, in the *Book of Thoth*, went so far as to assert that "the Tarot was designed as a practical instrument for Qabalistic calculations."

The point is simple: regardless of the actual origins of Tarot and Kabbalah, by 1890 Kabbalistic teaching was integral to Tarot design. It is my contention that the expanded understanding and use of Tarot has Kabbalah—properly understood—at its root.

The foregoing is presented only to suggest the rich history of the Tarot in relation to Kabbalah, fertile ground for exploration should readers' interests so incline them. The history of the Tarot, however, is incidental to the study of the cards themselves, so let us now return to them and to the Minor Arcana in particular.

The Minor Arcana fall into four suits: Pentacles, Cups, Swords and Wands. Pentacles became Diamonds (the word *pentacle* refers to a coin within which is a five-pointed star, or pentagram), Cups became Hearts, Swords became Spades, and Wands became Clubs. Often, if someone says, "I can read your fortune from regular cards," it's because they have learned to read the Tarot and are familiar with the correspondences. They are simply translating.

Of course, our deck of playing cards has fifty-two cards, and the Minor Arcana of the Tarot, as I have mentioned, number fifty-six. The disparity can be explained in that we have three royalty cards in our modern deck—the jack, queen, and king. But the Tarot equivalent is composed of four court cards—the page, knight, queen and king. The page and the knight collapsed into one another to make the jack, thereby eliminating one card from each suit and four cards from the deck.

The deck with which we will be working is, as I have mentioned, the Waite deck, designed by Arthur Edward Waite and executed by Pamela Colman Smith. Its designs are wonderful and have been published by a number of companies. The differences among them (with one exception that occurs in the Major Arcana) are in the rendering of color. The designs are identical. What the various versions share is Waite's innovation of depicting the cards of the Minor Arcana as people in action or process, involving the symbols of their suits. Thus, the Four of Wands, the Two of Pentacles, the Seven of Swords, and the Six of Cups show us not only wands, pentacles, swords and cups in the number named, but also human beings somehow interacting with them. Prior to Waite's designs, the pip (or numbered) cards of the Minor Arcana simply displayed the symbols of the suit in some abstract or geometrical design. It is for this reason that I have selected the Waite designs as a reference point for our work. The Universal Waite, delicately illustrated by Mary Hanson-Roberts and published by U.S. Games Systems, Inc., is reproduced here for the purposes of reference.

What we learn from the Tarot is very much akin to what we learn from Kabbalah. One of these important messages is that we need everything we've got. Everything we have is of value, which is why it was given to us. We don't have to get rid of anything. What we need to do is integrate everything.

If we look at the aces of the Tarot, we see in every case a similar image. We see the hand of God, a huge, oversized hand coming out of the sky, out of the heavens through a cloud, shining in a halo of white light. Doing what? Offering a gift. Kabbalah means "receiving." The aces are doing the giving, and the universe is doing the receiving. They give us the gift of pentacles, of cups, of swords, and of wands. There's one ace for each of these suits. Now, since this is the first deck of playing cards, it didn't have to be that way. If Wands were more valuable, for example, than Swords, the deck could have been designed so that there were seven Aces of Wands and three Aces of Swords. If Pentacles were not of very much value, that suit could have been designed without an ace. So there is something to be learned from the fact that each suit is represented by an ace, and one ace only.

This is important because each of the suits corresponds to what the ancients called elementals and also to what the great psychologist Carl Jung called the functions of consciousness. The Suit of Pentacles refers to earth, the Suit of Cups refers to water, the Suit of Swords refers to air, and the Suit of Wands refers to fire. Having announced that authoritatively, I must add that you can find reputable writers who disagree with almost every one of these associations: C. C. Zain pairs Pentacles with air and Swords with earth, and Stephan Hoeller relates Swords to fire, for example.

Of more interest, in Jungian terms, the Suit of Pentacles refers to the sensate function, information that comes to us through our five senses. The Suit of Cups refers to the feeling function, our emotional response to stimuli. The Suit of Swords refers to the thinking function, how we consciously process information. The Suit of Wands refers to the intuitive function, that mysterious way of somehow *knowing*, and to what Freud called *libido*, our primitive life force. Each of these is equally valuable. The four court cards have similar associations: pages with earth and the sensate; knights with air and the mental; queens with water and the feeling-toned; and kings with fire and the intuitive. Kabbalistically speaking, we don't want merely to get to a particular place on the Tree and stay there; we want to identify with the sap that moves all through the Tree. Similarly, we don't want to find our favorite suit or our favorite card, achieve an understanding or mastery of it, and live there.

The universe is in constant motion. Nothing in the universe is static. The chairs on which we sit are composed of molecules racing through the space between them. The blood circulates in the body. The air flows in and out of the lungs. If we lock our knees and say, "Now I've got the Truth! This is where I want to be and this is where I'm going to stay!" something will happen (instantly, in my experience) that forces us to make a readjustment. In order not to fall over, we have to be on the balls of our feet.

We don't want to be in our thinking mind when we're floating in eighty-degree water in the Caribbean, but we also don't want to rely on our intuitive function when we're trying to balance our checkbooks. As always, the key is appropriate response. If we can avoid rigid attachment to a single perspective, a single way of being, a single truth, we are more likely, as our universe continues to change, to be ready for whatever happens next and to answer the demands of the experience.

The Suit of Pentacles is my personal favorite among the suits, which means that I have a lot more work to do on some of the other suits than I do on Pentacles! (Pick your favorite suit and then ignore it! Work on the other suits; the ones with which you need to gain affinity.) It is a grossly misunderstood suit, the underdog of the Tarot. Many people think that Pentacles has to do with money, career, health—with the material world. That's not how I see it. The Suit of Pentacles has to do with how we relate to money, how we relate to our career, to our state of health, to the material world. If I get sick, how do I feel about that? What do I do about it? When I go to work, is it just a way for me to earn money, or is there a sense of service involved? Not the world, but how we interact with the world, is the domain of Pentacles.

The Suit of Cups has to do with our feelings: how we feel, how we express feelings, and how we respond to the feelings of others. The Suit of Swords has to do with our clarity, our ability to analyze, our capacity to think clearly. It also has to do with our courage. The Suit of Wands reflects the fiery energy that on one end of the spectrum expresses as frank physical sexuality and on the other end of the same spectrum as intuition, psychic knowing, and inspiration. Please note that you did not read the "lower end" of the spectrum and the "higher end" of the spectrum. There is nothing intrinsically "lower" in sexual expression than in any other expression of our life force. We were given the gift by God's own hand to experience fully .

That we need all the suits of the Tarot is clearly seen in the creative process. When we speak of the creative process, we do not limit ourselves to the writing of a symphony or a poem, or the painting of a canvas. We address anything we do, or any way we live, that involves creative thinking. Functional relationships require endless creativity, the ability to engage another in a way that enhances the lives of each rather than rigid adherence to old patterns that result in conflict. To be ourselves demands creativity, achieving what Jung calls individuation. Any time we free ourselves from preconception and habit we are engaged in the creative process.

If we look at the act of creation, we can see that it best begins with the Suit of Wands, with intuition. The first thing that happens is that something comes through for us. It's not the end of a logical process. If we want to write a poem or open a store, we don't begin by making a list of all the things we can write a poem about or all the different kinds of stores we can operate. An inkling flickers within us: a "What if . . . ? I wonder . . . Eureka!" phenomenon. The creative process begins with intuition, with Wands.

The second phase the creative process needs to go through is feeling, because if we don't feel very strongly about a new project, we're going to drop it. It takes so much effort to start something new that if we don't have a tremendous emotional investment in it, it will simply be abandoned or forgotten. We need the fervor of Cups.

Third, the act of creation must move to the thinking phase. Herein lies the difference between a dream and a goal. A goal has a plan. To have an idea about which we have strong feelings does not make anything happen. We have to think things through. If I want to open a retail clothing store, is it going to be high- or low-end clothing? Is it going to be for very young girls or mature women? In what part of town do I want to open it? Where am I going to find my buyers? Where am I going to find my suppliers? Only Swords will help us in this phase.

And finally, we need our Pentacles. We've got to *do* something. We have to take action in the world. That's the difference between a plan and a retail store, the latter providing a better chance of weekly income. We've got to get into the car and drive around and find a location, get on the phone, find out whether or not we can afford the rent, or whether a particular building is for sale. We've got to handle merchandise and deal with the public. A novel isn't a book until we set pen to paper. In the creative process, in all of life, we need each of the suits, each function of consciousness, and none is superior to any other.

I would like to make a final point about the Tarot. It is my belief that everything that is part of human experience can be expressed by, and is expressed in, the Tarot. One excellent way to work with the cards is to think in terms of Tarot, so that when you have a significant experience, you immediately ask yourself, "What would be the card for that? There's got to be a card!" If you follow that practice, you will find a much-enriched understanding of the cards.

Conversely, we are all capable of experiencing everything that the cards suggest. In fact, it is fruitful to assume that there's nothing in those seventy-eight cards we won't experience at some point in our lives—each and every one of us.

Finally, each card carries both a positive and a negative charge. What a card conveys is determined by a complex of factors. So how do you know? How do you know when you're reading the cards what interpretation to put on them? Ah, that's what makes the game so interesting. That's why, over the centuries and our personal lifetimes, the Tarot is never in danger of boring us. It demands our intuition as well as our knowledge. It requires feeling, perception, and an awareness of all the other cards in a spread as a distinctive pattern. It also exacts a sense about the person for whom one is reading. Sometimes things we intuit seem to be coming not *from* the cards but *through* them. When that happens, the process is amazing and wonderful.

If you are approaching the Tarot as a novice, be prepared for the adventure of a lifetime! If you are an experienced practitioner, the exploration of the Minor Arcana that follows will, I hope, serve to deepen your understanding, enhance your skills, and encourage you along lines of personal discovery as your intimacy with each card grows.

Having put the Tarot in this skeletal context, we can turn our attention to the central question of use. The Tarot can be used in a variety of ways and for a variety of purposes. It will be as important to understand what this book does not set out to address as to grasp what it endeavors to accomplish.

Tarot has often been associated with occult practices; the names that most readily come to mind are Aleister Crowley and the Deck of Thoth, which he designed. It is neither in that tradition nor in that spirit that this work is undertaken.

The Tarot cards can be used for meditation in various ways, and although the objects of this meditation are more usually the Major Arcana, this seems to me less a consequence of their intrinsic superiority for that purpose than a historical tendency to undervalue the Minor Arcana in general.

Although meditational practice will not be the subject of our study, such practice is most compatible with it and is enthusiastically recommended. There are two methods that work very well in this regard. The first is to allow the card to act upon us, to surrender our active, intellectual investigation and simply invite the image to do its work. The second involves entering into the card; this in turn can be done in one of two ways. We can assume the identity of any or each of the characters portrayed, or we can join the scene, otherwise maintaining our own identity, and confront or interrelate with any or all of the figures depicted. In either case, we can explore what spontaneously comes up for us, without an attempt at directing or controlling it.

By far the most popular uses of the Tarot, however, are prognostication, or fortune telling, and divination. I list these as distinct, for despite a superficial similarity, they are quite different. The similarities are that in each case a *querent* (or questioner) enlists the services of a Tarot-card practitioner for a reading. Cards are shuffled and generally laid out in a spread, a configuration in which each position carries a fixed meaning independent of the card that falls to it—"the past," "the obstacle," "the possible outcome," and so on. Here the similarities end.

What is the difference between divination and prognostication? Both involve foretelling future events through signs, but the former carries as well the suggestions of hidden knowledge, the aid of supernatural powers, unusual insight, and intuitive perception. The great difference between the two apparently similar modes lies in the more subtle, introverted question of what we bring to the process, the attitude with which we approach a reading.

People who want their fortunes told often approach their reading as entertainment or as a test of the reader. They are dazzled by specific information—the names and ages of their children, an accident injuring the left ankle that occurred three years previously, and other facts that we may safely suspect were already in their possession. So what have they learned from the encounter?

Sometimes people have their fortunes told at the insistence of others, at a party, or on a boardwalk. These people often approach the reading with the opposite but equally fruitless attitude of skepticism. Their posture is to dare the practitioner to tell them something true. Generally, their complaints are either a gleeful, "That's not true!" or a grudging "Yeah, but you could say that to anybody!" If something true and idiosyncratic emerges, the unruffled client generally asks for proof that it wasn't an accident or coincidence. This is expressed in the challenge for the reader to do it again.

Finally, there are those who approach prognostication with awe and trembling. "Your husband is full of cancer," a kindly fortune teller informed a trusting woman. This constituted proof to the loving wife of what she had long suspected—that Western medical diagnostic techniques were benighted and farcical. Seven years later, her husband continues his daily routines of work and leisure, but for the wife, some esoteric healing must explain it. Certainly so powerful a figure as a reader of fortunes could not have been wrong!

Although these attitudes are apparently radically different, they have an important element in common. Nobody learns anything. No growth or insight occurs. No meaning is derived. Whether the reader is perceived as a performer, trickster, or priestess, all of the attention is on her. It is to her that all power is relinquished. The querent is a passive recipient of information or a scoffing baiter, but never a participant.

Divination does not polarize querent and reader, but acknowledges that a valuable Tarot reading has three necessary components: a deck of cards, a competent and sensitive reader, and a right-minded querent. Every professional reader has had the experience of reading for someone whose cards fall into an instantly coherent constellation followed by a person whose spread is entirely opaque. Same deck. Same reader. Different querents. A person interested in divination approaches the Tarot with respect. There is a seriousness of purpose, an openness, and a wish to be seen, understood, known. There is a true desire for guidance, an integrity of self-perception, the honesty to face the difficult, the desire to learn and grow, the courage to change. The right attitude is that of active participation.

The humanistic Tarot, as opposed to the esoteric Tarot, concerns "who we are, how we act, what forces shape and direct us," according to Rachel Pollack. We use it to raise our level of awareness, shift our attention, and recognize our patterns of response—and our responsibility in those patterns. Because we, each of us, can look at the Tarot images, respond to them, and project on them, this interaction is possible. Unlike astrology, for example, we don't need to turn ourselves over to "the expert." We can dialogue with the reader of Tarot in terms of what we perceive in the cards, how we react to them.

But don't the cards foretell the future? If I ask about my job security, and the Ten of Swords—a prone figure pierced by ten swords—is the final outcome of my spread, doesn't that reveal my fate? Isn't my fate sealed? In a prognostication, such a card of death is the herald of doom. The querent has given away all power; the reader has made a pronouncement; the game is done. In divination, however, the entire purpose of the reading is to empower the querent. The reader, like the cards themselves, is an instrument of insight and growth. The querent can change the reading.

How do you change a reading you don't like? That sounds too good to be true! Well, the good news is that you *can* change a reading, and the bad news is that you *can't* change the cards. Let me explain.

One balmy evening, I was driving down the hill from my home at roughly twenty miles per hour above the speed limit. It is a rugged area with no cross streets and one that invites disregard of rules. On this occasion, however, several cars driving up the hill flashed their lights at me. It was still light out, so I checked to make sure my lights weren't on. I checked my turn signal. Then, from the dark recesses of my mind, a memory flickered. Flashing lights by passing motorists warn of a policeman in the area. I slowed my car, passed the policeman at the legal speed limit, and avoided a citation. That's how you change a reading.

A Tarot reading shows you where you are headed if you continue your present course of action. A Tarot reading is the flashing light of warning. The choice is then yours. I could have chosen to continue driving too fast, but the consequences had been made clear. If you want to be assured of job security, you don't lay the cards again and hope for a better outcome card. You change your behavior: get to work earlier, stay later, find ways of avoiding conflict, become more productive and valuable on the job. The reading tells you only what the outcome will be if you don't—if you choose to go on as if you hadn't consulted the cards at all.

Finally, let me address some of the most frequently asked questions about the Tarot cards themselves. The first involves their handling and what we do with them. Is it true that someone must give you your first deck? Is it true that you should never allow anyone else to handle your cards? Should you wrap them in silk? Is a sandalwood box better? Or a gold one? How can we use them? I like to suggest baking with the cards, using the Minor Arcana as a sugar substitute, one card per tablespoon of sugar. Or shred them like confetti and add them to a bubble bath. Am I making my point? Put the cards to whatever use works for you. If your understanding is magnified by sleeping with a card under your pillow, who am I to call it nonsense? If your deck feels more vital for having been lovingly wrapped in Japanese silk or sheltered in Arabian sandalwood, why not store it in that way? The cards are little cardboard pictures, to be protected or destroyed by you. They are *only* little cardboard pictures. They have no power other than the power you invest in them. They are the instrument. The power is in you. The power is in each of us, in the glorious human psyche, with its infinite capacity to search and sense and stretch and unfold.

Having said this, we are now ready to turn our attention to the Tree of Life, an instrument of great power that will prove invaluable to our understanding of the cards.

Each vessel, or sefirah, on the Tree is named for an attribute of the infinite, unknowable God. Each bears an archetype of that manifestation of the divine. The Minor Arcana may be seen as pictorial expressions of those archetypes. Underlying the historical association of vessel and card is a potent, mysterious psychological truth: The Kabbalistic Tree of Life provides the archetypes by which the Tarot can be understood. This observation is well made by Stephan Hoeller, drawing on the teachings of Carl Jung, in *The Royal Road*: "The coincidence of the two systems . . . is not a mere haphazard concurrence of unrelated circumstances, but is a meaningful coincidence of great psychological, or if you prefer, mystical power and purpose."

As Gershom Scholem conceded privately to Stephan Hoeller, and as the latter emphasizes in *The Royal Road*, "the combined system of Kabbalah and Tarot works. . . . Past history matters less than first-hand experience." If the proof of the pudding is, indeed, in the eating, then sample the wares herein and be your own best judge.

CHAPTER TWO
Kabbalah: The Ultimate Gift

*K*ABBALAH is a sophisticated and mystical system of thought that deserves a lifetime of dedicated focus, study, meditation, and prayer. So, in a sense, to *talk* about Kabbalah briefly, as I do here, is to do it a disservice. To *experience* Kabbalah is quite different.

It is impossible to talk definitively about mystical experience, which is of course what Kabbalah is. It is like trying to describe chocolate to one who has never tasted it or the color red to someone who has never seen color. Having said that, we do want to say what we can about Kabbalah, because, for our purposes, it seems to be better than saying nothing. But we must always remember that we are not dealing with the immediate experience of Kabbalah, which is a nonlinear, noncognitive experience—a mystical experience.

Originally, there were three requirements for the study of Kabbalah. Number one, you had to be a man. I will refrain from commenting on that particular stipulation. Number two, you had to be at least forty years of age. And number three, you had to be married. Can we clear our rage at the sexism this involves and at the bias that only married people are capable of studying Kabbalah appropriately? How are we to react to the restriction on age? "I'm thirty-nine years, eleven months, and two weeks old; can't make it. In two weeks, when I am forty, all of life will open up to me with clarity. Can't wait!"

If we can put aside our offense at what seems to be both insulting and silly, however, we can question what might have been at the heart of those restrictions. The answer becomes clear when we remember the *midrash*, the interpretive story, about four rabbis who entered paradise. One of them dropped dead on the spot. Another became apostate, losing his faith in one God. A third went stark raving mad, and the fourth departed paradise in peace. That was Rabbi Akiba. He left in peace because he entered in peace. He entered paradise centered, serene, and balanced within himself, so that is the way he left.

Similarly, what we're actually confronting in these apparently foolish restrictions is the need for groundedness and preparation. First, if we are going to enter the mystical realm of Kabbalah, which draws so heavily on the female side of us—the intuitive, the psychic, the mysterious—we have to approach it with a highly developed male part of ourselves. To use Jungian terms, if we are going into *anima* activity we need a strongly developed *animus*. If we do not have this, whether we are male or female, we are going to be yanked way off balance. We can understand the necessity of being a "man" in these terms. Each of us, male or female in body, is androgynous. To study Kabbalah, we require a strongly developed male side, so that logic, reason, objectivity, and the capacity for analytical thinking will balance the experiences we may encounter in this pursuit. Secondly, to be "married" may be understood to mean engaged in life on Earth. We must have the kind of commitment that will keep us present and actively, enthusiastically relating in our lives. Marriage is, I believe, a metaphor. Finally, to say that we have to be forty years old is to say only that we need to have had some experience of life. We have to be grounded. We need to have made necessary preparation.

Many are the horror stories of inadequately prepared people who play around with powerful forces. In Hindu and Buddhist tradition, the life force coiled at the base of the spine is called *kundalini*. The benefits of raising kundalini energy are legion. I know of one man who was extremely successful in getting his kundalini to rise, but he did not then know what to do with that energy. He had an idea of how to go about the process, and he was successful at it as a craft, but he was not grounded in any belief system and had no understanding of what he was doing. He is now paralyzed from the waist down.

More common are the people who take drug trips. They are catapulted into realms of tremendous excitement, exploration, and discovery. Yet very often these experiences pull people off the deep end. They find themselves unable to function anymore. The difference between the acidhead and the prophet is preparation. The former have experiences that are transitory and ultimately of no use to anyone, including themselves. Of the many societies in which mind-altering drugs have played a role, ours alone is plagued with problems of addiction and deviant behavior. Mystical experience, regardless of its source, must, if it is to have meaning, occur in appropriate context. Maturity, balance, and the wish to use these experiences to enhance rather than to escape from life are wise criteria to apply here. These are, I believe, how the traditional requirements for the study of Kabbalah are to be understood.

Having made this apology, let me begin by saying that the most important thing to know about Kabbalah is very simple: Kabbalah means "receiving." That tells us a number of things. First, that God the Creator chooses for us to receive. We are dealing with an explanation of the creation in terms of a generous God. The concept here is that God, being perfect and complete, has as His essence the desire to impart; He creates the entire universe so that there will be something to receive what is given. (Kabbalistically, the godhead is twofold. There is *Adonai,* the male aspect of the godhead, the Lord. And there is the *Holy Shechinah,* the female aspect of the godhead. We are dealing with an androgynous spirit. For the sake of grace as well as brevity I sometimes use words like *He, His,* and *Lord.* That is not to be understood as male but as the divine ruling spirit, the Eternal One. Similarly, to avoid both the sexist *he* and the awkward *he or she,* I have opted for the ungrammatical *they,* pending the evolution of a genderless singular pronoun.)

God then, however we conceive that spirit energy, has as His essence the desire to impart, since He needs nothing. He therefore creates a universe that is meant to receive. The animals can receive, but not with conscious awareness. The angels don't need to receive in the same way that we do, although they have conscious awareness. Human beings alone were created to receive with conscious awareness what it is that God the Creator has to offer. Therefore, we are the only ones who can sanctify, who can bless the creation.

The implications of this are rather staggering. One is that human beings are the crown of creation! We are the point of it all. There would be no creation if it weren't for human beings. Basic to the Kabbalistic system, then, is that the universe is created by a loving God whose wish is to give and who has created us specifically as creatures who can receive, with loving awareness and conscious appreciation.

This is very different from certain Christian beliefs in which we are born in a state of sin. We are all responsible for and guilty of the so-called original sin and come into the world apologizing, trying to make it up to God. There are systems of Christian belief in which we cannot be saved by good works, but only by grace, God's gift to us, because we are, in our *essence,* sinful and therefore incapable of earning our own salvation. This is totally different from the Kabbalistic view. In Kabbalah, human beings are born to receive; we are the fulfillment of all creation and exactly as we should be. We have choices to make, and we can fall into evil ways, but we are born perfect.

That Kabbalah means "receiving" involves another important implication: receiving is not associated with selfishness. We are here to receive, we have been created to receive. If we come into this world screaming and wailing and crying, "Make me comfortable! Make me warm! Feed me! Take care of me!", it is exactly what we're supposed to do! God is rubbing His hands in delight, thinking, "I've done it again! Another perfect person!" And if we go through our lives screaming, "Give me! Give me! Give me!" this does not make us selfish or evil. This is what we are designed for.

Does that mean there's no such thing as selfishness in Kabbalistic thought? Does that mean there is no such thing as evil? Not at all. What it does mean is that the distinction between good and evil, or the unselfish and the selfish, occurs after the desire to receive. The impulse to good, or *Yetzer Ha-tov,* is the desire to receive in order to impart, to share, to bring forth into the world. The evil impulse, or *Yetzer Ha-rah,* is the desire to receive for oneself alone. To receive and retain, to hold back, is selfish. The desire to receive in itself, however, is blessed.

Another important concept in Kabbalah involves the relatedness between ourselves and the universe. This must be understood in terms of how God created the universe. We come again to a marked departure from many other systems of belief.

God created the universe by emanation. God allowed His own essence to flow forth, to radiate forth, and in so doing filled the world with His own being. What does that mean? What are the implications?

First, if everything that exists partakes of God energy, then each of us has not something godlike within, but has *God* within! God is within each of us. It can indeed be said that each of us is God, that we are God.

And what does that mean about our relationship to one another? It is not that we are all sisters and brothers; that doesn't tell the half of it. We are clones! We are spiritual clones of one another. We couldn't be more closely related to one another. If what is in me is what is in you, we are indeed one.

We now have a new understanding of the central prayer of Judaism, the *Shema*. The Shema says, *"Shema Yisrael Adonai, Elohenu, Adonai Echod."* That means, "Hear, oh Israel, the Lord is God, the Lord is One." What does that truly mean?

Let's begin with "Hear, oh Israel." How did the universe come into being? Many physicists now say it was with the Big Bang. The sound of that bang, we are told by scientists as well as spiritual leaders, reverberates throughout the entire universe and will continue forever. There's no limitation to the universe. There's nothing to stop those sound waves. So we are being asked to hear, to tune into that moment of creation in which all was clearly one. "Hear, oh Israel." Who are the people of Israel? Does this refer just to people born of Jewish parents?

The word *Israel* first appears in the Old Testament when Jacob wrestles with an angel. All day and all night he struggles, and he says to the angel, "I will not let thee go until thou bless me." At dawn he wrests his blessing from the angel, and at that moment he is called Israel because Israel means "one who struggles with God." The one who struggles with divine energy. Everyone reading this book is an Israelite. Everyone who sees these words is a part of the people of Israel.

Adonai, Elohenu, Adonai Echod. Adonai means "the Lord." Adonai is the Creator God. Elohenu means "the God within," the God that I experience in my everyday life, the God I experience as my share of the emanation. Echod means "is one." What's up there and what's within is one God. The remote godhead and my own soul, all our souls, are one.

The metaphor that is often used to explain this is light. This is appropriate for a number of reasons. First, we all have a great love of light. Plants gravitate toward the light and need light for photosynthesis. If we drive by the ocean at sunset, we see all of the seagulls lined up facing the sun, getting the last rays of sunlight. Second, light is unique in that, in shining forth, it is undiminished. Unlike water, for example, the source is unaltered by the pouring forth. And most importantly, light is a principle of union. If I light a candle and then with that candle I light another candle, I have two candles and I have two sources of light, but I have one light. Light is light. It's the same light. So to speak of God's nature as light which emanates forth is to remind us that while there may be many different candles, the light within each of us is the same.

This notion of oneness, of a total and complete unity, is the basis of Judaism and the basis of Kabbalah. It is easy to say, one would think it would be the easiest thing in the world to grasp, and yet living as if we are all one is the greatest challenge we can undertake. Living as if we are one with even immediate family seems impossible most of the time: the promiscuous daughter, the alcoholic mother, the irresponsible father, the stingy son, the sister on drugs, the smug grandmother, the self-righteous grandfather, the manipulative brother, the uncle whose rage terrifies everyone. How are we then to live our belief in oneness with strangers, or worse, those crazy, peculiar, dangerous foreigners who can't even speak English? Further, it is not enough, Kabbalistically, to live as if we are one with the majestic lion. We must also strive to feel at one with serpents and scorpions! At one with not just the family dogs but with their ticks and fleas. That's the challenge. That's a message that takes a lifetime of understanding and practice.

Let us turn our attention now to the heart of Kabbalah, *Torah*. Torah, the first five books of the Bible, is held by Kabbalists to be the blueprint of the universe. The idea is that God didn't create a universe on the spur of the moment but first laid out a plan. Then He created the universe by that blueprint. Now this may sound like a very radical and strange idea, and in fact, it is a wildly exciting one. But it's not unique to Judaism. How does the Gospel according to Saint John begin? "In the beginning was the Word, and the Word was with God, and the Word was God." It makes the hair on the back of your neck stand up, it's so exciting, this relationship between the Word, the Torah, and everything else that exists. As Rabbi Mordecai Finley puts it, "If the world was created by the word of God, we are God's poetry."

There is as well a blueprint for all human beings, for all experiences, and for any system that one can imagine. This universal symbol, central to Kabbalah, is the Tree of Life. The original human, the blueprint of humankind, was called "Adam Kadman." By this blueprint of the celestial human, human beings were created.

The first thing we notice when we look at the Tree of Life is that it certainly is a strange-looking tree. Any one of us, regardless of our artistic capabilities, could draw a better tree than that. Clearly then, this is not meant to be a representational tree. The Tree is conceptual. What does that mean?

What is of extreme importance about a tree is that it is a single organism. We can't look at the beautiful crown of the tree with its brilliant green shining leaves and its bright pink-and-white blossoms and say, "Well, that part of the tree I like. But these filthy roots down in the dirt? I don't see what we need those for!"

We have the roots, the trunk, the bark, the branches; we have the twigs, the leaves, and the blossoms: what we see here is diversity in oneness. That's the message of the conceptual tree. Isn't that what the universe is, the *uni* being the oneness and the *verse* the diversity? So it is true that we are all one and that the universe is a single organism. It also true that there is great diversity.

This is certainly true of ourselves as well. If I am walking from one room to the next at two in the morning and I stub my toe, where does the scream come from? Not from my toe, but from my head, from my mouth. I am one organism. This is true psychically and spiritually as well. What we are is a single wholeness, and we cannot separate out the parts of ourselves that we think are unworthy or that we don't like or that we think are bad or evil. Our challenge is acceptance, recognizing that everything we have is a part of one whole and that everything we have enables us to function. Perhaps the aspects of ourselves we like least will turn out to be as valuable to us as the roots are to the tree. We are not in a position to judge. The conscious mind is not the brightest organ of the body.

This is so very important because I don't believe there's anyone reading this passage who doesn't secretly believe they could do a better job on themselves than God did. Each of us would like to sit down at a large dining room table—close the door—and spread it all out! We'd like to look over everything that's inside of us and with a pair of tweezers, pick over and remove the things we don't like, the things we think are unworthy, sinful, weak, or even disgusting. You know, disgusting, like those ugly roots down in the dirt crawling with worms and bugs! Let's just get rid of the roots! Isn't that a good idea? Let's just chop them off. That's not the part of the tree I like. And then what happens to the tree? The tree depends on those "disgusting" roots much more than it does on the beautiful crown. We have to remember that we, like the tree, have dark energies within us that we may nonetheless need in ways we can't even suspect.

Another cardinal message of Kabbalah, then, is *integration*. We are not here to get rid of anything. If it didn't belong here, God wouldn't have put it here. We are here to integrate everything we have and everything we are in order to put it to its best possible use. Whatever we feel guilty about or ashamed of or embarrassed about, we are challenged to think of in a new way—as an energy that has the potential for positive thrust. The challenge, as always, is toward oneness. We are challenged to be at one with God, at one with one another, and at one within ourselves. Perhaps this last is our most difficult endeavor.

Before we begin examining the Tree and its relation to us, we must be clear that when we talk about right and left on the Tree, it is as if we are looking at the back of the Tree or at a mirror image of ourselves. *Right* and *left* refer both to the Tree and to ourselves. It is not, in other words, as if I am facing you, my right being on your left side. Let us now turn our attention to this great, universal glyph.

First, we see that the Tree has three pillars. The right-hand pillar is called the Pillar of Mercy. It is the pillar of energy flow, and it is called male or masculine and positive. The left-hand pillar is called the Pillar of Severity. It is the pillar of form. It is called female or feminine and negative. (Here we must interpret "negative" in terms of a necessary "nothing" in the same way that a socket is a nothing, an emptiness which receives a plug.) A connection is required to make the energy flow. We need both the energy and the form. Again, if you want a drink of water, the water is the energy flow. But you can't just have water. The water must be in something, even if it's the banks of a river. You need something to give water form; for example, a cup. Yet what gives form also restricts. A six-ounce cup limits the water you can receive to six ounces, and if the cup didn't resist the water, it couldn't receive it. It would be a sieve. The left-hand pillar is called

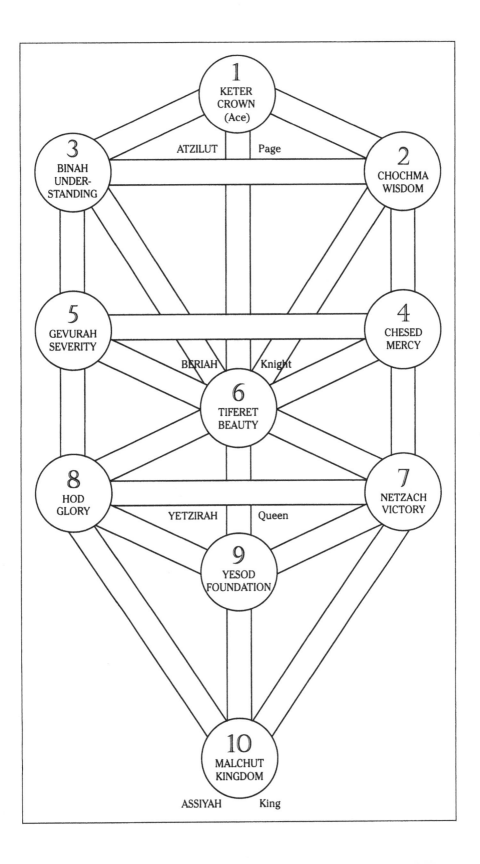

the Pillar of Severity because in giving form it brings limitation. The two are inextricably related. To give form is to restrict, and yet without form we can receive nothing at all.

Put more simply, in our own lives we experience the need for balance between energy and form. People who have a tremendous amount of energy and no structure are very exciting to be around—but not for long. After a while they start to make us crazy because they're flying off in all directions. These are the people who tend to be a little on the flaky side. They've got all kinds of wonderful ideas and great vitality and nothing ever gets done.

On the other hand, people who have too much formative energy in relation to their energy flow are very solid and dependable and boring. Our own lives fluctuate between pillars. Sometimes we feel we're bursting with enthusiasm to create and express a tremendous amount, but we're not accomplishing anything because we're lacking in discipline or structure. Other times when it seems everything is absolutely under control, but there doesn't seem to be much point to getting up in the morning. So we need both energy and form; they're equally valuable, which is why they're represented on the Tree as being perfectly balanced.

The central pillar is the Pillar of Harmony. It is the pillar of integration. The importance of this cannot be overemphasized. Once again, we encounter the radical! We are dealing with a worldview whose ethic is not binary but triune.

When we are children, we are taught to be good, not bad. We are told to be generous, kind, compassionate, loving, clean, and polite. We are raised to believe there are rules we must live by, laws we must obey. We are to shun dishonesty, violence, selfishness, bullying, cruelty, hatred, and, in some traditions, even jealousy and anger. We are raised to seek the light and eschew the darkness: in short, to be positive and not negative.

While these are indisputably worthy goals, they do not seem to have improved human conduct appreciably over the millennia. Further, it can be argued that the guilt and shame to which such a code subjects us have effects on our behavior contrary to those intended by its principles. In place of these polarities, Kabbalah suggests a view far more sophisticated and with far greater psychological validity, stemming, as always, from the message of the One.

The right and left pillars of the Tree of Life are not called good and evil, but merciful and severe. As a symbol of the universe, the Tree represents what is—not what we wish were the case. In fact, those of us on a spiritual path have long known that it is not ease and comfort but transformation and enlightenment that are our goals. Sometimes the lessons by which we attain higher ground are painful and severe. The Pillar of Mercy yields blessings of delight; the blessings of the Pillar of Severity tend to be less delightful, but the blessings are one—all propel us toward our chosen end; all are part of a single journey. Our task is to acknowledge the darkness—in the world, in ourselves—and, on the central pillar of the Tree, invent ways to balance and integrate it with the light.

The Pillar of Harmony is the place where these energies come into perfect balance. Why don't we just forget the Pillar of Mercy and the Pillar of Severity (which are extremes), get on the central pillar and stay there? Hey! Show me how to do that. I'll do it. Show me how to do that and guarantee me that the phone will never ring at four o'clock in the morning with some very bad news. We would do it if we could, but we can't.

When we talk about Kabbalistic meditation, there is a way of working the Tree that is called the Way of the Arrow. From the base of the Tree we shoot up to the very top! Of course we just want to stay there forever. It's a place of ecstasy and union and oneness and serenity and perfection. Why don't we stay there? Why doesn't the arrow stay in the sky when we shoot it from our bow? Because that's not the law of gravity, and that's not the law of the universe. We all know from experience that when we catapult up that fast, we come down almost as fast, and we usually land on our heads. That's the way of the arrow. We've all had ecstatic experience listening to music, walking on a beach, witnessing the birth of our first child, making love, reading and understanding something critical for the first time, or having a powerful religious experience in a church or a temple. But the experience fades.

Ram Dass makes this point with his usual power and humor. He talks about working on his spiritual growth and going to church at Christmas time, singing the wonderful hymn "Holy, Holy, Holy," and feeling that he "just loves everybody so much" and that he'll always be in that place of loving union. He says that feeling lasts until "we sit down to Christmas dinner, and somebody else gets the drumstick. . . ." We can be thinking of ourselves as holy, spiritual beings, and over food, we can be reduced to feeling competitive and resentful. "He got the drumstick last time too! Why didn't they pass the plate the other way this time?"

We would like to stay in what we think of as a spiritual place, a high place, a holy place. We would like to remain on the central pillar in a state of perfect balance. But life doesn't work that way. We have to work the Tree in the way that is called the Way of the Serpent, which winds all around the Tree and slowly, gradually, and patiently experiences and integrates every energy on the Tree.

As we continue our examination of the Tree of Life, we can best direct our attention to the series of circles that make up these pillars. As you will recall, these are called *sefirot,* the singular of which is *sefirah.* A sefirah is a vessel, created to contain the divine energy that emanates from the godhead. The Tree may be perceived as a many-tiered fountain. As God allows His energy to flow forth, the energy is caught up in the first sefirah. When that overflows, it fills the next two sefirot, and when they overflow, they fill the following two sefirot, down into the sixth sefirah, and so on.

We can imagine that the sefirot at the top of the Tree are lighter, thinner, more transparent and more fragile; as we move down the Tree, we move into sefirot which are thicker and stronger, but through which the light (God energy) shines more dimly. When we're down on this earth plane, we need the stronger vessels to contain the divine essence, because we know what it's like on the freeway if we're driving in Baccarat crystal. We're going to get shattered. In order to get to the clearer energies, the sefirot through which the light shines more easily, we need to do our meditations working up the Tree. But the most important thing to remember is that the light at the base of the Tree is the same light as the light at the height of the Tree. The light itself is unchanged. The difference is in the container, but Dom Perignon tastes the same in a Baccarat crystal goblet and an earthenware mug.

There is a place between the first sefirah and the sixth sefirah in which there seems to be an empty space. There is, in fact, an uncreated sefirah there, which is called *Daath.* (That is the sefirah that God is waiting for us to create.) But you can see very clearly that if there were a sefirah in this place, we could fold the figure any way we chose and the number-six sefirah would always be in the center of it. Again, the message that we get from the Tree of Life is that of balance and symmetry.

We can see that the Tree of Life also forms three triangles, each described by three sefirot, with a single remaining sefirah at the base. These triangles delineate three *olams*—realms or worlds. There is *Atzilut*, made up of the first three sefirot, which is the realm of emanation. It is an upward-pointing triangle. The second triangle forms the olam called *Beriah,* the world of creation. Next on the Tree come the three sefirot that form the realm of *Yetzirah,* the realm of formation. Finally, all by itself, we have *Assiyah,* the world or olam of action. We should be starting to wonder right now why there is only one sefirah or vessel in this realm.

So we have now looked at the Tree in terms of its three vertical pillars and its four horizontal olams or worlds. We can see that there are ten sefirot or vessels. Additionally, there are twenty-two paths which connect these sefirot. As we shall see, each aspect of the Tree relates to the Tarot.

In fact, the sefirot of the Tree of Life have been related to everything from pagan gods to scents, wild flowers, curative herbs, and gem stones. These represent a great departure from Jewish mysticism and complicate our original intention. We will therefore limit the correspondences we explore as we talk about the sefirot of the Tree to two modalities that have long supported the spiritual seeker—the chakra system of the East and the planets of astrology.

Let us now turn our attention to the sefirot themselves. The first sefirah is called *Keter,* and Keter means "crown." It is the first place where divine energy enters the Tree, and in terms of our own bodies, it represents the crown chakra. (This explains why orthodox Jewish men wear *yarmulkes,* the little skull caps, all the time. You don't bare the crown chakra to the entrance of divine energy without preparation. You show humility by covering your head. What is not explained is why only men wear yarmulkes.) Keter carries the energy of absolute unity. It is the first something of the universe. It represents pure existence and perfection, and, astrologically, it represents the swirling nebulae, the entire cosmos.

We move from Keter to the number-two sefirah, which is the first sefirah on the Pillar of Mercy—the right-hand, masculine pillar. This is

Chochma, which means "wisdom." Chochma represents the full potential of creative energy, infinite expansion. It is dynamic, the stimulator of the universe. It is also the supernal father. It is associated with the right temple and the right lobe of the brain, and astrologically it represents the entire zodiac.

The first sefirah on the Pillar of Severity is called *Binah.* Binah is sefirah number three, and Binah means "understanding." The more alert among you will have guessed that Binah is called the supernal mother, since she balances the supernal father on the top of the right-hand pillar. She is the giver of life and of limitation. We can't take those two apart. The mother who gives life also pronounces our death sentence.

No one gets out of this world alive. Once we enter into life, it is with the understanding that life will come to an end. So at the same time that we are given form, we are given restriction. This is always the case. If electricity is going to pass through a wire so it can be of some use, the amount of electricity will be limited by what the wire can conduct.

Binah is the first place on the Tree where we have rest from force, which has come swirling down into Keter from the *Ein Sof Ohr,* the limitless light, and continues tumultuously into Chochma. Binah, then, is receptivity and resistance. Astrologically, Binah is naturally associated with Saturn, the planet of constriction and restriction. Like the birth canal through which we all must be squeezed into birth only to find ourselves human and therefore mortal, Saturn disciplines and limits us. In terms of our bodies, Binah is associated with the left lobe of the brain and the left temple. If we bring the right temple and the left temple, Chochma and Binah, together at the central pillar, we arrive at the third eye. Certainly third-eye insight depends on our balancing wisdom and understanding.

In these first three sefirot, we have been in the olam of Atzilut, the world of emanation, which is called the supernal triangle. These are the most mysterious of the energies on the Tree. In fact, there is a special meditation beginning on the second night of Passover in which we move energies around the body according to the bottom seven sefirot on the Tree. This is because the supernal triangle is far beyond what we can achieve alone. Even among the sefirot themselves, the unattainable nature of these three is recognized.

We now move back to the Pillar of Mercy and to the fourth sefirah on the Tree. This sefirah is *Chesed,* sometimes called *Gedulah.* It means "loving-kindness and mercy." Since it is the central sefirah on the Pillar of Mercy, and since we're dealing with issues of balance, it is the most merciful place on the Tree. It is associated astrologically with Jupiter, the planet of expansiveness and expansion. It can be thought of in Catholic terms as the state of grace. It brings a flow of blessings and compassion and sweetness, goodness without end. And in terms of our own bodies, it refers to the right shoulder and arm.

Stephan Hoeller has described Chesed as the soft-ice-cream machine that never turns off. There's just all this rich, sweet, creamy, delicious, gooey stuff that keeps flowing into our lives forever, and we all know what happens when we have too much soft ice cream. If we don't actually get sick on it, it at least becomes sickening. And obviously what we are going to need, in order to keep the Tree in balance, is something as difficult as Chesed is merciful. So we kind of know we're in trouble here. If Chesed represents the energy that is entirely positive and wonderful and compassionate and loving, then what are we going to need to balance it?

We move to the number-five sefirah, which is the central sefirah on the Pillar of Severity, and therefore the most severe place on the Tree. It is *Gevurah*, called "severity." It has also been called *Pachad,* "fear and trembling." Finally, it means "judgment." The word *judgment* has two meanings. One suggests that discrimination needs to be exercised. How much soft ice cream shall I eat? There has to be containment here. But there is also the implication on the Tree of Life that judgment means being evaluated—judged by God.

Remember always that we are created in God's image. So our left shoulder and arm are the left shoulder and arm of God. It's the left hand with which God smites us. It's the most severe place on the Tree. And it's associated astrologically with the fiery planet Mars. Gevurah has been called the Great Limiter. Why, in a spiritual system, do we have to have this energy on the Tree? Isn't spiritual study supposed to be uplifting? Why introduce this harsh energy? Why? Because it's there! Do you know anybody who has gone through life without experiencing agony? Have you gone through your life so far without experiencing the anguish of Gevurah? It's impossible. Cardinal to Kabbalistic thinking is the understanding: As above, so below. As below, so above.

It's here—so it's on the Tree. We're experiencing it in our lives; therefore, it's reflected in the Tree of Life. It's part of the universe. That's the way it is, unfortunately. Unfortunately? Perhaps. Really, this depends on our perspective.

In mystical Judaism, there is a concept called *Gilgul,* which means "reincarnation." For those of us who believe that the soul's journey extends beyond the life of a single body, a host of questions arise. Let us, for the purposes of our discussion, restrict ourselves to just one of these: Given the facts of pain, deterioration, loss, and death to which we are exposed on the earth plane, why does the soul reincarnate?

One answer suggests that between incarnations the soul (self, spirit, or higher consciousness) looks down at the havoc wrought by it's behavior during its most recent incarnation and despairs at the ramifications of its choices. It sees how its infractions of karmic law have led to imbalances in the universe, and it cannot rest until it avails itself of the opportunity to make it right. The soul carefully chooses the incarnation that will make it possible to redress balance and correct evils that have resulted from the infractions.

It is at the place of Gevurah that these corrections are made. From the perspective of ego, personality, Gevurah is the place of fear and trembling, the dark night of the soul. But from the perspective of spirit, Gevurah offers the greatest, if the most severe, blessings of the entire Tree. Without its harsh judgment, how could we restore balance? The incarnation—with all of its sorrows—would be wasted.

We can consider from this point of view what is arguably the most misunderstood line of the entire Bible: An eye for an eye and a tooth for a tooth. From the viewpoint of our ego consciousness, this is retributive justice. But from a higher view, isn't this simply a statement of the law of karma? Aren't we hearing a rule of thumb about how the universe operates? Gevurah, then, is the corrector to breaches of karmic law. If we take the right shoulder and the left shoulder, which are represented by Chesed and Gevurah, and bring them together on the middle pillar, we arrive at the place of the throat chakra, which is the place of communication.

We move next to *Tiferet,* the sixth sefirah on the Tree, and Tiferet means "beauty." Tiferet, as you can see, is the exact center of the Tree. And since we're dealing with a system in which balance and symmetry are so important, you can well understand why Tiferet is called beauty. It is perhaps the most beloved of the sefirot. It is the place where all of the brilliant energies from the higher sefirot and all of the dark energies—the good, rich nutrients of earth that move upward through the Tree—meet. Here soul and body, self and ego, higher consciousness and personality come together. The angels can't come down this far because they are disincarnate, and the animals can't come up this far because they lack the necessary conscious awareness. Tiferet, associated astrologically with the Sun and with the heart chakra, is the place of our humanity.

It is also the place of the Messiah. It represents Mount Sinai where, after forty years of wandering, the man Moses climbed to the summit of the mountain. God, satisfied that Moses had come as far as he could, descended as far as was needed for Torah to be given.

Tiferet is also referred to as the place of the sacrificed god. In the Christian religion, it is often called the place of Christ consciousness. Because it was not enough, in the Christian system, for Jesus to say, "Gee, I really feel sorry for all those guys down there. I'd really like to save them. How about it, God?" It didn't work that way. Jesus had to come down into the world and sacrifice himself in order to save it.

God chose to make Himself incarnate in the person of Jesus so that He could experience what it is to be in a body, what it feels like to wear a crown of thorns, to be crucified, to have one's side pierced. He had to know from within a body the rage of righteousness, the stench of a leper colony, the loneliness of Gethsemane.

Tiferet is the descent of the divine into the realm of the human, which we see in all mythologies. Orpheus was the love of Euridice, who was tempted down into the underworld by Hades, the god of that realm. Orpheus couldn't call her from a safe place above the earth: "Hey, Euridice, come on back!" He had to go down into hell to get her. He had to place himself in danger in order to save her.

Tiferet is the place of the wounded healer, a concept on which all the twelve-step programs—AA, Narcanon, Overeaters Anonymous, for example—are based. You've got to have been there to help somebody who's there now. You can't do it from a detached place. You can't do it from a safe place.

If I get up in front of an AA meeting and say, "Well, look, I've never had a problem with alcohol, but I'd like to tell you what I think about drinking," I'm going to be booed right out of there, as well I should be. Nobody cares what I think. What do I know? What could I know?

Tiferet is the place of the *Bodhisattva,* the one who has achieved *nirvana* and returned in order to help those who have not yet reached that place of peace. It is the place of the guru. It's the place of the one who, through the loving heart, brings human experience to the help of others.

Finally, Tiferet is the place of paradoxes. It is the place where life is death and death is life. If we cling to life—the life of the ego and the life of our conscious minds—that spells our death. What do we do then, when consciousness comes to an end? We lie in a coffin. Clinging to that kind of life, that ego, that everyday, conscious life, is our death. But death is life. If we're willing to make the sacrifice of ego consciousness, then we like Jesus will have life everlasting.

Tiferet, as we can see, is a complicated and marvelous place, the place of perfect balance of spirit and matter. It gives a new meaning to the phrase so popular these days, "Get centered." Tiferet offers us the best way to get centered.

Now we move from Tiferet to *Netzach,* and in so doing, leave the olam of Beriah, the realm of creation, and enter *Yetzirah,* the olam of formation. We're back on the male, energetic side of the Tree. Netzach means "victory" and represents feeling, emotion, and the flow of energy. It is associated with the top of the right hip and the planet Venus. Every relationship, every creative project, every undertaking is energized by Netzach.

We move from Netzach to the eighth sefirah on the Tree, called *Hod.* What would you think we would need to balance all the feeling, all of the emotion from Netzach? Hod refers to that much maligned part of us called the logical, thinking mind.

Now the mind has gotten a bad rap, I think, because people are aware of the problems it can cause when we use it to the exclusion of other parts of ourselves. The mind, as we all know, makes a fine servant but a poor master. We don't want the logical part of us making all our decisions and running our lives. But we certainly want clarity when we're working through issues, analyzing, solving problems.

I don't want to be in my logical, thinking mind when I'm listening to Brahms or the sounds of the waves on the shore. But I don't want to be in my ecstatic mind when I'm analyzing my finances. And I certainly don't want to be in my mystical state when I'm preparing a lecture. When we're trying to communicate, we need our logical minds. Hod means "glory," or "splendor"—which in itself provides insight into mystical Jewish values. The crowning glory and the splendor of the human being is Hod, the mind.

Hod is both the principle and the function of intellect, and it can involve us in deceit, intrigue, illusion, and skepticism. There is that negative side to Hod. But those problems arise for us when? When we get out of balance! There's a reason why Hod is balanced by Netzach just as there is a reason why Netzach is balanced by Hod. We need both. If we cut ourselves off from our intuition and emotion, we can get involved in illusion, obsession, and deceit. These can occur when the mind doubles back on itself. But if we keep the mind in balance, then it becomes a wonderful servant.

Hod is associated with the planet Mercury, the quick mercurial communicator of the gods. Mercury, the Roman equivalent of Hermes, was the messenger of the gods. In terms of our bodies, Hod is associated with the top of the left hip. The tops of the right and left hips, represented by Netzach and Hod, come together at the place of the solar plexus.

Now we move to the final sefirah in the olam of Yetzirah or formation, *Yesod.* Yesod is called "the foundation," and it is associated with the unconscious. What a good name for the unconscious: the foundation. There's a great deal of psychological truth to that. What we believe, not in the fancy front part of our minds but deep, deep in our unconscious, is what our lives will express. What we hold unconsciously is what will manifest in our lives and what will prove to be the foundation of our lives. I may drive a Rolls Royce and wear designer clothes and live in a mansion in a swanky part of town, but deep inside myself I may not feel very good. I may feel that I'm not very bright, or not so good looking, or not as accomplished as my brother, or whatever. If in my unconscious I feel unworthy, my life will manifest that belief, and sooner or later I'll crack up the Rolls Royce, lose the house, and destroy every good relationship. I'll find a way to squirrel every career opportunity. If I believe deep in my unconscious that I'm no good, that I don't deserve good things, I will find a way to be unhappy all my life. There are people who go through grieving periods, through terrible trials, but within themselves have a sense of their own goodness. Their foundation is positive and strong, happy and joyful, and that is what their lives manifest. Such people are resilient because they know they deserve good things—abundance and success.

You know, it's really interesting. When I worked in the advertising industry, I sometimes dealt with people who had learned all the new feminist jargon. They would never refer to their secretaries as "girls" and would always be careful to say "Ms." rather than "Miss" or "Mrs." But fundamentally they were sexists in their hearts, and you could feel it and see it in the way they treated people.

Again, on the surface, I may not approve of anger and have no conscious awareness of my anger. But if unconsciously I am filled with rage, am I going to come across as a loving person? Probably not! I may say the right things, but I'll say them through gritted teeth. What we have in our unconscious is the foundation that will manifest in our lives. It's as simple as that.

Yesod represents our instinct. It is below the place of Hod, intellect. It represents our libido, our desires, and our intuition. Some of you crafty people have already figured out that in the astrological system it would be related to the Moon. It is associated in the chakra system with the axis between the base of the spine and the genitals. There's a reason why we need to combine these, because the final sefirah, *Malchut,* represents a departure from the chakra system which I think many of you will find fascinating.

Malchut is the tenth of the sefirot, and it means "the kingdom." It is associated with the planet Earth, this planet on which we live. It is the material, the incarnate. Malchut is the only sefirah in the olam of Assiyah, the world of action. And Malchut, in terms of the body, refers to the soles of the feet. Why? Because without our feet, as Kabbalist Stephan Hoeller says, we aren't going anywhere. Without our feet, there is no action.

Here we have an area in which Kabbalistic thinking markedly departs from the Eastern systems. Kabbalistically, the planet Earth, the real world as we know it, the incarnate material world, is not *maya.* It is not illusion. It is not a distraction. It is extremely important. That is why it is called the kingdom.

We are not here only to sit cross-legged and chant and meditate. Part of the time, sure, but not all of the time. Part of the time we're meant to get out there and do something, make things happen.

Judaism traditionally raises the question, "How are we to live in the presence of God?" I know how I used to behave when I was a school teacher and the principal came to visit the classroom. I know how I used to behave when I was selling advertising space for magazines and my publisher would come out from New York. I wanted to be prompt, look my best, and make sure that my appointments were all lined up properly. He was just a publisher. But God is *God,* and He's *always* in town. How are we to live in the presence of God? The traditional Jewish answer is threefold: prayer, study, and good works. Where do we pray? We pray in Malchut. Where do we study? We study in Malchut. And where do we perform good works? Where is the only place in which it's possible to do good? Malchut! This planet Earth, where we are right now.

Now we can reraise the question of why, among the four olams (the world of emanation, the world of creation, the world of formation, and the world of action), is there only one sefirah in the world of action? The answer is, because it is so important. I would go so far as to say that the first nine sefirot are like the first nine months of a being's life—gestation. Pregnancy is meant to be followed by birth. Anything which does not find its way past the first nine sefirot is stillborn. Whatever the potential is, whatever the power is, if it doesn't find expression in this world, on this Earth, who profits by it?

There is work to be done in this world. There are homeless people who need to be sheltered. There are hungry people who need to be fed. There are scientific discoveries crying out to be made. Somebody's got to find a cure for AIDS; somebody's got to find a cure for cancer. We need energy sources that will protect our planet, ways to ease drought, famine, and poverty.

These gifts are not going to be carried by a choir of angels descending upon us, singing "Glory, Glory, Glory, God Almighty!" They will be provided by scientists working in their labs so long that they are a little "pitty," people who need a shower so badly that you wouldn't want to socialize with them. People obsessed by their work. It's all going to happen right here on planet Earth with all of its limitations, created by human beings with all of our limitations, and with our feet, like the roots of the Kabbalistic Tree, in the earth. Malchut may be the densest sefirah, through which the light has the most trouble passing, but it is also the strongest. It's where the work of the world gets done.

And it is so important, this world of ours, that it has an olam entirely to itself.

It is our hope in these studies not to find a particular spot on the Tree with which we particularly identify and say, "This where I want to be. This is where I am going to stay. This is the best place, and I've now achieved it. I'm never leaving." We don't say this because we can't. That's not the way the universe functions, and that's not the way life is. We know that from our personal experiences. How many of us have reached a point over and over and over again where we feel that we have finally learned the truth, or we have finally worked out the relationship, or we have finally decided on the most rewarding way to spend our time—just before everything changes? Wherever we are, however desirable and long sought the place, if we are standing with our knees locked, we will fall over because the universe is not static. The universe is always in motion. What we need to do is keep the weight on the balls of our feet so that whatever it is the universe offers us, we are in a position to respond to it. And sometimes that requires being in a severe place, or being in a painful place on the Tree and in our lives.

This constitutes the Kabbalistic Tree of Life. As we turn our attention to the Tarot, we can only be amazed at the ways in which these two totally distinct and disparate systems of thought converge, leading us to a single great teaching.

For a start, we must be struck by the fact that there are ten sefirot on the Tree of Life and ten *pip,* or numbered cards, in each suit of the Tarot. This numerical association alone invites us to connect the ace through ten of each suit with the sefirah corresponding to its number. Keter, as the first sefirah on the Tree, corresponds to the aces, for example, while the fifth sefirah, Gevurah, lays claim to the fives, Hod to the eights, and so on. We will find as we explore these connections card by card that the associations do not seem to be those of chance. Rather, there seems to be an intentionality, a rightness, even a clear fit in some cases between the sefirah and card that share the same number.

This synchronicity, in Jungian terms, benefits the student of Tarot in a number of ways. First, it separates the forty pip cards from the sixteen court cards, making each more conceptually manageable. Instead of being accosted by fifty-six random images to memorize, we begin with forty that break neatly into four groups of ten. Ten cards numbered one through ten, each of which seems to have a sefirah governing it, is a reader-friendly proposition compared to fifty-six disorganized images clamoring for our attention.

SEFIRAH	CARD	ASSOCIATION	BODY PART	CHAKRA
Keter	Ace	Entire Cosmos	Crown of Head	Crown
Chochma	Two	All 12 signs of zodiac	Right Temple	Third Eye
Binah	Three	Saturn	Left Temple	
Chesed	Four	Jupiter	Right Shoulder	Throat
Gevurah	Five	Mars	Left Shoulder	
Tiferet	Six	Sun	Heart	Heart
Netzach	Seven	Venus	Top of Right Hip	Solar Plexis
Hod	Eight	Mercury	Top of Left Hip	
Yesod	Nine	Moon	Axis between base of spine & genitals	Base and sexual
Malchut	Ten	Earth	Soles of Feet	

In assigning the pip cards to the sefirot of the Tree of Life, we introduce a further suggestion that facilitates both understanding and remembering the cards. The implication is that similarly numbered cards of each suit have something in common. And, indeed, what they share is their association with one of the ten sefirot and the distinctive character of that sefirah. If we have understood what the energy of Chesed is, for example, in assigning the fours of each suit to that sefirah, we can say, "Look at the image of the Four of Cups. How does what I know about Chesed color my perception of that card? Can I detect the quality of that vessel in the Four of Wands? How does it help me to understand the Four of Swords? How does the nature of Chesed challenge my initial impression of the Four of Pentacles?"

The appropriateness of the match between sefirah and Minor Arcanum is more powerful in some cases than in others, or at least more obvious. The coincidence of sefirot and pips challenges us to seek meaning and connection, to grasp why the image of the Four of Cups and that of the Four of Wands belong to Chesed, to find what, in essence, they share. Even at its most arcane, the connection between the sefirah and the cards that belong to it by virtue of their numbers is worth pursuing and exploring.

The sixteen court cards also break into four clear groups: kings, queens, knights, and pages. Once again, we are confronted with a numerical correspondence in the Tree of Life, this time with the four olams or worlds. Understanding the nature of each world will inform our understanding of each set of court cards. Again, seeing what the pages of each suit have in common, how they are manifestations of the olam that they all share, enables us to remember them more easily.

The process is reciprocal. The nebulous flavor of the sefirah or olam is rendered intelligible when we see, in the image of a Minor Arcanum, a palpable expression of it. Conversely, we find deeper meaning in the cards as we come to understand how they are characterized by the sefirot and olams of the Tree of Life to which they are assigned. (That there should be twenty-two Major Arcana in the Tarot and twenty-two paths connecting the sefirot of the Tree of Life is the final mysterious connection between the two symbologies. The discussion of that subject, however, is beyond the scope of this work and is reserved for another time.)

CHAPTER 3
Pentacles: The Soul of Bread

*T*HE SUIT OF Pentacles, as the alert reader may recall from my introduction, is my favorite suit of the Tarot. Like the sefirah of Malchut, the lowermost sefirah on the Tree of Life, it has to do with things incarnate and material: health, money, career, sensuality, work, home, cars, maintenance, clothes—anything observable by other people as opposed to anything that is going on within ourselves.

Ideally, we would not have a favorite suit. If we could, we would relate to every card of the deck with equal energy because they are all equally important. All of the suits have value. However, anybody who tells you that they relate to every card with equal energy probably lies about other things, too. We are on this earth to work through our imbalances. That's what we are doing on this earth plane. If we already had it totally together and totally integrated and totally in balance, what would we be doing here? We would be on the plane of angels. We are here because humans alone, of all God's creations, can improve, and we are here to improve. One of the ways in which we make improvements is by learning the most appropriate, the best responses to whatever the universe offers us. And the way in which we achieve that point of development is by getting ourselves in balance.

The pentacle, you will recall, is made up of two parts: the pentagram, which is a five-pointed star, and the coin that surrounds the pentagram. For those of us who can picture the Leonardo cartoon of a man circumscribed in a circle, we can see how easily the pentagram represents that figure. We see here the body and the soul. The soul is star stuff. That is what we are. That is what we are made of. And the coin is the body that houses it.

The challenge of Pentacles is the challenge of always remembering that, whatever the body, there's a star inside. There's a soul inside. Whether it's a bird or a flower or a rock, there's divine energy within. The challenge is not to get caught up in the externals of things. This is very much the message of *The Little Prince* by Saint-Exupery: always see with eyes of the heart.

If we recollect a cardinal lesson of Kabbalah, that creation is the result of divine emanation into the ten sefirot, or vessels, of the Tree of Life, we can see the pentacle in a new light. The coins—our outward forms—may be different, but the star stuff is the same within each of us. As Ram Dass says, "Only the packaging is different. You look into the eyes of another being—you see another being looking out at you. 'Wow! How'd you get in that one?'" I particularly like Ram Dass's choice of the word *being* rather than *person*. It reminds me of what may be my favorite line from any movie. Rocky, in the first film of the saga, turns to his wife and says of his dog something like, "You know, sometimes when I look at him, he doesn't look like a dog to me." Many of us who have deeply loved animals have had that experience— seeing in their eyes the divine spark, feeling the shared creaturehood, rather than fixating on the body and seeing the difference of species. Seeing, in fact, the One manifesting as many.

We have suggested that for balance we need all four functions of consciousness, all four suits of the Minor Arcana. Each involves a way to spirit and an obstacle to spiritual growth. What, then, is the way of Pentacles? It is twofold. One is the way of gratitude and appreciation.

At some time in a college dormitory, at the age of nineteen, many of us had heated discussions until four in the morning regarding whether a tree falling in the forest makes a sound if there is no ear to hear it. What is much more interesting to me now is whether a tree blooming in the city was created in vain if people pass by but don't notice it. If there is the sound of a bird, if there is anything wonderful in the world—a sunset, a pebble, an animal ranging through the grasslands, whatever it is that turns you on—if we are there, but do not relate to it in any way, is that wonder of natural beauty created in vain? And does it bring God sorrow?

Blessings are being showered upon us uninterruptedly. The Suit of Pentacles is the suit through which we can appreciate what we have been given. It is easy to get used to blessings and to take them for granted, and it is easy to fixate on things that are wrong. (I speak from experience.) It's so easy to pick, pick, pick at the things that aren't right and accept without acknowledgment the most important things. Anyone reading this book can count on waking up in the morning, opening their eyes and seeing—that's a blessing. Anyone turning these pages doesn't need someone to dress them because they're paralyzed. Yet how many of us awaken to the day exclaiming, "Not one nerve in my entire body hurts!" How often do we rejoice at the miracle of our daily lives? Only the first day after a three-week bout with the flu do we experience the wonder of feeling normal. Otherwise, we think *perfection* is normal.

We're not entitled to healthy bodies. They are gifts. Yet we are so focused on the things we "need" in order to feel we are getting "enough" that we either overlook, or think there is nothing very special about the fact that all of our senses work, our muscles work. We take for granted that we can interrelate with people and make a new start if we don't like what we have been doing. We can function in the world.

In the Jewish tradition, we are enjoined to say one hundred *baruchas,* or blessings, a day. God doesn't need that; we need that. When we say a blessing, it puts us in touch with the good things in life.

The first blessing of the day is for elimination. At first, this may seem too trivial a subject for prayer. At best, it may seem comical; at worst, blasphemous. *Pray* in the *bathroom?* Let's just keep religion out of the toilet, shall we? But on reflection, why not? It's the first thing we all do on awakening—let's start the day off right! And no one hesitates to say, "Thank God!" after surgery when elimination first occurs naturally and the dread catheter is removed. Yet the process—the miracle of the system of elimination—is the same. Only our attitude toward it has changed.

We have said that, Kabbalistically, human beings are the crown of creation, because we alone can receive God's gifts with conscious awareness. We alone can sanctify the creation and with our blessings make the mundane holy. By our blessings, our baruchas, we make the world *kadosh,* holy. If we thank God for the good feeling of the sun on our backs, for the sound of the breeze, for the smile in a friend's eyes, we become *aware* of it. I am reminded of my first trip to Chicago, a city I loved on sight. On a public bus I found myself sitting across from a woman whose demeanor radiated good spirits. Although clearly of advanced years, her twinkling blue eyes were clear and alert. Everything about her proclaimed vitality and joy, right down to the white hair bouncing out from under her woolen winter cap and the way she held her cane. I couldn't resist speaking to her, so I said, "Excuse me, but you seem to be such a happy person, I have to ask, 'What is your secret?'" She replied simply, her laughing eyes animating her smile, "I've always been a grateful person." At the next stop, still smiling, she limped off the bus, looking expectant and enthusiastic as she entered a shoe-repair shop.

The blessing is the shift of focus onto our gifts. And we must all agree that the happiest people we've ever met are not the ones who have the most, but the ones who appreciate the most.

A couple of months before my marriage fell apart, I was on vacation with my family. It was a dream vacation. We had just finished almost two years in England where my husband had been working for the London office of his company, and if we wanted to get away for the weekend we could go to Paris, or if it were a three-day weekend we could make it to Copenhagen. I had gone from teaching seven days a week to not being able to get a Green Card. I had no choice but to go to museums and parks and theaters all day. It was terrific! It was a great life and the marriage was ready to be flushed. As if those two years abroad weren't wonderful enough, we then bought an English camper and screwed the big square wooden canary's cage to the back wall and loaded on our two mongrel dogs and our little daughter and traveled for six months all over Europe. We had our transportation, we had our food, we had our accommodations; nothing could touch us! We literally turned where we saw a rainbow. My husband had his trip, and I had my trip, and we were very unhappy and lonely.

I can remember driving along a road in Italy just as the sun was going down and seeing some women returning from the fields where they had been harvesting grapes. Backbreaking work all day in the hot sun of August. Their arms were around each other's waists, and they were singing. And I was jealous, because whatever it was they had, they were capable of really appreciating it and enjoying it. They would have changed places with me in a minute, and they would have been stupid to do it, because I was unhappy and they were happy. It's not what we *have* in the external world, it's how we *experience* it. That happens within the Suit of Pentacles. It happens in Malchut.

Malchut is called the kingdom. What is it that turns the earth plane, with its innumerable woes, into the home of kings? Why is it Malchut that is "fit for a king" rather than Keter, the topmost sefirah of the Tree? Malchut, like the Suit of Pentacles, offers us the opportunity for blessing. When we recognize all we have been given in this life, our gratitude makes Malchut a kingdom. And our power to transform it, by blessing it, makes us monarchs in return.

The other aspect of the Suit of Pentacles that makes it so precious is that, as we have suggested, it is the only place where we can be of service. We can take these bodies of ours, these brains of ours, these hands of ours with opposable thumbs, these mouths of ours that have the gift of speech, and our imaginations and dreams and creativity, and we can do something with them that benefits other people. What a great feeling! So the second part of the way to spirit for the Suit of Pentacles is service.

I couldn't wait to get out of advertising. I was making a lot of money, and I had an interesting expense account: If I didn't send Dom Perignon to someone who got a promotion, home office would say, "No wonder she didn't get the business. She wasn't treating her clients right." It was my job to go to restaurants where lunch for two was a hundred dollars. But I kept thinking back to the days when I was a high-school teacher. I had to be at work by 7:45 A.M. and grade papers all night. I had felt then that I was imparting something to young people who were vital, vulnerable, and receptive. And I thought to myself, "If the entire advertising industry slipped from the face of the earth, what would be lost? Who would be the loser?"

Anyone on a spiritual path wants to be of use, but few recognize how many and simple the opportunities are. A *Chasid* (devout Jew) once asked his *rebbe,* "How can I best serve God?", expecting an esoteric reply. But the rabbi responded, "With whatever you are doing at the moment." This little story introduces the notion which in Hebrew is called *kavanah,* or intention. When we cultivate an attitude of appreciation, an awareness of our oneness with others, a desire to sanctify, to make kadosh all that we encounter and perform, our intention is holy, and the opportunities for service reveal themselves.

Martin Buber, in his great work *I and Thou,* distinguishes between the I-Thou and the I-it relationship. In the former, we address the soul of another from the place of our own soul. We see another as a sister star, not merely a coin. In an I-it relationship, our focus is on the coin: This is a washing machine; it cleans my clothes. This is an answering machine; it delivers my messages. This is a waitress; it brings my food. On an elevator, in our cars, at the checkout register in a market, the opportunities and challenges abound. We can experience impediments and express impatience—or we can look into the eyes of another being looking out at us. We can hold the "Door Open" button, create a space for the car waiting at the stop sign, and ask, "How long have you been on your feet? Off tomorrow? Hope the weather holds up for you." As the Zen Buddhists teach, "Before enlightenment, chop wood, carry water. After enlightenment, chop wood, carry water." The shift is internal—to kavanah, to making kadosh, to appreciation and awareness of our oneness. The shift is from I-it to I-Thou, from coin to star. The Suit of Pentacles teaches us that we don't have to withdraw to a religious place to experience life spiritually, that spirit can manifest in the here and now.

Being of service is so important to us that we had to leave the Garden of Eden! It is why we had to ask God to withdraw some of the energy He sent forth into the Tree of Life so that we too could make a contribution. And it is in the Suit of Pentacles and the realm of Malchut that the contribution is made. However, we must now turn our attention to the problem of Pentacles.

The flaw of the Suit of Pentacles, the obstacle to spiritual growth inherent in the suit, is forgetting that there is a star in every coin. We can grow greedy and selfish; we can get caught up in superficiality and form. How many relationships fail because what is loved is the coin rather than the star? F. Scott Fitzgerald depicts the misery and tragedy that must follow when we love only the material form of another.

It is staggering to recognize how many people well out of their teens continue to choose the mate who will impress others. The aging man who wants the young beauty on his arm, the one who turns every head and makes him "the envy of every man in the place." The young beauty who chooses the aging gentleman, not for his wisdom or kindness, but for his new Mercedes and the expensive gifts he showers upon her. The small child, an embarrassment to her mother because she stutters or limps, who is left alone with her loneliness. Is the best job opportunity always the one that pays the most? Is the best companion the one who can afford to travel with us in the style to which we are accustomed?

I used to think the women in Los Angeles were a breed apart: on any beach on any day in summer, all the bikini-clad bodies were Amazonian, goddesslike, toned and beautiful. How, I wondered, could all the women in this huge city achieve such perfection? One day the answer occurred to me. Not all Angelinas are Venusian, but the imperfect ones don't come to the beach. Don't dare. They forego the joys of sea and sand, wind and sun, because the bodies housing their responsive souls are not trim and golden.

We will see how both way and obstacle to spirit manifest in the cards of the suit.

Ace of Pentacles

It certainly makes sense that the aces belong to Keter. Keter is the topmost sefirah of the Tree, the point of entry for original energy. It is the first sefirah on the central pillar, the Pillar of Harmony, the pillar in which mercy and severity find perfect balance. Keter means "crown"; if we view this Tree as representing the human being, it is the place where divine energy moves into the crown chakra.

We see a picture of something very similar in the Tarot. We see a larger-than-life hand, which is the hand of God, coming out of the heavens through a cloud, shining in a halo of white light. And what is it doing? It's bringing something into the world, a gift. If Kabbalah means "receiving," here is the first gift we are to receive. And the gift of the Suit of Pentacles is the gift of incarnation and materiality.

What is the first gift we receive from the hand of God, pictured in the Ace of Pentacles? What is the first gift God gave to the first humans, Adam and Eve? The gift is the Garden of Eden, and the garden in the Ace of Pentacles, replete with red roses and white lilies, certainly suggests this. The gift of the palpable comes to full flower in Malchut, the earth plane, but its inception comes to us through the earthy aspect of the hand of God, the Ace of Pentacles. From the swirling nebulae of Keter, the chaos of the entire universe, the hand of God emerges to create the world and the first garden.

We begin with this wonderful gift! We get to be on this earth, where green grass grows and blue water flows and stars shine at night. And the message and the challenge of the Ace is to know when to pass through the mystical arch out of a garden, a sequestered place—perhaps the garden of Eden, perhaps our own little home environment—to the stark, high, snowy mountain peaks, unsoftened by verdure, which represent the pinnacle of pure truth. (Mountains throughout the Tarot refer to reaching a higher level of unadorned truth, facing the objective truth.)

The path that leads out fortunately also leads in. The Ace gives us the gift of knowing that we can venture forth and then retreat to a place of safety and comfort. We can move out with courage and confidence knowing that we have a place to which we can return.

Rounded archways are mystical. Many of us, I think, have had the experience of passing through an arch and feeling that we have entered a different level of consciousness. It's one of the reasons that Romanesque cathedrals have always been more spiritually moving to some of us than Gothic ones whose arches are vaulted. On Pacific Coast Highway in Los Angeles as you drive north to Malibu, you come through a dark tunnel and suddenly find you are out in the light, seeing the shining waters of the Pacific Ocean. At the right time of day, the light on the water is blinding. It is as if you have transcended to another level of being. What is suggested in the Ace is that when we move out of our garden of familiarity and habit, we move to a place of higher understanding.

Two of Pentacles

When we look at the Two, which is Chochma, the supernal father, and the right temple, we are reminded that Pentacles have to do with the earth. The farther down the Tree we move, the closer to earth Pentacles come, the more comfortable the energies seem to be. (When we look at the Suit of Wands we will find the reverse. Wands, being airy and refined in their nature, grow increasingly troubled as we move down toward the earth.) But up here, in the supernal triangle, the top three vessels of the Tree of Life, we see that the Two of Pentacles is an uneasy figure. If we recall that the number-two sefirah is the place of relatedness, this becomes even clearer. In a relationship, what is harder to balance than material resources? What causes more difficulties than the sharing of funds, financial responsibilities, physical space, and privacy issues? The divorce of two lovely people who can no longer live together may be perfectly amicable until it comes to the division of the property. The boundlessness of Keter has given way to the zodiac, the infinite is now the finite number twelve. Allocation of resources is suddenly necessary.

What are we to make of this Two of Pentacles? What we see in the image is a somewhat foolish-looking young man with an absurd hat. He is out of balance; he is trying to juggle and not doing a very good job of it. Maybe he's trying to figure out how to pay Peter without borrowing from Paul. There is a turbulent sea behind him. The ship looks as if it might capsize. And he is dancing as fast as he can just trying to keep it together.

Obviously this is not a place any of us would choose to be. It's the card of ambivalence, of disorganization, of not having things in balance. The image suggests not knowing which foot our weight is on. Do we want to stay in or get out of this job, situation, relationship? Interestingly, the pentacles are held loosely within what looks like a figure eight of green yarn. What this is, in disguise, is a figure called the *Holy Lemniscate*, the infinity symbol that appears, among other places, above the head of the Magician, the powerful number-one card of the Major Arcana. In that card, the Holy Lemniscate appears firm and taut. What it represents is the eternal balance of opposites and the creative energy that moves back and forth between dark and light, male and female, positive and negative, odd and even, Eastern and Western. It's a dynamic, challenging force that invites creative approaches to the resolution of opposites. By its shape, it represents an energy that never dissipates but which cycles back and forth forever.

So why is the Holy Lemniscate we see in the Two of Pentacles so slack and useless? Because the figure is interfering with it! The message is "Get your hands out of the way! Let the universe work!" Part of the meaning of this card is, "Have a little more faith in the universe. You do not have to do it all. You are not personally responsible for the law of gravity. Things will fall where they're supposed to fall without your help."

This can be a card of confused sexual identity or of bisexuality, if the person is uneasy with being bisexual. The card can represent any kind of confusion and the acute discomfort ambivalence brings.

The Two of Pentacles is the first of what I will call the separation cards. Unlike the figures in most of the Minor Arcana, the figure in the Two is not pictured in the landscape, but on a stage before it. He has literally separated himself from the action. Although it might seem necessary that the card be drawn this way since no one can stand juggling in a raging sea, we will see many other images in the Tarot involving the critical meeting place of water and land that reflect integration and union rather than clear-cut demarcation. Further, the platform on which the figure is standing is not drawn to suggest a boardwalk, much less a beach. It is clearly the artist's intention to show an abstracted stage, so we must ask why. What is she conveying here?

It seems to me that the separation represented in the Two of Pentacles is more than just physical. It is not that the figure merely happens to be set apart from the sea. The isolation feels existential, a deep truth about the very existence of the juggler. Sensing the danger of the rolling waves (being overwhelmed by debt, unable to solve the problems of some imbalance of his life) he does not ask the relevant questions: "Why is this happening? How am I responsible?" and "What am I to learn from this?" His response is consistently inappropriate. First, he separates his being from the perceived danger and his feelings about that danger. Second, his mitts are in the midst of the Holy Lemniscate: he exacerbates his difficulties, perseverating in obsessive, nonproductive behavior. He can juggle them from left to right; he can juggle them from right to left. There they still are—two, but only two, pentacles. Could this be why he is wearing a dunce cap?

Interestingly, an important principle of the Tarot in general comes across in the Two of Pentacles. From a Jungian view, each of us has everything pictured in the entire Tarot deck within us. In addition, every card represents polarized extremes. This is why it is very difficult to say that a card is a good card or a bad card. Each card, properly understood, is both.

Let's talk about this principle in relation to the Two of Pentacles. How can ambivalence possibly be positive? Ever? The answer is that sometimes the best thing we can do is stay confused and stay off balance. Because this condition is so uncomfortable, we often move out of that state just to be out of it. We'll make any decision at all, just to avoid being with our ambivalence, just to be free from the discomfort. That's always a mistake, even if the decision happens to be a good one.

When we're in a place that is ambivalent and uncomfortable, we are in a place of enormous growth potential. Inertia is the enemy of growth. Comfort, uninterrupted, is the enemy of growth. If we are not thrown a little off balance from time to time, what is going to move us to the next level of understanding? What is going to motivate us? When we are uneasy, if we can stay with it long enough to hear the sound of our own higher self—higher consciousness, soul, spirit, divine energy, whatever we want to call it—then and only then growth can occur.

There are people, for example, and we've all known some, who move from one relationship to the next. Sometimes they don't even move out of one relationship until they have another one in place. They find it too painful to close the door at night and hear no sounds except their own and to know that they are truly alone. Some people find that experience so frightening that instead of staying with it and exploring why being alone is so threatening, they move immediately to a more comfortable place. Nothing is learned, nothing is gained, nothing has changed, which is why second and third marriages often last less and less long. It's not unusual for a first marriage to last ten years, a second four years, and a third six months. But when we are willing to stay uncomfortable, off balance, not in control of the situation, we can learn something about ourselves and not continue replicating our mistakes. This growth can fairly be called wisdom, which is what Chochma means. On the earth plane, which Pentacles represent, our wisdom often comes to us at the price of our ease.

Three of Pentacles

We move to the Three of Pentacles and to Binah, the supernal mother. The Three of Pentacles, like all threes, is very magical: the union of opposites to bring forth something new. We have male and we have female, and when we bring them together, we bring forth a child. That child is half its father, half its mother, and at the same time uniquely and distinctly itself. This is magical, mysterious, beyond explanation. So the Three always represents that which comes forth from the dynamic interchange of opposites that is more than either of the two by itself. The whole is greater than the sum of its parts. It represents a step forward in growth: the synthesis in the Hegelian formula of thesis and antithesis coming together to form a synthesis (which is also a new thesis). Further, we shall find that the threes of the Minor Arcana always represent the fulfillment of the suit.

What we have in the Three of Pentacles is a wonderful image of being of service in the world. Kahlil Gibran tells us that work is love made visible. In the Three of Pentacles, we have someone who is working in the world—a sculptor, an artist. As he is working in a cathedral, the spiritual symbolism is explicit. Furthermore, he is standing on a bench that literally elevates work, raising it to a higher level. The artisan is not alone. The remaining two figures are representatives of the clergy and the court. Clearly, the orientations and values of the three must be different and perhaps at odds. The interest of the artist is purely aesthetic and of the priest, religious—is the work in keeping with church doctrine? The perspective of the court may be the aggrandizement of the monarch—will this cathedral be the finest in all the land? Or perhaps the concern is "How much is this going to cost the king?" (We must say it. He may be holding the blueprint or plan, but the guy is clearly a clown.) We have then a great challenge depicted in this card. For the first time in the Minor Arcana, there is the suggestion of community—relatedness, contact, communication. People are getting together and consulting as to the best way to do something that will be of benefit to all. It is, however, a situation fraught with great danger. If accommodation cannot be reached among the three, the great work goes undone. What is needed for the cathedral to be completed is the willingness of each to restrict the exercise of personal will and to discipline the ego for the sake of the greater good. Binah, we are reminded, is associated with Saturn, the planet of restriction and discipline. (As Binah refers to the left temple, it meets Chochma, the right temple, at the place of the third eye in the chakra system. A useful, if challenging, meditation would be to bring the images of the Two and Three of Pentacles together and release into what is revealed at this energy center.)

We find as well in the Three of Pentacles a specific symbol of the union of opposites. The three pentacles themselves form an upward-pointing triangle representing the "element" of fire, spirit, that which moves up and strives to attain higher planes of being. That is male energy. Below it we find a downward-pointing triangle suggesting water, that goes not higher, but deeper, deeper, deeper, to the deepest of mysteries, deepest of feelings, the depths of the unconscious. That is female energy. If we slide them to a point of overlap, we discover the Seal of Solomon, the Star of David—the incredible symbol of uniting polar opposites. Miraculously, the water does not put out the fire; the fire does not boil out the water. Instead, we have something new and therefore a symbol of totality, union, and oneness.

As always, the most profound meaning of the card relates to our internal growth. From a Jungian perspective, the three figures represent different facets of ourselves. Each of us has within a creative being, and each of us also has a part of ourselves concerned with protecting our spirituality and a part that is practical and worldly. As we seek our true work in the world, how are we to juggle, coordinate, resolve these three sides of ourselves? If I paint, can it be the pure vision of my fancy? Suppose what is expressed is dark, bizarre, or violent? Can the part of me that wants to serve God accept such work? And will it bring me fame and prestige? Will it sell well enough to pay the bills?

We have said that each card of the Tarot carries both a light and a dark possibility, a positive and a negative charge. (As Rachel Pollack says, the good cards are the ones that tell the truth.) The negative of the Three of Pentacles is the suggestion of interference. In that case, the demands of church and state prevent the artist's full expression—indicating not cooperation, but compromise. We all remember that a camel is a horse put together by a committee.

Finally, however, the Three of Pentacles is an inspiring card, a true three in fulfillment of the suit, and a card of genuine service in the world.

Four of Pentacles

Now we move to Chesed, loving-kindness, which is the fourth sefirah and the central vessel on the right-hand pillar. It is the place where we give and receive. This is another troubled energy in the Suit of Pentacles. Here we see a figure, once again isolated, clinging to a pentacle. He has two others trapped under his feet and a fourth balanced on his head. This is the guy with the brand new Jaguar. He can't drive it anywhere because someone might run into him on the freeway. He can't park it anywhere because someone might rip it off. He can't even take it to the supermarket because a careless person throwing open their door might scratch the new paint job. So he's got this new car, and what he can do with it is wax it every weekend. Wash it and wax it and polish it. So does he have it, or does it have him?

Not to be sexist, the Four of Pentacles is equally the woman who has the large diamond solitaire. She wouldn't dream of wearing it to work. That would risk arousing the envy of her coworkers, who have nothing so grand, and alienating her from the group. She certainly isn't going to wear it when she goes out in the evening to the theater; there could be someone in any public place whose purpose in being there is to scout for such treasure! (Then they follow you home, knock you over the head, and rip you off—unless of course you're on the subway or a bus, which saves them the time and trouble of following you home.) She can, to be sure, keep it in her night-table drawer, wear it at home, or simply look at it. After all, she didn't buy it to show off; she just loves looking at it for herself. But then she has to clean her own house—can't have a cleaning person poking around while you're at work, not with a two-karat diamond in the house. Unless you hide it. But you have to hide it really well. And remember where you hid it. (I have a cousin who hid a rope of pearls with an opal catch so well that she couldn't find it for three years!) Because you can't write it down—someone could find the paper. Finally, what she can do is wear it locally when she has dinner at the homes of wealthy friends. She just has to leave work early enough to get to the bank forty-five minutes before it closes so she can get to her safe-deposit box. Sometimes that's stressful—her boss calls an unexpected late meeting and traffic is heavy. Talk about having fun! Does she have it, this brilliant square-cut diamond, or does it have her?

The figure in the Four of Pentacles should listen more carefully to Gershwin's Porgy: "Got no car, I got no house, I got no misery! . . . The folks with plenty o' plenty" (as opposed to "plenty o' nothin'"), he sings, "got a lock on their door. 'Fraid somebody's a-goin' to rob them while they're out a-makin' more. What for?" The problem with the material world is that when we forget the star that is within the coin and we start clasping the material object for itself, *it* starts to own *us*. We know so many people, all of us, who are house poor. What's that all about? "I have this wonderful house. I love my home. Of course I can't afford to go anywhere or do anything because I couldn't make my house payments if I did. I haven't traveled or gone to the theater or bought any books or records in five years, but I did buy a new couch. I dust the piano three times a week." So do I have a wonderful home, or does this wonderful home have me?

The Four of Pentacles figure cannot move, cannot even move his head without losing what he has accumulated. What he has gotten for himself has cost him his expression, his freedom, his growth.

Let us remember the words God said to Moses before the burning bush: "Take off your shoes, for the ground on which you stand is holy." This is being said to each of us all the time. It is the same message: "Be aware of the star in the coin." Be aware of the holiness in the earth on which you stand. We are always in the presence of the burning bush, in the presence of God. Yet here we see a figure who has separated his feet from the holy ground with things. He has let the accumulation of material things come between him and his divine relationship with the creation. His crown chakra is covered; he's got a pentacle blocking it; nothing can come through. His heart chakra is covered; nothing can touch his heart, and he can express no feeling. In locking out the energy flow between chakras and the universe, he has isolated himself with the things he has garnered.

This separation is represented as well in the background of the Four of Pentacles. It is in fact the second of the separation cards. The immobilized figure, of service to no one, sits far from the city and therefore from potential danger. He has not retreated to the country, however, and the healing powers of nature. He has retreated from life.

The Four of Pentacles, then, is a card of rigidity, a card of overwhelming need for stability and security. Of course the approach of hanging on doesn't work. The crown and heart may be covered but the back remains exposed and vulnerable. You can make sure you have enough, in material terms, and you can guard your security in any way you like, but there is absolutely nothing to guarantee that you won't be struck by lightning, or that a phone call won't come at four in the morning, or that you won't be hit by a car while crossing the street. If our primary concern in life is retaining gifts, maintaining the status quo, we are out of harmony with the flow of the universe. Gifts are meant to be used, shared, imparted (the *Yetzer Ha-tov*, or impulse toward good). When we hold back what we have received for ourselves alone (*Yetzer Ha-rah*, evil impulse), we sacrifice ourselves to a goal that is both unworthy and unrealizable.

What good thing can we possibly say about the Four of Pentacles? Well, if you're somebody who has been bankrupt most of your life, somebody who can never manage to get the light bill and the gas bill paid in the same month, someone who lives from hand to mouth, this is a good start to getting yourself together. It's a move toward marshaling your resources, being aware that these resources aren't infinite, and taking responsibility for budgeting what you have. So for someone who has just come out of drug or alcohol detox, or for someone who has been unemployed for ten months and is heavily in debt, this is a terrific energy. Discipline! Control! Yeah, hold on tight!

The message of Chesed is simple: Tap into this energy when you need it, but don't get stuck there. Know when it's appropriate to use this energy and when it's appropriate to let go. Know how to receive and also how to give. There is another important lesson we learn from seeing the image of the Four of Pentacles in Chesed. It has to do with the question of "enoughness" with which we all deal throughout our lives. What is enough? When have I received enough? How do I know it is enough—enough love, enough money, enough security? Is my wardrobe fashionable enough? Are my grades good enough? Is my house high enough in the hills? Does he bring me flowers often enough? Does she spend enough time with me? Is he thoughtful enough? I remember my amazement in learning that people can be broke at different levels. If my cash outlay exceeds my cash income, I'm broke, even if that means I can't make the payments on my second house, my third car, and my daughter's finishing school education!

Many would say the figure in the Four of Pentacles has more than enough, four times what he needs. Clearly he doesn't feel he could do with any less, and if he has enough, it is barely so. We are reminded then that Chesed, bountiful as it is, linked to the expansive energy of Jupiter, is not on the central pillar of the Tree of Life. There is a reason that it is on the right-hand pillar, the Pillar of Mercy, and not the Pillar of Harmony. Chesed by itself leaves us out of balance. The right shoulder, arm, and hand of God, tenderly dispensing compassion, can well be taken for granted. Without the balancing force of Gevurah, we don't know what emptiness is and so cannot gauge how full we actually are. The young protagonist of Marjorie Kinnan Rawlings' *The Yearling* is always complaining of being hungry until his return from several days of self-imposed isolation in the woods. When asked later, "Are you hungry?" he replies to his mother, "I ain't never been hungry but once."

I am reminded, too, of an interesting complaint registered by a Swedish immigrant about the weather in Southern California: "In Sweden, there's so much rain and cold and snow, we wait for the sun to shine. Here it's always sunny—you can't even appreciate it!" He missed the miserable weather, not because he liked cold and rain, but because it was miserable. Without the austere force of Gevurah, the sweetness of Chesed seems normal—unremarkable—and for the Four of Pentacles, barely sufficient. When the universe isn't giving us enough, perhaps we should look more to ourselves than to the universe.

Five of Pentacles

We move next to Gevurah. Gevurah is the fifth sefirah and carries fiery Martian energy. It is the place of severity and judgment, the toughest place on the Tree, the place where infractions of karmic law are corrected. The fives of every suit are terrible in the truest sense of the word. It is not difficult to remember that they refer to the sefirah of Gevurah.

We find here one of the most profoundly important cards of the entire Suit of Pentacles, and from my perspective, the whole Tarot deck. It is a card that has many meanings. What we see on first glance are two ragged people, perhaps beggars, walking either barefoot or barely shod through the snow in a fierce storm, huddling for warmth inside their clothes, and not even in contact with one another. One is lame, as we see from his crutches, and a leper, as we see from his bell. Oddly, they are passing a cathedral. Why don't they go in? What are they doing out there in the cold and dark when there is a place of refuge, with light shining through the window, that is there for them? This has to be the first question that occurs to us.

One interpretation addresses organized religion. There's the cathedral; where's the door? How are people supposed to find their way to God when organized religion slams doors against them or, worse, doesn't build doors to their houses of worship? I read once for a client who had been raised in a household where the Christian virtues were held second in importance only to the eschewing of sin. At thirty-seven, beautiful, sensual, and vital, this woman was involved in her third marriage and still tormented by having experimented sexually as a teenager. She felt forever tainted and longed for God's forgiveness, but from the age of fifteen had been too ashamed ever to cross the threshold of a church. How terribly sad.

Another meaning, of course, is the experience that many of us have who don't follow an exoteric form of religion. There was a program on PBS in which religious fundamentalist ministers in Texas were telling Bill Moyers, who is a Christian and a Texan, that if he didn't believe every word of the Bible was the inspired word of God, he was no Christian. I made an instant decision to strike that town from my "must visit" travel list. I suddenly felt what it must be like to wake up some morning with a cross burned on your lawn because you're a Jew or a Christian who happens to think that the Bible is not the literal word of God. I was suddenly aware that, for example, when we read in the Bible, "Thou shalt not suffer a witch to live," God wasn't advocating the murder of bag ladies, Tarot card readers, people who talk to animals, or whatever someone decides constitutes a "witch."

Clearly, too, in the Five of Pentacles we are looking at an image of impoverishment. On the most literal level, this can be monetary. If this card shows up in a reading about troubled circumstances at work, you may have to prepare to hit the unemployment lines. The check you are expecting to cover your next rent payment may be delayed with the disastrous consequences of the homelessness depicted. But the impoverishment may be of a totally different kind—lack of mental stimulation, spiritual barrenness, or emotional isolation. Certainly the figures are friendless, unable even to touch one another.

There are many meanings to this card, then, but for me, the most profound meanings are always the ones that go deepest within. Not the extroverted ones but the most internalized ones. And what this card finally means is lack of self-worth. The reason the paupers do not go into the cathedral is that it doesn't occur to them that this beautiful place of refuge is for them. Maybe they think they can't go inside because they aren't rich enough. Maybe they think they can't go in because they aren't smart enough. Maybe they think they aren't good looking enough. Maybe they think they are of the wrong socioeconomic class or the wrong ethnic background or don't wear stylish-enough clothes. Maybe it's, "I can't go in there. I used to beat up my little brother every day when my parents weren't home. I don't belong in a house of God. I feel too guilty."

What's wrong with these people, thinking that they aren't good enough, in some way, to receive comfort? Are they crazy? If so, we're all crazy, because we all have some issue with self-worth, and most of the time we don't even know what it is. I'm too fat, I'm too thin, I'm too bald, I'm too hairy, I'm too old, I'm too young, I'm not intellectual, I intellectualize everything—whatever it is: I don't belong in there.

I spent my freshman year at Bryn Mawr College having come from a neighborhood in Brooklyn where 95 percent of us were Jewish. Suddenly I had friends with first names like Whitney and last names like Rockefeller. They were all excited about cotillion balls and coming-out parties. If I didn't feel like Cinderella, I don't know what Cinderella felt like. That was the Five-of-Pentacles place for me—the place of not even pressing my nose against the window to peek in at the debutantes.

But that cathedral is there for everyone. When we can bring to light what it is about ourselves that makes us feel we don't deserve to go into God's house, we can begin to deal with it. When we bring to consciousness whatever our own *mishigas* (our own craziness) is, we can begin to resolve it. We can find creative ways to work with our feelings about ourselves as worthy and our feelings about ourselves as worthless. None of us is a leper, unfit for human kindness and contact, and each of us is crippled in some way. An optimistic slant on the Five of Pentacles is that in circumstances of extreme adversity, the figures have not given up. They are not sitting passively in the snow, waiting to freeze to death. They are moving forward.

The dark force of Gevurah is the left hand of God, the hand with which He smites us. But we are not smitten out of cruelty, and the poverty we experience in our own lives is not gratuitous. Our material disadvantages, our ill health, our impoverished self-esteem are no less blessings than the generously bestowed gifts of Chesed. Less enjoyable, granted, but no less blessings. They are given to us as opportunities for psychological insight and spiritual growth. They are the painful offerings that enable us to correct infractions of karmic law and grow in compassion. They are no less for our ultimate good than the vaccinations that prevent smallpox and tuberculosis in our toddlers—and just about as enthusiastically welcomed. The left shoulder of

Gevurah and the right shoulder of Chesed meet at the throat chakra of communication. At a quiet time, hold the images of the Four and Five of Pentacles together in your mind and begin to speak. Allow what you perceive to find its true voice, whether it comes in words or sobs or screams or muffled whispers. Experience the jovial generosity of Chesed more fully for the Martian destruction of Gevurah.

When the Five of Pentacles turns up, take a good look at what in yourself you find most loathsome or shameful and find a way to forgive yourself. To love yourself. To accept yourself. Think of the person you love best in the world and ask yourself whether, if the problem, fault, or behavior was theirs, you would give them the heartless, harsh, unrelenting message you give yourself. Then determine never to say anything to yourself that you wouldn't say to the person you love most in the world.

Six of Pentacles

With the Six of Pentacles, we move to Tiferet, the place of the heart chakra. Here we find another card of enormous complexity in levels and depth of meaning. What we may see at first glance is a middle-class person who has achieved a degree of wealth holding a scale, distributing coins to two kneeling beggars. So we may first see this as a card of generosity—of sharing, fairness. The scales are nicely balanced. But at some point, we may ask the question, "How generous is giving that is done with a scale in hand?" If we measure and balance how much we give, have we lost the essence of giving? Isn't giving open-handed and full hearted at its core? Mother Teresa has said that true giving has to hurt a little bit. Her example is of a small child who once offered her a packet of sugar—the size we use in a cup of coffee—which was his allotment of sweets for the day. In giving it to her, he went without the delight of his day.

The next question that comes to mind is, "Who likes to receive down on their knees?" When this card turns up, one of the first questions to ask is, "Am I involved in a relationship in which there are energies of domination and submission, of superiority and genuflection? And if I am, with which of these three figures do I identify? Do I have all—or at least too much of the power? Do I have to get on my knees and beg in order to get what I need and want? Or is it even worse? Am I on my knees begging and not getting anything anyway?"

Whether it's a personal or professional relationship, it's essential to raise this question when the Six of Pentacles card comes up. I actually once read for a blissfully unselfconscious client who volunteered, on seeing this card, that he "only hires emotional cripples" so that he can control them easily. In less extreme cases, it can represent the doling out of time, affection, attention, or sex—or pleading for any of these, possibly without success. "You look great," "I love you," and "I missed you" all lose their sweetness if they are responses to "How do I look?" "Do you love me?" and "Did you miss me?" If we have to ask, the giving is at best blemished. Sometimes, however, we suffer the humiliation not just of asking, but of less rewarding responses: "OK—Why?", "Don't keep asking me that!", and "Stop pressuring me with your insecurities" are some blood-curdling examples.

Another interpretation of the Six of Pentacles, and a profound one, is that if what we really want is to give, we have to be very clear on what and how much a person can and wants to receive. True giving is not simply an outpouring of what we want to impart. Unsolicited advice may be unwelcome, regardless of its wisdom. Statements that begin "The trouble with you is . . ." are often more accurate than helpful. A wealthy interior decorator may not delight her newly wedded daughter by surprising her with a fully furnished new home. (I am reminded of the Christmas when my brother presented my mother with the most wonderful gift he could imagine. A cap gun! He was seven years old at the time, but some generous people never get beyond that level of awareness.)

Additionally, the issue may not be one of desire but of readiness. A four-year-old comes up to us and asks, "Mommy, Daddy, where do I come from?" How much information do we want to offer? We have to measure what the child is really asking and how detailed and explicit we want to be. Do we need to tell a four-year-old about desire and passion and the dangers of lust? Probably not. Generally a four-year-old is satisfied with, "You came from inside my tummy." And when the four-year-old turns six and asks the question again, we again have to evaluate, measure, and weigh what the child is ready to receive.

Another meaning of the Six of Pentacles is to keep someone in an uncomfortable, demeaning, or even humiliating relationship by giving them "just enough." Not enough to satisfy them, but just enough to keep them in tow—stuck, hoping for more. A small raise, instead of the large one promised, that comes after two years instead of six months. The flowers that arrive after the fifth broken date; the dinner invitation just when we have decided to seek companionship elsewhere. Only a masochist could be comfortable in the place of the crouching beggar who pleads and implores and never gets anything. That way, they know that the person they are begging from is really important, because they are able to withhold so completely. How lucky to be with so powerful a partner!

Let us turn now to a completely different view of the Six of Pentacles. The standing figure can be seen to hold the scale of law and justice, and the law we're looking at is the law of human nature. There are rabbis and priests who look at the evolution of humanity in terms of the prophets who were recognized in various stages of history. Why, for example, did Moses place such an emphasis on law and Jesus such an emphasis on love? Huston Smith notes that Christianity bears the same relationship to Judaism that Buddhism bears to Hinduism. In each case all the elements of the latter can be found in the former. The former, however, are religions that are ethnically or societally based and therefore restrictive in some way. As Smith puts it, "I could never be a Hindu because I wasn't born into a caste." The newer religions open the theologies of the older to a universal audience, but the truths developed by the offspring are contained within the parent.

There was a time in human development, going back three thousand years, when the human race was not ready for the message of Jesus. We were ready for the message of Moses, the lesson of law—rules and accountability. We required the message of fairness before we could temper that justice with mercy. Perhaps Moses, himself an adept, understood everything Jesus taught. In fact, there was probably someone very like Jesus who was a contemporary of Moses but never made an impact because we were not ready for him.

When Jesus taught the law of love, he was not alone. Rabbi Akiba, roughly contemporaneous with Jesus, also taught that the key to the entire Torah was "Love thy neighbor as thyself." (Like Jesus, Akiba died a martyr's death, and his last words were of love. As the skin was flayed from his living body, he said, "Now I know what it means to love the Lord my God with all my heart, with all my soul, with all my mind.") We are given what we are spiritually ready to receive.

We can see in the Six of Pentacles a powerful symbol of this divine judgment in the hand dispensing the coin. It is the hand of a priest making the sign of the cross, the last two fingers of his hand folded over his palm. The suggestion of the partially open palm is the same in each case: something is offered, but something is held back, too. There are gifts that are gifts only when the recipient is prepared to receive them; until then, wisdom withholds them.

There's a final interpretation of the Six of Pentacles that goes within and to me is the most profound, the most moving, and the most challenging. The soul is infinite while the body exists in time and space. If we see the standing figure as the self, soul, or spirit, we may see the crouching figures as different aspects of our soul, the different roles that we play. Who among us has not faced the challenge of deciding where our time and energy will go? If I'm a nurturing mother, it's dollars to doughnuts I'm not a diva or a ballerina. If I'm spending a lot of time at my job, doing it as well as I can with an eye to promotion, I'm probably not spending a lot of time with my dog. If I'm a meticulous housekeeper, I'm probably not a seductive courtesan to my husband; and if I'm a gourmet cook and fabulous hostess, I'm probably not working out at the gym. We have just so much time and so much energy, and it's difficult for us to set priorities and to be satisfied with the decisions we make. It's tempting to do always what is most urgent instead of what is most important. These bills have to be paid now, so when do I write my poetry? The refrigerator's empty, but the light is perfect for painting. There's always a leak in the dike. Somebody's always got to go to the pediatrician or the vet, or the plasterer has to come in, or the toilet is leaking, or the checkbook doesn't balance. Something is always making demands on our time. So when does the soul get to dance? When do I get to be all that I am?

I'll never get to be all that I am. No wonder Leonardo da Vinci didn't finish most of his paintings. He was busy inventing airplanes

PENTACLES

and writing strange manuscript you can read only if you hold it up to a mirror. The more gifted we are, the more difficult the challenge.

It becomes clear now, I believe, why this image appears in Tiferet. Here, at the center of the Tree, at the place of perfect balance, we see the perpetual challenge of balancing in our own lives the divinely in-spired soul, and the necessary body. It is as well the place of the sac-rificed god. The choices we make always involve sacrifice, usually sacrifice of a divine part of ourselves. I once did a reading for a young woman who could not understand why the Six of Pentacles showed up for her. She was involved in a relationship with a respectful, loving man who was her writing partner and whom she was about to marry. Together they developed scripts for television and film, and she swore that she was entirely happy. By "chance," it emerged later in the read-ing that the writing had left her with no time for her first love—pho-tography. As she put it, the scripts might never be produced, but in the darkroom, she could always see the fruits of her labor within a matter of hours. Her God-given talent as a photographer was being crucified to her personal relationship and her gifts as a writer.

Of course the Six of Pentacles can operate on a mundane level. Should I cook tonight or go through the filing cabinet? Will I explore a new friendship or spend the time in meditation? The card suggests setting up schedules within which we can function comfortably so that our lives are in order—yet not at the expense of creative expres-sion. How do we know which interpretation to put on the Six of Pen-tacles? That is where the fun comes in. That's up to you. It's a matter of intuition, experience, sensitivity.

The interactive reader will already have noticed that the Six of Pentacles is another separation card, the third we have seen in the suit. How the separation is to be interpreted depends on the interpre-tation of the card as a whole. If what we see is disparity of power in a personal or work relationship, the separation can be seen as a want of empathy, a lack of compassion, an inability or unwillingness to experi-ence the situation from the perspective of the disadvantaged. It is in fact the ultimate I-it relationship in which human beings are reduced to objects, useful or not, deserving or unworthy, but whose feelings are never acknowledged, much less considered. If, on the other hand, the standing figure is seen to be exercising judgment with the inten-tion of appropriate, balanced action, the separation can be understood as detachment. We then see the crucifying of ego for the sake of cultivating a larger perspective, the recognition—in my brother's case, for instance—that it's not right for me to give you a cap gun if it is I, and not you, who wants it. Again, the Sun of Tiferet gives us a lucid view of the situation as it really is, while the heart chakra is moved to care for the less fortunate or less evolved.

Seven of Pentacles

We move now to Netzach, the seventh sefirah associated with Venus and the top of the right hip, and to the place of the Seven of Pentacles. I think what we see here is best expressed by saying, "Is that all there is? There must be more to life." This is not a card of failure; it is a card of *success without fulfillment.* Here we see a gardener. He has sown, he has cultivated, and he is reaping a bumper crop of pentacles, so plentiful that they cover the vine. Gee, does he look happy! Not exactly. His whole demeanor, from his facial expression to the heaviness of his body as he leans on his hoe, conveys dejection. But *why* isn't he satisfied? Could it be that it's time for that caretaker to move out of his carefully cultivated garden and climb the mountain?

The dark side of the Seven of Pentacles is the inability ever to feel satisfied. Here we see the perfectionist, the person of such ambition that nothing will, nothing ever can, be enough. That's a sad place to be. The "Desiderata" very wisely advises us to enjoy our accomplishments as well as our plans. For some people perfectionism is a curse. It seems impossible for them to say, "Boy, I really did that well. It came out just right. I feel good about that." It's always "But there could have been . . ." or "I should have done . . . ."

The positive side of the Seven of Pentacles is the budding of self-awareness. In the Rider deck the figure is depicted wearing one brown boot and one that is distinctly orange. Even after I had focused on this peculiarity, it took years for its meaning to reveal itself to me. A man who wears boots that don't match must be considered a nonconformist. Perhaps his dissatisfaction stems from his being successful at work that does not express his values, gifts, and desires. Perhaps this is the wealthy third-generation neurosurgeon who always wanted to be a jazz saxophonist. When we realize that material gain and success in the eyes of others leave us empty, we have taken the first step to discovering what Joseph Campbell refers to as our "bliss."

Netzach, we recall, is called "victory," but it is also the vessel from which our passion flows. The success of the morose gardener challenges us to examine our preconceptions about what constitutes victory in our own lives. Making a lot of money? Outdoing a perceived competitor? Achieving a stated goal? How about graduating from college? Any of these may be victories, but none carries that guarantee. In *The Graduate,* Ben, the protagonist, celebrates his triumph in scuba gear at the bottom of the family swimming pool to escape the party being held in his honor. In the Seven of Pentacles, we see the hollowness of victory without passion and the moment at which we experience the need for passionate involvement in our lives.

Eight of Pentacles

We move on to Hod, the eighth sefirah associated with the top of the left hip and the mercurial quality of intellect, and to the place of the Eight of Pentacles. We see here quite a simple image compared to some of the others we have looked at. It is a workman, diligent and skilled. Look at his body language. He likes what he's doing. He's comfortable with it. And he's working at something he does well, something in which he has developed expertise. His pentacles, all perfectly crafted, hang before him and lie at his feet as he works away happily at his chosen occupation. This is a very nice card. It is a quiet card. In some ways, it's the best that the Suit of Pentacles has to offer. It's a card of finding the way to be content in this world, to enjoy our work and to do it willingly and happily.

I am blessed with a cleaning woman who sings while she works, and you should see her eyes light up when she tells me about a new product that really makes things sparkle. She is not a stupid person. She is extremely bright, perceptive, insightful, and quick. At twenty-seven, she has four children. She loves her work. I am sure she is a wonderful mother, a wonderful wife. She knows how to enjoy whatever it is she does. She does it as well as she possibly can and takes pleasure in what she achieves. What a blessing!

What's the negative of this card? What we see here is that a formula has been derived for doing something very well, perhaps perfectly. If you're an artist, this can be a dangerous card. We've all gone, for our sins, to outdoor art shows and seen the same face that Keene decided was endearing appearing on different bodies: huge round eyes and perhaps a single falling tear. Everything in the painting changes except the face, because Keene derived a formula that he thought worked. That is not the artistic process. Art is the process of taking chances, leaving the garden, going up to another level on the mountain of truth. Between shows, Jackson Pollack used to leave off painting for months to assure breaking any habits he might have slipped into. Jim Dyne speaks of wanting to paint, "not with his left hand—but resisting the movement of his right hand with his left." The artist's work is to push the envelope of experience and creativity, to experiment, explore, and seek a truer mode of expression. So if you are an artist and this card shows up, examine very carefully whether you are becoming facile.

However, if you are a craftsman, a scientist, an engineer, and you've come up with a reliable formula, the Eight of Pentacles praises you for your work. If you are a cardiac surgeon and you have perfected a procedure, this is a reassuring card. If I were undergoing open-heart surgery, I would want the doctor who had performed ten thousand operations, all the same way, all with the same result. I would not seek out the creative soul who, at 6 A.M. on the Tuesday of my surgery, might choose to get inventive. "I'm tired of this same old procedure. Today I want to try something entirely new. I wonder will happen if I go in through . . . the back!"

If you have attuned yourself to the concept of separation cards, you probably noticed at once that the Eight of Pentacles falls into this group. How are we to interpret the nature of the separation of the craftsman from the town? He has positioned his work bench far from others as well as setting it on the hallmark stage of the separation cards. Here I believe the separation is a mental one; the physical distance is the artist's way of suggesting distance of thought. What we see in the figure so absorbed in his work is how focus and concentration isolates us from the mundane surroundings that would otherwise distract us from our work. Those of us who have been deeply involved in creative or scholarly work have had the experience of finding ourselves suddenly famished, only to realize that it is 5:30 P.M. and we haven't had breakfast yet. Immersion in the process has cut us off from the sounds of traffic, the passing hours, the foot we've been sitting on since noon that has fallen asleep.

We can now see the association of the Eight of Pentacles with Mercury, the mental planet, as well as with the sefirah Hod, which means "glory" or "splendor." Only the glorious human mind is capable of the sustained and concentrated attention without which work of consistent quality cannot be produced.

The top of the right hip, associated with Netzach, and the top of the left hip, associated with Hod, come together in the chakra system at the solar plexus. This is the chakra of our groundedness, our solidity in the world. It is interesting to think about, as well as to feel the relationships between the Seven and Eight of Pentacles, in terms of the work we undertake in the world. Perhaps the cards suggest that we must know in a conscious way what our true work is. If we do not, the work, regardless of its evaluation by others, will never express our true feelings and therefore never engage our passion. Consequently, it is destined to leave us empty and dissatisfied.

Nine of Pentacles

We come next to Yesod, the Foundation, the place of the unconscious, and the Nine of Pentacles. Attentive readers among you may have noticed that this is the image that appears on the cover of the book you are reading at this very moment. This is because the Nine of

Pentacles decided that she was my card. When I started working with the cards and read the handy-dandy handbook that came with the deck, it said things like "Choose this card for yourself if you are under forty and have hazel eyes and brown hair," or "Choose this card for yourself if you are a very young woman or a young man." I tried to figure out my coloring and gauge the answer: "Am I a Queen of Pentacles? No, I'm not that dark. I'm too old to be a page, and I'm not male enough to be a knight." While I was worrying and calculating, the Nine of Pentacles just kept turning up, turning up, turning up. In every reading, there she was. Finally I thought, "Oh, so that's my card!" And it feels absolutely right.

While the Tarot-for-simpletons pamphlets usually direct the novice to "find their card," the only benefit I can see accruing to this procedure is to involve the newcomer with the deck early on. Any device that encourages time with the cards and scrutiny of detail will pay off for the reader. If identifying with a card immerses you in the magic of the Tarot, so much the better. My caution is against simplistic formulae for choosing or discovering a card to represent yourself, based on superficial externals like age and coloring. If you long for a card to represent you, invite one to declare itself. Ask the deck to get into cahoots with your own unconscious and produce the synchronicity that will answer your need.

It's important when we're working with the cards to remember that we are the final authority. Our intuition is king and whatever it is we see is the final truth. There is no way to make a mistake. It's very helpful to know something about the cards, but we learn more by perceiving the cards than by looking to someone else.

The Nine of Pentacles: what is there about her which is so appealing to so many people? The first thing I see, because of my feelings about the physical world, is someone who is totally at one with nature. She is in a garden, and the garden is producing a great harvest of grapes and pentacles. There is a feeling of abundance. On her hand she holds a member of the animal kingdom, a falcon, with whom she is on easy terms. Fierce and powerful, he sits quietly and gently on the hand of his mistress. There is an elegance, grace, and serenity to her demeanor, an air of peace, a quiet appreciation and joyfulness.

What many fail to notice, however, is that there is another animal in the card. It's a snail. Yuck! What is he doing on the card?

No, not "Yuck." He's part of the natural world. She accepts him in the same way she accepts the bounty of the garden and the falcon. He's welcome. He's part of it all. He's part of us. You can't be at one with nature unless you are at one with all of nature, and being at one with the nature "out there" is a metaphor for being at one with your own internal nature. If you can't enjoy a garden unless it is free from snails and other pests, unless each leaf and flower is perfect, you will never enjoy a garden. Similarly, if you cannot accept yourself because of your flaws and failings, if you cannot accept yourself as worthy of abundance and love unless you are perfect, you will never enjoy yourself. The snail represents our human failings; the serenity that the lady's demeanor expresses is the peace that comes from really being comfortable with yourself, really liking yourself just as you are.

In the far distance on the right of the card is the lady's manor house. She wears patrician dress. There is no feeling here of the holiness of poverty. In certain Christian sects there is a belief that we have to give up the material world in order to get closer to God. We have to mortify the flesh. That's not part of the Kabbalistic tradition, it's not part of the Jewish tradition, and it's certainly not at all what we see in Tarot. Abundance is wonderful! God gives us the world to enjoy and luxuriate in. There is no apology for being successful and well dressed, for having a big, beautiful house and magnificent gardens.

Now, what about the falcon? The falcon represents, I believe, the soaring human spirit. Why is it hooded? The falcon flies when the lady decides that the falcon may fly. She is capable of intense feeling, of enormous creative and emotional expression, but she is not a slave to her passions. She is not addicted to them. The hooded falcon is the symbolic representation of *choice through discipline.*

What does it takes to train a falcon? What does it takes to train a puppy? To train the dog, you first train yourself to be aware of what the dog is doing all the time, because if your attention wanders he will surely have an "accident." You train yourself to get up at five-thirty or six o'clock in the morning to take the puppy out whether you want to or not. That's how you train a dog. First you train yourself.

The way to train a falcon is first to train yourself. The mastery and the discipline are over the self first. The bird does not fly free and terrorize the lady's doves and pigeons and pluck out the eyes of her pet dog, but neither has she strangled the falcon, caged it, or clipped his wings. She has created the choice of when to let that falcon—that spirit, creative energy, emotional intensity—fly free and express itself and when to control, restrain, and deny it. What a wonderful capacity to have in a relationship, in creative work, in anything we do.

Ted Falcon, a Seattle-based rabbi, talks about responsibility as *response* and *ability*. What he tells us is that the more aware we are of our lack of self-worth (Five of Pentacles) and our insecurity (Four of Pentacles), the more we are able to respond to what we see. If I am aware of my violent tendencies, it doesn't mean I have to act them out. Being aware that I would like to pick up a heavy object and fling it through a window doesn't mean I have to do it. My awareness gives me a choice. If I'm not aware of my rage and violence, I'm much more likely to be inflamed to action. Once I know what my nature is, whether it is sexual, spiritual, aggressive, or creative, I can decide when to let it free and when to contain it. That's what the falcon means.

The Nine of Pentacles, then, represents self-realization, abundance, and creativity through self-acceptance and self-discipline. What can be the down side of this card?

Well, the lady is all alone. I'll bet she gets lonely from time to time. I'll bet it would be very nice for her to have some companionship. The problem with the Nine of Pentacles is the problem of isolating ourselves from other people. We may cut ourselves off from communication and contact and relatedness, sacrificing all of that for our own development. Perhaps we even use our own inner development as a screen for feeling uncomfortable or inadequate out there in the world. Many are the so-called intellectuals, scholars, and scientists who sequester themselves to pursue their research, but in so doing avoid the human contact of which they feel incapable or terrified. Their isolation perhaps frustrates the people who are around them—their children, their wives, their husbands. The negative aspect of the Nine of Pentacles can represent people who are always working on "something greater" in a very disciplined way, but who, unable to accept the snail, never seem to have the time to take the hood off the falcon. (Can you find the other person in the card? Is the lady's isolation about to end?)

How does the Nine of Pentacles relate to Yesod, the Foundation, and the Moon? The moon, you will recall, has long been associated with the unconscious, casting an eerie light that cuts through our ordinary way of looking at things. Objects at hand lose their familiarity and seem to demand a fresh look. What we perceive by the pale white light of the moon is often what we project. The imaginings, fears, demons, and imps of our own shadow conjoin with the shadow of the sun, the underside of the sun, the reflected light that is invisible by day. As the moon is the hidden light of the sun, so the unconscious is our own hidden light and, as we have previously discussed, the foundation of our lives. What we hold to be true in this hidden shadow of our being is what will manifest in our lives—modern depth psychology has its basis in this truth. The Nine of Pentacles holds out the assurance to us that, if we can truly accept and know ourselves well enough to discipline our passions, we are assured of serenity and abundance.

Yesod is associated with the axis that runs from the base of the spine to the genitals. In the chakra system, this encompasses our most deeply rooted instincts: survival and procreation. How safe do we feel in the world? How comfortable are we with our sexuality? Our most profound and least understood feelings are buried in these least-conscious chakras, yet they constitute the foundation of the lives we manifest. The Nine of Pentacles, in fully accepting herself, magnetizes the abundance of which she feels worthy and is serene in solitude.

Ten of Pentacles

Finally we come to Malchut and the Ten of Pentacles. It's one of the cards in the Tarot we have the most difficulty seeing. We keep feeling that we want to get around behind the pentacles so we can see what's going on. They seem to be in the way. This is the danger of the Suit of Pentacles: allowing material things to become so important that we lose track of the animating force within. We are all capable of letting the money or the beautiful home or the brand new car get between us and our relationships with other people.

In the Ten of Pentacles we see a multigenerational family and a grand manor house. Inspection of these images reveals many symbols, but the card remains unclear. We see another Romanesque archway—we have seen one in the Ace of the suit—beside which sits an old man. Is he sitting at the entrance to a courtyard, looking in, or is he looking out from a courtyard at the couple and child? It is a perspective that can shift.

What is the relationship between the man and the woman in the Ten of Pentacles? They seem to be saying something to each other, but we don't get the feeling that it's necessarily drawing them closer together. Quite the most interesting question for me is, "Is the lady arriving or is the lady leaving?" Is she being lured into a relationship with family, or is she saying, "Good-bye, Charlie, I've had it! I can't take this anymore! I need to be able to stretch out my arms without knocking my elbow on a pentacle!" And why is the young man holding a spear? Is he going to accompany her as protector, or is he barring her entry?

The Ten of Pentacles is cluttered. There is a sense of unrelatedness among the people. Nobody is paying any attention at all to the old man, who at least should be acknowledged as an authority figure and almost certainly as one of wisdom. Surely his robe is more than opulent; it is mysterious and covered with provocative symbols. Is that a lyre we see? A throne? Where in fact does the cloak leave off? Perhaps he is a magician, a wizard in disguise. The gods of Mount Olympus often came to earth in disguise to see how they would be treated when taken for ordinary humans. In any case, we see wisdom ignored and age isolated.

The little child clings, perhaps, to the woman's robe, but he seems in his own world, lonely. The only actual touching involves the two dogs, hunting dogs, generally held to be the most loving. This is a family that seems unable to reach out to one another. Both the child and grandfather depend, for basic animal comfort, on their canine friends.

We have much wealth here. We have a family crest in which there is also a pair of scales. How much weight is being given to the coin and how much to the pentagram, the star within? We see depicted the belief that "more is better," when in fact *appreciating* more is better. Accumulating more is worse.

On the positive side, we find that the ten pentacles form none other than the Kabbalistic Tree of Life. We will find this image nowhere else in the Tarot. What can this be meant to convey? The suggestion, I believe, is that with appreciation, all gifts can be transformed into what they should be, spiritual riches far beyond their material value.

In the Ace of Pentacles we found a Romanesque archway leading from a sequestered garden to the mountains of pure truth. In the Ten, we find another of these mystical gateways leading to the Tree of Life. The truth to which this gateway leads us is that by flipping our perspective, we can recreate the Garden of Eden at any moment. When the ten pentacles forming the Tree of Life become the focus rather than the distraction, when we see the holy pattern rather than the individual coins, we restore blessing to our lives and love to our relationships. We do this simply. We do it with a *barucha,* a prayer, and with *kavanah,* holy intention. We make the moment *kadosh,* holy, by remembering who we are.

Malchut, the kingdom, is the earth plane and the planet Earth. It is a dangerously comfortable place for Pentacles. We are involved in a study of balance in this work; pentacles in the place of Earth, while offering us the only Kabbalistic Tree of the Tarot, can also clutter our lives with the material and mundane.

Malchut is associated not with a chakra but with the soles of the feet. Malchut is the sefirah to which action is appropriate. Whether the lady is departing or returning and accompanied or alone, action is implied. She is setting out upon or coming back from some quest in the world at large.

The danger and challenge in Malchut is exacerbated by the Suit of Pentacles: the danger on this earth of accumulating things while forgetting the Creator of all we treasure most and the animating force that is its true value. But with this danger comes the opportunity to remember the star in the coin, to remember who we are, and to set out in the world bearing the Kabbalistic Tree as our shield and guide.

CHAPTER 4

Cups: Plumbing the Human Heart

W E HAVE SAID that each suit of the Tarot represents a way to spirit. The way of Cups is the way of love. Love is so powerful an energy that Emmet Fox, the Christian theologian, tells us that with enough love, there is absolutely nothing that cannot be accomplished, no barrier that cannot be broken down, no wall that cannot be scaled, no situation that cannot be reversed. If we look around us in our everyday lives, we see expressions of this all the time.

I don't know how many of you have seen the film or read the book *My Left Foot*. They dramatize a clear example of the power of love in the perfectly true story of a man born with so crippling a disease that he had no control over any part of his body but his left foot. Eventually and with great difficulty he taught himself to speak, but as a child he seemed mentally defective as well. Here was someone who might have been tossed aside as a total loss, a human being the Spartans would have abandoned on a mountaintop to freeze or starve to death within hours of his birth. Yet this person became an accomplished writer and painter. He married and lived as normal a life as the restrictions of his physical body allowed. The limitations on his life were all physical; they weren't spiritual, they weren't emotional, and they weren't mental. What freed him? The love of his mother. It was her refusal to give up on him, her refusal to believe that he was hopeless, her insistence that he be treated with respect, and her patience in the way she spoke to him, even before she believed that he could understand, that ultimately redeemed him.

However, the Suit of Cups does not represent love alone. It represents emotions in general, negative as well as positive. I am not in favor of hatred. I am not in favor of jealousy. I do not advocate resentment. I am not saying that it is wonderful to be in despair. What I am saying is that all of these emotions exist. And because they exist, they must be acknowledged and permitted expression along with all the rest of human experience pictured in the seventy-eight cards of the Waite Tarot.

There is a problem with the positive thinking and affirmations so often advocated in popular self-help books. While they have a place, they can pull us off balance. Balance—that's all we see in Tarot; that's all we see in Kabbalah. The central Pillar of Balance in the Tree of Life serves as a gravitational focus between the two extreme Pillars of Mercy and Severity. When we are not striving for balance, when we are striving only for perfection, we are prone to what I see as the most dangerous psychological state possible: denial. A woman I know recently said, "My boyfriend wouldn't make a commitment to me. He said he loved me, and I was crazy about him, but he just couldn't make a commitment. Now, one year later, he has made a commitment to someone else. I keep thinking I have forgiven him, but I find I have to keep doing it over and over again." Although she is a good person, clearly on a spiritual path, and although it is wonderful that she has affirmations on her bathroom mirror about forgiving and being entitled to abundance, she is subject to all the emotions of the rest of humanity. There is a time to forgive, and it comes after honestly experiencing harsher, darker feelings.

We want to open ourselves to good things. We can miss them if we are not open to them. But to expect life to be a symphony, to imagine that we're going to leap from bed every morning feeling refreshed, joyful, bountiful, and loving to our enemies as well as our friends, is to set ourselves up for frustration and disappointment at best. We must be aware of all of our feelings, and we must be honest with ourselves about those feelings whatever they are: discouragement as well as hope, despair as well as euphoria, and fury as well as serenity. So if I say the Suit of Cups is the suit of emotions and that it covers all the negative emotions as well as the positive ones, I'm not saying that this is the way things *should* be—only that this is the way they *are*. To deny the truth is to invite trouble.

Of course it is important to forgive, and it is healing for us to let go of anger. But when? When do we expect to forgive the mugger? While we're being stabbed? We need time to process our feelings. We have a multitude of reactions and we have to allow them all. After we have them, after we experience them fully, after we go through them completely—only then can we release them. But we can't take the short way around; there are no honest shortcuts. The Suit of Cups is the suit of *all* emotion.

As we have observed in relation to the Suit of Pentacles, every suit and every card has its shadow side as well as its light side. Every suit has its way to spirit as well as its flaw. The way of Pentacles to spirit, we suggested, is the way of service and appreciation; the flaw is the tendency toward accumulation—getting caught up in the material, forgetting the star and remembering only the coin.

In the Suit of Cups, there is a twofold flaw, a twofold danger. One is getting caught up in negative feelings. We'll talk about these in detail when we look at the court cards. The other flaw of the Suit of Cups is passivity. Cups, representing emotion and associated with water, seek their own level, and we can feel and feel and feel more and more deeply and never do anything about what we are feeling.

There are people who are so enormously compassionate that they faint at the sight of blood. These are the last people we need around us if we are wounded. If you were bleeding to death, who would you rather have at hand: a skilled and insensitive surgeon who would put down their sandwich, sew you up, and go back to their rare roast beef on rye, or someone who is so full of feelings that they tremble, cry, scream, or faint but can't even get to a telephone to call for help? We want compassion, we want sympathy, we want deep feeling, we want intense emotion in our lives. But we don't want feelings alone. Cups need to be married to the other suits. We've talked about Pentacles; we saw how Pentacles need Cups. Earth needs water to be fertile. Without water, the earth becomes dry and cannot bring forth life. But without earth, the water runs off and is useless. Cups need Pentacles, too. If there's no action, if we don't make some difference in Malchut, the plane of earthly existence, then our most intense feelings aren't going to help anybody.

Ace of Cups

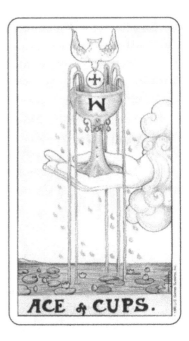

ACE ⚜ CUPS.

Let's begin now looking at the individual cards of the suit. We begin as before with the Ace. You will recall that the number-one sefirah is Keter, the crown of the Tree, and our own crown chakra. It is the place where the divine emanation of God's essence first enters the Tree. And it refers to the Ace, the number-one card in the suit.

What we see again is an oversized hand, which can only be the hand of God, coming out of the heavens through a cloud, shining with white light, offering us a gift. The gift is a cup, and the cup is overflowing. If there is an image for the line of the Twenty-Third Psalm, "my cup runneth over," it would have to be the Ace of Cups. There is a sense of joyfulness in this card, of buoyancy and unlimited love. To me it brings to mind Handel's *Water Music*, music a friend once described as joy more profound than any sorrow. What a magnificent notion!

The symbolism of this card is enormously rich and highly spiritual in that it combines the symbols of three great religions. The most obvious of these is the Christian symbolism. The cup suggests the Holy Grail, the goblet from which Jesus drank at the last supper and which caught his blood when his side was pierced at Golgotha. It is the cup for which the knights of the round table went in search. There is, therefore, the suggestion of the Holy Eucharist. We see as well a white dove—a Catholic symbol of the Holy Ghost, the Holy Spirit—dropping a communion wafer into the cup. The wafer represents the body of Christ just as the wine represents his blood. The myth is that every year the wine is refreshed and renewed in its power by the presence of the Holy Spirit dropping the Eucharist wafer into it.

The cup we see literally overflows. There are five streams. The number five represents human beings with our five digits and five senses. There are five streams because the gift is for us, for human beings. We are the ones who can receive the gift with awareness. This then is the great Christian symbolism.

When we look at the bottom of the card we see the waters that we know run deep because floating at their surface is the lotus, or water lily. Water lilies have very long stems whose roots, like the Tree of Life itself, are buried in the good, rich, moist earth at the bottom of the water. The lotus grows upward from this dark place, representing the movement of spirit up into a place of divine light. This is Eastern symbolism, associated with both the Hindu and Buddhist religions.

Finally, there is the symbolism of Judaism in this card as well, in the little droplets of water. To understand these droplets requires a digression from the Ace of Cups of some length. However, the symbolism recurs with sufficient frequency and import in the Tarot to justify a full exploration of its significance.

The name of God in Hebrew is never pronounced, or as Rabbi Don Singer would say, "God is nameless." He can have no name because we cannot know His essence. When we name something, it suggests that we know what it is. It confers a kind of power over what is named. I can say, "Bring me the chair," if I know the word for chair. I now have control over the chair and the way in which it is manipulated. But since there is no way for us to grasp what or who God is, there is no way for us to give a name to that energy, that being.

God first speaks to Moses from a burning bush, commanding him to lead the children of Israel out of Egypt. Moses asks this voice, "Who shall I say is sending me to lead the children of Israel out of slavery?" God replies, "I am as I am," or "I am that am," or "I am Who am." In other words, "You can't put a name on Me, because if you name Me, you distinguish Me from something that I am not. If you say, 'That's a chair,' you distinguish the chair from what is not the chair. I am 'Amness.' You can't distinguish Me from anything, because I am everything; everything is in Me." Rabbi Ted Falcon understands this to mean, "Everything that partakes of being is an expression of Me. How could it be if it did not partake of being, which is My essence? I am being!" Martin Buber translates this mysterious reply as "I will be there for you."

Because we cannot name God, we represent His name by the Holy Tetragrammaton, four Hebrew letters: *Yod He Vav He*. As an interesting aside, pronunciation of *Yod He Vav He* as "Yahwah" or "Jehovah" reflects a fundamental confusion since as Rabbi Falcon puts it, the rules of the Hebrew language do not allow the necessary placement of vowels in order to make the Holy Tetragrammaton pronounceable.

Rabbi Steven Robbins concurs when he says that "the rules of vocalization in Hebrew are almost impossible to apply to the *Yod He Vav He*." He refers to it as "the most nebulous of pronunciations—two breaths, as insubstantial as it can be."

Rabbi Stan Levy interprets the *Yod He Vav He* as a formula, an abbreviation. He explains that Moses is really saying to God, "Tell me who you are," and the answer, as each of us knows, can never be a name. God responds to Moses' real question, which is not for a label, but for the reassurance we all need in times of crisis. God seems to be saying, "I will be there for you" or "I will be present is who I am." Rabbi Levy likens the *Yod He Vav He* to Einstein's $E=MC^2$. Is it a name? In a sense, it is the name of an equation. But, as Rabbi Levy asks, "How would you pronounce it? It is not designed to be expressed or pronounced."

Again, Rabbi Singer reminds us that scribes writing the *Yod He Vav He* entered the vowels from *Adonai* or *Aloheynu* as a *reminder* that this was not a name to be pronounced but an "ineffable name" to be replaced by "Adonai" or "Aloheynu" when we read or speak! So holy is this combination of letters, and so powerful, it could be breathed only by the high priest of the Temple of Jerusalem (before its destruction two thousand years ago) and only on the Day of Atonement. As an aside, Rabbi Mordecai Finlay refers to *Adonai,* which means Lord, as a code word. The *Yod He Vav He* that it signals, however, he translates as "Cause of All Being." He then reflects on the consequences this confusion has had on all of us in the history of Western civilization and the lives of women in particular. You don't have to be a feminist to imagine the effect of a Bible rendered with that single change.

The presence of any letter of the Holy Tetragrammaton, but particularly the first, carries with it divine energy. Yod is that from which everything is created. Hebrew is called the flame language. Myth has it that if we begin with just the little tiny Yod, roughly the size and shape of an apostrophe, and a wind blows through it as if it were a candle flame, every other letter of the alphabet would emerge from it.

Finally, as you may recall, there is a Kabbalistic belief that Torah (or *Pentateuch*, the first five books of Moses) is the blueprint for the creation! Torah is held to have existed before the universe. If Torah is the blueprint by which God created the universe, there is clearly a complex relationship between the word and its manifestation.

Part of what this means is that we must be very careful of what we say because words create reality. "Abracadabra!" What does that mean? We all heard it as kids. Magic! Magic! If I say it, something is going to happen. If I say something, and then I say "Abracadabra," it's going to happen. *Abracadabra* comes from Hebrew or the related Aramaic and means "As it is said, so shall it be." (Literally, the translation is "that which is created is that which is spoken," *abra* being from the Hebrew *boray* [to create] and *dabra* from *deber* [to speak], according to Rabbi Stan Levy.) As it is said, so shall it be! The power of the word belongs to every breath we emit with sound. It floats to the top and above the Tree of Life to the highest realms of heaven—and changes things. It shifts energy.

Why is one of the Ten Commandments "Thou shalt not take the name of the Lord in vain"? If you could give your offspring, a son or a daughter, ten crucial pieces of advice on how to live life, would one of them be "Don't swear"? If you were limited for some reason to ten, would you waste one by saying, "By the way, don't curse"? Isn't that roughly on a par with "Always carry a clean handkerchief"? In exploring the mystical relationship between words and reality, however, the true and profound understanding of that command emerges: we are not to take the name of the Lord in vain because it can't be done. When you say God's name, energy shifts. Something is changed. If I look at you and say, "God bless you," a flow of love goes out into the world. "God bless you" is a powerful thing to say. If I say, "God damn it!" something changes, too. We want to be very careful about saying that. Is that what we really mean? Do we really want anyone or anything to be damned by God? In summary, the relationship among letters, words, and reality is potent, magical, and central to human life.

We can now return to the Ace of Cups and recognize that the little drops of water form Yods. God's own energy spills over through the initial letter of the Holy Tetragrammaton, the unpronounceable name of the unknowable Cause of all Being.

So we have in Keter (the crown) the Ace of Cups, the overflowing of joyful love. God reaches into the universe, the entire cosmos of Keter. He has already given us the gift of the material world in the Ace of Pentacles. Now He presents us with another crowning gift, the capacity to love it. His gift to us through the Ace of Cups is the capacity to respond with love and to feel emotion in this world.

Two of Cups

As we move now to Chochma, which is the second sefirah on the Tree, the supernal father, wisdom, we see the lovely card of the Two of Cups. We will recall that the position of the Two represents the place of relatedness and introduces the possibility of relationship. In Keter, the place of the One, or Ace, everything is everything else, and everything is one and we're all united. There is no possibility of relationship. Only when we get to Chochma, the place of the Two, does relationship becomes possible. I-Thou becomes possible. The Suit of Cups is the most hospitable place for the energy of the Two. Relationship is natural to the suit of feeling. We consequently see here a very comfortable card in the place of Chochma, a balanced and beautiful one.

We see in the Two of Cups an expression of the magic that can take place when two come together, not just in passion but in spiritual love. We see a man and a woman; the woman, magnetic, remains still; the man, dynamic, approaches. Each, handsomely dressed, is crowned with a garland, the woman's distinctly the laurel of victory. Each then is a winner. This explains why the two are not sharing a cup: she has hers; he has his.

The suggestion here is that this is not a codependent relationship. The woman does not come to the man saying, "I'm desperate! Still my terror, ease my pain, or I'm not going to make it! Let me drink from your cup because I don't have one." The man does not say, "At last! Someone in worse shape than I am! Compared to her, I'm a bloody hero! She can't even tie her own shoelaces. She needs me. If I have her in my life, I don't have to deal with my own stuff. Dealing with her crises—just ensuring her survival—will take all my time and energy. So what if I can't get through a day without a couple of six-packs? I function great compared to her!" What we see, rather, is that the man approaches the woman saying, "I have a full cup, and I would like to share it with you." We may imagine her reply to be, "I too have a full cup, and I would like to share it with you." The relationship suggested is that between two independent people. *Chochma* means "wisdom"; the wisdom they have achieved as individuals has prepared them for the relationship.

Because of their mutual independence, a cordial distance that is almost chivalric can be maintained between the two. There is a gentleness and caring; rather than risk intrusion or offense, the two keep a respectful distance. In recent years, we have seen a return to the gradual development of relationships. The madness of the late sixties through the early eighties seems to be gone. People no longer think that instant physical intimacy is an expression of freedom. We seem again to recognize the need for preparation, whether in cooking or spiritual development or relationship. We cannot achieve true intimacy without putting in the time and work. I was present to witness a moment of consciousness raising after a party in 1978. An agitated young man told me in confusion that he had met a woman at a party the night before, who after twenty minutes of "What's your sign?" dialogue and three dances, had gone home and to bed with him. Then she got up, got dressed, and left. "So what did she really give me?" he asked. Were I a cartoonist, I would have drawn a lightbulb over his head.

Over the figures in the Two of Cups we see a winged lion head, the red, leonine energy of passion. The spread wings unite the two as one so that the relationship is more than the sum of its parts. The whole is something entirely different. A fiery angel has been created by the feeling between these two: there is the suggestion of being uplifted as well as merging in passion.

Finally, between the two we see the caduceus, the symbol of the medical profession; and therefore the symbol of healing. This is an important and lovely concept, that relationships have the power to heal. The caduceus, for those of you who may not be aware of it, was created when the Greek god Hermes was walking down a dusty road and saw two snakes tangled in battle. He threw his staff down between them to keep them from harming each other, and they wound around his staff in the now-familiar pattern. By virtue of having prevented harm, Hermes became the god of medicine and healing, and the caduceus a symbol of the healing arts.

The suggestion of healing is particularly interesting when we consider an old Hebrew midrash, or interpretive story, about the creation of Adam and Eve that Rabbi Steve Robbins tells most beautifully. It is similar to the more exoteric forms of the myth in the Bible, but different enough to make a lot of us (especially feminists) very happy. The original creation myth is that God, having completed the rest of creation, made a being in His/Her own likeness and called it Adam. Because everything that was in God was also in Adam, it was possible for Adam to communicate with God at any time. But Adam wandered around the Garden of Eden and saw that each creature had a mate unto its kind, and Adam alone had no mate. The earthling was lonely and said to God, "Of all the creatures in the world, I alone am without a mate, and I cannot function in this world." (Interestingly, the word in Hebrew for sexual intercourse has the same root as the verb "to function." So much for any notions of sexuality as sinful.)

God replied, "I can make a mate for you, but if I do this, our relationship will never be the same because then you will be only half of what I am, and you will not be able to relate to me in the way you do now." Adam said, "It would be worth it. I must have a mate. I must feel that I am a part of this world." So God put Adam into a deep sleep and divided this first human down the center and, as the story goes, the two danced apart. Adam the androgyne was divided into two beings, the male and the female. (This story is very different from the version in which woman is created only from Adam's rib, the implication being that his heart, or even a lung, of which he had two, was too valuable to sacrifice for the creation of a mere woman. Apparently, even a finger would have constituted too great a cost to Adam's dexterity. So what does Adam have so many of and so little use for that he'll never miss one? The suggestion is that a woman is worth the concession of a single rib, and not an earlobe more.)

This moving midrash enables us to understand in a new way the tremendous yearning we each have within us to find our mate, because what we are really looking for is our own other half. This is what we feel when we talk about looking for our soul mate. We are looking for the one who will make us feel complete, whole.

Now, I want to stress here that this is, of course, metaphor. We each have male and female energies within us. It may be that my other half also takes the physical form of a woman. Or it may be that a man's other half takes the physical form of a man. That doesn't matter. When we talk throughout Tarot or Kabbalah about marriage, love, or union, when we talk about male and female, we're talking about male energy and female energy. It's very important to remember that. All varieties of love are valid to the heart. What is important is that two come together as one and create a relationship through healing and love that is both passionate and spiritual, the whole of which is greater than the sum of its parts. Between the two figures of the Two of Cups we see mutual respect. Recall for a moment the Six of Pentacles. That is an image of domination. This is an image of partnership.

We have said that Tarot cards all have both positive and negative charges. What could be wrong with the Two of Cups? Perhaps it's a little too good to be true. There is something so idealistic, so pristine, so perfect about the partnership represented that it sets people up for disappointment. You know, when you have this kind of entirely lovely relationship, you don't want to be around the other person when your hair needs washing. Yet sooner or later everybody's hair needs washing. And if you're actually going to set up house with someone about whom you feel this way, inevitably that person is going to see it all, and so are you. He will see you, bloated and short tempered with a touch of acne, roughly once a month. You will watch in horrified fascination as he laughs at moronic jokes on his favorite sitcom. He will wonder why you can cook only three different dishes. You will wonder why he drives ten minutes out of his way to save three cents a gallon on gas. And everyone has some personal habit fit only for total privacy in which we can be surprised, to our mortification and our mate's disillusion, if only perfection will do. Laughter at such moments is not an option for the figures in the Two of Cups.

The Two of Cups, then, is a card often associated with the *beginning* of relationships, because as they develop it becomes clear that no one on this earth can be our perfect counterpart. That is our ideal, but it is not realizable. We begin to find the little flaws and to see the grating inconsistencies between our image and what that person really is. That's when highly romantic love gets tested. In *The Road Less Traveled*, M. Scott Peck actually goes so far as to say that you can't begin loving someone until you fall out of love with them! You can't begin loving someone until you see and accept that person as they genuinely are.

There is another aspect of the Two of Cups that can be seen as negative: it is, as you have probably noticed by now, a separation card. As idyllic as the little house and rolling green hills of the background may appear, the couple pictured have separated themselves from it. They are in the early stage of their relationship that involves what John Bradshaw calls "primal gazing," the kind of mooning absorption appropriate to nursing babies and their mothers. This state of total infatuation separates the couple from everyone else. They are in their own little world, which, like a cocoon, spares them any awareness of troubles and sorrows "out there." We will see more mature images of love as our work progresses, but the couple in the Two are complete unto themselves. May they savor the exquisite fleeting moment. May we all.

Three of Cups

We move next to the number-three card, which is at Binah, the place of fulfillment. Representing the creative resolution of opposites, the three is always the completion of the suit. The fulfillment of the Suit of Cups is the rejoicing celebration, total lack of competition, harvest, warmth, and unbounded good spirits pictured in the Three of Cups. Binah means "understanding." A profound understanding of what is valuable and important in life is reflected in this image. Most of these cards, I think we will see, are relatively simple in relation to the Suit of Pentacles. Because the Suit of Pentacles has to do with perception, there is a lot to notice and see. The Suit of Cups has to do with feeling, and therefore how we react to the cards is more important than what we notice by way of detail. In fact, we will find in general that the best approach to a suit is with the function of consciousness that it represents.

What we have here are three women dancing in a way reminiscent of figures in Botticelli's *Primavera*. It's interesting that they dance not in a line but in a circle. None is the leader. None comes last. They are all women, because women represent loving and sharing rather than aggression and competition. Does this mean that only women can rejoice in this way? Of course not. When we talk about the female, remember, we're not talking about people, we're talking about energy.

When men do come together in this kind of loving, sharing way, they're coming from their own female nature. This is not the kind of friendship that's expressed in the locker room when one guy slaps another guy across the butt with a wet towel and asks about the ball scores. It's the relationship among men who can put their arms around each other and talk from their hearts, from the feminine parts of themselves.

This is a harvest card. We see the gourds, pumpkins, and squash, the flowers in the maidens' hair, the loosely held dangling grapes. The number three again brings together the best of the suit: rejoicing, celebration, and an outpouring of love. The Saturnian influence of Binah manifests here as the willingness simply to be part of a group, without individual ego expression, without the need to be exceptional. The Two and Three of Cups, the right temple of Chochma and the left of Binah, come together at the chakra of the third eye. The best of the Suit of Cups is love; we could have few more inspiring mandalas for meditation than the images of these two cards.

Four of Cups

We move next to the number-four sefirah on Tree, which is the place of Chesed, of mercy and loving-kindness. It has, perhaps, a warm, golden light that infuses, fills, and surrounds us, bathes us in loving comfort. It imparts the feeling of being connected to everything else around us. This is one of the more complex cards of the Suit of Cups. We see what most perceive as a young man (but it might also be a young woman) sitting cross-legged and cross-armed on a green knoll under a tree. In the background is the suggestion of a barren mountain. There are three full cups before him and a fourth cup coming out of the sky through a cloud, held by a small hand. This is not the hand of God, but perhaps the hand of an angel. Why isn't he taking the cup? That is the interesting question. The answer is manifold, and it's what gives richness and interest to the card.

There are some who feel—and I believe this is the most popular interpretation of the card—that this figure represents surfeit and satiation. Jupiterian expansiveness has become cloying. There is already such abundance that there is no enthusiasm or need for anything further. There's a kind of lethargy to the card, a sort of indolence—it's just not worth the effort to reach out for this next cup; it will just be more of the same. This ties in very well with the message of Chesed. We are reminded again that Chesed, as wonderful as it is, is not on the central pillar of the Tree. It is an extreme. It needs to be balanced. There's nothing more wonderful than going out for a delicious, beautifully prepared, multicourse gourmet meal when you're really hungry. It is less wonderful to go out for a delicious, beautifully prepared, multicourse gourmet meal right after one has just finished a delicious, beautifully prepared, multicourse gourmet meal. We need to hunger as well as to be satisfied. So one of the interpretations of the Four of Cups is that this is someone who is just spoiled; someone who is subject to the danger of Chesed: having more than enough.

However, there are a number of other very interesting interpretations possible. Many of these have come from students of mine. I love to look at these cards, these same images year after year, and have someone just blow me away with an interpretation that I've never thought of and that is obviously correct! One person said, "Oh, he's going to take that cup all right—when he's ready! But if that's his cup, he doesn't have to grab at it, because nobody else is going to get it. It will wait for him." There's a lot of wisdom in that.

Another interpretation I like is that this card represents a temptation. Perhaps the figure sitting under the tree is meditating, and when we're meditating, the last thing we want is to be distracted by some cup that comes along. Yes, it may be a good thing, but how good would it have to be to make it worth interrupting our meditation? What is more valuable than inner peace, discourse with the divine? We are even reminded of the temptations of Jesus. Refusal may not be a sign of lethargy.

Still another interpretation is that this person, far from doing nothing, far from being indolent, is bringing this cup into his life, as indeed he has attracted the other three. This then becomes an image of centering ourselves, so that we know what we really need and want, and then attracting it—sucking it out of the universe, quietly drawing it into our life instead of scurrying around, getting involved in a lot of activity, and raising a lot of dust. Magnetizing our desires, rather than chasing them. You know, we go back to the notion of Abracadabra: as it is said, so shall it be. And isn't that what affirmations are? After all these years, finally we come back to affirmations: the notion of the relationship between what we say and what happens to us. So this is a card of sending out the kind of mental energy that pulls into our life what we want and need.

There is in the Four of Cups the suggestion of the Buddha sitting under the bodhi tree in meditation, cross-legged and undistracted. But there's also the suggestion in the crossed arms of holding back and keeping ourselves safe from the world. There is a defensiveness in this posture, the suggestion of being closed off at the heart chakra, the solar plexus, or somewhere in between. Perhaps the figure is too recently out of a relationship (or three) to be ready to receive the love now being offered—not because the love is flawed, but because there has not yet been enough healing to risk further vulnerability. It is unclear whether the eyes are closed or the eyelids merely lowered, but the figure in the Four of Cups is clearly turned within, feeling rather than looking out. He is unaware of the mountain, always the symbol of pure, objective truth, truth beyond subjective feeling. Again we are off balance in Chesed, in need of form to balance feeling.

Five of Cups

We move on to Gevurah and the Five of Cups. Gevurah, we will remember, carries a force that is difficult and painful. Gevurah means severity, strength; it means judgment and is related to the left hand of God. It forces us to deal with the judgment we need to exercise in our own lives.

We have in the Five of Cups a terribly sad image men invariably see as male and women as female. In fact, most people I know relate to

it as a photograph of themselves. What we see is simple and clear: a figure shrouded in black, head hung in a posture of grief, faces three overturned cups while two full cups remain behind.

This is clearly an image of mourning. There is a river, perhaps the River Styx, the river of death, which runs through Hades in Greek mythology. Or maybe it's the River Lethe, the river of forgetfulness, which also runs through Hades. We see a little bridge that crosses the river to what looks to be a quite comfortable house. So one very common interpretation of the card is that there is no use crying over spilled milk. "If you would just turn around and see every-thing you still have to be grateful for, ev-erything you don't have to be unhappy about, if you would just recognize that you haven't lost everything, you could cross that river and get on with life." That is both true and extremely important.

It also very much misses the point. The question is not *whether* this figure should turn around, see what life still has to offer, cross the river, and get on with life. The question is *when!*

If I'm a mother, and I see my four-year-old son run over by a truck, what is my reaction? Do I throw up my hands in joy and proclaim my good fortune that I have three other children? Do I skip back into the house to play with them? To take denial to this extreme reveals it for the unauthentic response it is. Yet in more subtle forms, many of us are subject to it.

What I have described is an enormously painful place, and there is no one reading this book who hasn't been there, and there is no one reading this book who will not be there again. The question is not whether we're going to be there; the question is whether we're going to allow ourselves to feel the appropriate feelings when we are there.

Pain hurts! We can't wait to get out of it! When we're little kids and we see something we want on the hot stove, we reach out to get it and our hands get burned. Nobody has to tell us to pull our hands back! Nobody has to explain to us why we should! Ow! That hurts! Our natural response to pain is to get away from it. And that's true for suffering, too.

Am I advocating wretchedness? Should we ache forever? Of course not. But most people don't have that problem. The problem most people have with grieving is not that they stay in it too long. The problem most people have with anguish is that they won't stay in it at all. We can't get away from it fast enough! There is another reason we are all so anxious to get away from pain (as if we needed one). It makes us feel helpless.

What is the first thing many people do with hurt? Convert it immediately into anger. Anger makes us feel powerful and strong! "Look at me! I'm charging around screaming! I'm yelling; I'm raging; I'm swinging at things! I'm frightening people! They are reacting to me. I'm no pathetic victim, reduced to useless crying and passive suffering." That's the way a lot of people deal with pain. They flat out deny it, turn it into rage. We can see it in their eyes, in their body language.

There is a final problem with pain, apart from the present misery that reduces us to inaction and humiliating impotence: when we are in it, *we don't know how long it's going to last.* I always think when I look at this card of the signs on the Los Angeles freeways: three miles to Fairfax, two miles to Fairfax, one mile . . . . Where are these signs when we really need them? What we need is a signboard that says, "Three years until you never think about this again, six months until it becomes bearable, two months until you have a two-hour stretch when it doesn't occur to you at all." We might be able to stick with it then and go through the agony we have to go through. But we can't count "how many days" until we get over the loss of a child or the death of a parent. We are only told how many shopping days there are until Christmas.

Yet somewhere, unmarked on the calendar, is the day we get through unscathed. We look back on it and say, "You know, I didn't think about him once all day!" If we knew when it was going to be, even if it were years away; if at the end of each day of suffering, we could cross a day off the calendar and say, "I'm one day closer to being free of it," we could somehow find a way to make it without falling into despair and running away from the torment. But that day is there. We've got to believe it's there. That is the meaning of the Five of Cups: to stay in pain as long as we need to.

I once did a short reading in which the card turned up reversed. When this card turns up reversed, you know the person is in trouble, because the reversal suggests denial. I said to the querent (the person asking the question), "Have you recently lost someone you loved?" and she said no. I asked, "Have you suffered any loss?" and she said no. "It doesn't have to be recent," I persisted. "Can you think of anything?" She thought a while, and finally said dispassionately, "Well, my mother died, but that was a year ago." Muffling my astonishment, I asked, "How long do you think you should (and I purposely used the word *should*) grieve for your mother?" To my further amazement, she answered me with a *number*. She thought about it and said, "A year." "I don't agree with that at all," I told her. "You grieve until you're through grieving, and the place in you that mourns doesn't care what your conscious mind thinks about it. Your conscious mind does not get a vote. Your rational mind does not get to decide how long you 'should' grieve." At that point, she suddenly broke down, and she said something that made me cry, too. It was naive, but it expressed an emotional truth. She said, "I worry about her sometimes. I worry about her being in the ground, and I worry if she's cold." Now, of course it's only the body that's in the ground. We know that. But the fact is that it was the body of her *mother*. That was the feeling the card reflected, and it appeared upside down because she had been repressing it.

When the bloody warrior planet Mars strikes, we have to mourn, to allow ourselves to hurt. We have to stay with the pain until it changes something in us and releases us. Only then can we release *it*. But we can't decide from a logical, quantifying place how much pain we're going to allow ourselves to feel. We just have to be brave enough and have enough faith—in God, in the universe, and in ourselves—to know that somehow, if we allow the process to complete itself, we will come through. So yes, this is a card of grieving. First we have to cry, "I have lost the use of my legs! He was the drunk driver! *He* walked away! *I* lost the use of *my* legs." Then we can turn around to the two upright cups and say, "Life isn't really over. I still can see; I can communicate; there are still good things in my life!" Only then is it time to cross the bridge and begin again. When we have experienced Gevurah's dark night of the soul and submitted to God's judgment for the restoration of karmic balance, when we have endured the severity of the experience and exercised our judgment to stay with our pain until we have learned the spiritual lesson, then we can be released from suffering.

The right shoulder, arm, and hand of Chesed and the left of Gevurah meet at the throat chakra, the chakra of communication. In the Four and Five of Cups, we see images in which there is no avenue of expression. We may chant to the Four of Cups and sob to the Five or bring the images together in spontaneous song. Perhaps we can use the voice of our pen to express what these images release from our unconscious. For most of us, the left hand offers us the opportunity for automatic writing; the right, more directed, conscious pursuits. Both efforts would be well spent in relation to these powerful cards.

Six of Cups

Now we move to Tiferet, beauty, which is the sixth sefirah on the Tree, and we find the Six of Cups, a card that is apparently simple at first glance. We see two children in the courtyard of what looks like a wealthy estate. It is a card of unutterable sweetness; it is not only filled with cups, but the cups are filled with flowers! We see a little girl three or four years old, looking up adoringly at her brother, who is five or six. He is offering her white flowers. She thinks he's wonderful, and the card is just as sweet as can be—until we look a little more closely.

The first thing many of us notice is that there is something odd about the figure of the little boy. We begin to wonder whether he is a child or whether we are in fact looking at a dwarf. That would explain the disproportionately large upper body. If that is the case, the meaning of the card changes dramatically. What we are actually seeing then is a dwarf adored by someone who is too little to know that he is "abnormal." We are reminded of Ghirlandaio's painting of the loving upturned face of a child who sees only his beloved grandfather and not the disease that has ravaged the old man's face. Sadly, the dwarf cannot expect to receive such love except from a very small and unquestioning child.

Who is the figure retreating in the background? Is he the caretaker, his work on the grounds completed? Or is he an abandoning parent, leaving the children entirely on their own, in their sweetness and innocence? Let us turn our attention next to the shield bearing the diagonal cross of the martyred Saint Andrew. The suggested martyrdom forces us to focus on the question of why the image of the Six of Cups shows up in Tiferet.

Tiferet, as we may recall, is the place of the sacrificed god, the place of Christ consciousness. It is the place of the wounded warrior. Why is the cross of the martyr in the card of children? The shocking answer is that children are always martyred. William Wordsworth, in his magnificent "Ode: Intimations of Immortality," tells us that we come to Earth "trailing clouds of glory." The god-spirit, fresh from Keter, is suddenly subjected to all the pain and harshness of Malchut. The soul is sacrificed to the rigors of conformity, socialization, arbitrary rules, rigidity, rejection, disillusion, and "all the natural shocks that flesh is heir to," in Shakespeare's words. Between incarnations we choose our wounds. We choose to be wounded so that the warrior we emerge to be is feeling, as well as strong. Often the martyrdom is of such proportion that it is beyond bearing. My practice as a Tarot reader affirms John Bradshaw's assertion that one in three children is sexually molested. When we add to this figure other forms of physical abuse and to that, emotional and mental abuse, the reality becomes staggering. It takes a lifetime of work and great faith to believe that there is a matrix from which we chose our experiences for our own karmic growth. So yes, children are always martyred.

As appalling as this notion is, what I am about to say is still more horrifying. There is one sense in which the children must be martyred.

When children are very small, we have to promise them that we will always be there for them, that we will always take care of them, that we will never let anything bad happen to them, that they are 100-

percent safe. I have a five-year-old niece whose closest friend was recently killed in an automobile accident. She is plagued with nightmares and in such terror that she doesn't want to leave the house, much less get into a car. Her parents have to tell her, "It's not going to happen to you! It can never happen to you! You don't have to worry about it."

When small children first see someone in a wheelchair or a blind person walking with a cane, they become very frightened. They feel their own vulnerability. They are so little. They don't know how to cross the street; they don't how much a quarter is; they can't read. Children are so helpless that unless their parents tell them, "You're all right, you're safe. I'd never let anyone hurt you," they wither. Research has shown that very small children, two or three years old, give up on life if they don't get reassurance and nurturing. It's too scary for them. They either die or they become schizophrenic. They totally withdraw from the world. We have to make them this promise of total safety.

What happens when little Georgie is no longer four years old, and I'm no longer putting a bandage on his knee and kissing his boo-boo and telling him it's all better now? Now Georgie is sixteen, and he says, "Oh, Mom! I didn't do my term paper, and it's due tomorrow. You know a lot about the Civil War. Just type something for me fast, will you?" I say, "Excuse me? Whose term paper is this? You mangled it. Fix it! You stay up all night and type it, or you explain it to the teacher." And he says, very rightfully, "But you said you'd never let anything bad happen to me! If I go to school without the paper, I'm going to fail! Are you going to let that happen to me?" And I say, "You bet." And that's betrayal. I lied. I promised him something, and I was lying, and I knew I was lying at the time.

When our kids are busted for drugs and hauled off to the police, what is the devoted parent to do? We remember what we swore to our children; shall we go down to the police station and say, "You've got this all wrong! Actually, my friend and I were having a little party and it was our stash; it had nothing whatever to do with my son."

If we don't lie for the boy, he'll be arrested, and he may go to jail. We promised him we'd protect him from anything bad. To be honorable, not to mention consistent, don't we have to spare him the terrible consequences of his behavior?

We could follow this course. That's how we raise nice little socio-paths, people who have no sense of responsibility. So what are we to do? Do we tell kids when they're two years old, "Stand on your own two feet. Yes, you could be killed in a car crash. You just have to take your chances"? Or do we, when we are dealing with teenagers who are being irresponsible, say, "Don't worry. I'll hide you; I'll take care of it"?

There is only one remaining alternative. We have to martyr our children. We have to lie to them; we have to betray them. There is a time in their lives when they have to *feel* totally protected although they aren't, and there is a time when they have to take full responsibility for their actions.

The Six of Cups is a card of sacrifice for the parent as well as for the child. The retreating adult carries a spear. A time comes when we cannot protect our children, no matter how much it hurts us to do what we know is the right thing to do. No, I will not write a sick note for you saying that I had a cold compress on your forehead all day if you were at the beach surfing. I won't do that. It hurts me to refuse, but I know I must. Our crucifixion as children is to be betrayed. Our crucifixion as adults is to betray the ones we love most.

The good news is that resurrection follows crucifixion, and the sacrificed gods—Osiris, Balder, Jesus—don't stay dead. Even Orpheus and Proserpina returned from Hades, the kingdom of the dead. The variety and meaning of sacrifice notwithstanding, all these myths share an ultimate meaning: return brings a new perspective, a new understanding, a lucidity that comes to us in no other way. With Tiferet comes the sun in all its blinding brilliance. With the sun, our hearts re-emerge from the darkness of our sacrificial night, and there is beauty in the transformation we have survived.

Seven of Cups

Next we move to the Seven of Cups, which is in Netzach. Netzach is an energy of movement and passionate Venusian feeling. The Seven of Cups shows a figure standing in silhouette with seven cups hanging in the air. Some of them hold overflowing jewels, castles, victory wreaths, and angels. In the others are a dragon, a serpent, and a ghost-like figure. On one, a skull seems to confront us. This is the card of projection and fantasy. We see here someone who stands with his head literally in the clouds! He has no reality check. This figure in the Seven of Cups is operating totally on feeling; there's no balance. Netzach carries energy which needs to be balanced by Hod. Without the balance of rational mind, projection results.

The projection seems to be of a negative sort. The figure is in silhouette, and the raised hand is stiff and suggestive of fear. Leonardo da Vinci's *Last Supper* depicts such a hand.

The painting reveals the dual nature of Jesus: the left hand, representing his divine nature, is upturned as a gift. It says, "I will be betrayed. I will be crucified. It is part of God's plan. I must suffer." The right hand represents Jesus' humanity. Palm down and tense, like that in the Seven of Cups, it shows his fear of what lies ahead.

In the Seven of Cups, then, is the suggestion of fear and of unrealistic hopes. It is a card of expecting something that is totally beyond the realm of reality. The good *and* bad news is that whatever we anticipate is coming from within; it's not a reflection of anything in the world external to our psyches. Suppose the Seven of Cups turns up when you are trying to envision your first day of work on a new job. Any number of fantasies can go through your head! "Gee, maybe this will be *the* career move for me. After six months, there'll be promotions and raises, and by the end of my life I'll be president of the company in the big corner office with windows on both sides." Or else, "Maybe nobody will like me, and I won't have anybody to eat lunch with. Maybe I'll be fired within a week, or maybe they'll cut my pay." All of these hopes and fears, the Seven of Cups tells us, are our own projections and imaginings. If you are awaiting the results of your medical exam, and you just *know* the lab tests are going to come up positive, hope for the Seven of Cups. It tells you that what is masquerading as intuition is only fear. On the other hand, if you meet the man of your dreams at a party some Friday night and just *know* that he is the man who will marry you and father your five unconceived children, temper your expectations if the Seven of Cups presents itself.

A positive aspect of this card deals with creativity. Novelist Vladimir Nabokov has said that the first fiction writer was the boy who cried wolf—the one who had the imagination to cry, "Wolf! Wolf!" when there was no wolf. This is the card of creative imagination.

Finally, some see the figure of the Seven of Cups as a magician conjuring the vision before him. If this is so, his strained demeanor suggests that he is a novice. Yet until we can conceive what it is we wish to create, until we can envision what we mean to manifest, we have little hope of realizing it. The victory of Netzach resides in our successful reification of our fantasies. What we see more powerfully represented, however, is the danger of being out of balance, even if it is on the right pillar of the Tree, the Pillar of Mercy. Netzach and Cups both carry our emotions. We have the suit of feeling in the sefirah of feeling, and that's simply too much unchecked feeling. When we look at the Eight of Cups (which combines the feelings of Cups with the mental energy of Hod) or the Seven of Swords (which places the mental suit in Netzach, the vessel of passion), we can see the benefits of balancing thought and emotion.

Eight of Cups

The Eight is associated with Hod, the sefirah of reasoning and intellect. It shows a figure walking away from eight cups that are stacked nicely, but in a formation that suggests lack of completion. He's walking alone, but with determination, courage, and great energy, as suggested by the red of his cape and boots. He is walking to a place of higher ground, to a dark mountain at the edge of indeterminate waters. He walks by night in the light of the moon, which is shown in two phases. Or perhaps it is day, and the darkness is due to a solar eclipse.

Is it a partial eclipse, or will the moon completely obliterate the sun as his journey progresses?

The first question we must ask about the figure in the Eight of Cups is, "Why has he turned his back on eight cups? Why is he walking away from so much?" The most persuasive positive answer is that he is the consummate idealist, someone who will not compromise his ideals. He is not willing to settle for what most of us would see as plenty, and he has the energy and intent to climb higher. On the other hand, there is an equally persuasive answer that reflects the negative charge of the Eight of Cups, and that is that the figure is the consummate perfectionist. As the cups are stacked, there's a gap in the middle. The pattern is not perfect. "Not perfect? Not good enough! I'm out of here. I'm leaving, and I'll keep going until I see something perfect." Herein lies the flaw of the Eight of Cups, because there is no perfection in this world. If you're going to leave your job because the water in the cooler isn't cold enough, or if you're going to leave a relationship because you don't think your lover is tidy enough, you may keep walking away from good things all of your life.

There is a place for perfectionism in our lives. If in our efforts we strive for that standard, knowing it is not attainable, we may achieve a quality beyond what we would otherwise manifest. The problem with perfectionism is in viewing it as a realizable or even *necessary* goal and applying it in the wrong areas of our lives. Nothing, for example, needs to be perfectly clean, and no one can expect be perfectly happy, or kind, or serene.

An interpretation I particularly like, which never would have occurred to anyone with my temperament, is knowing when we've had enough of something. "I'm leaving, not because it's not wonderful, but because I've done that. I've had that experience. And now it's time to move on." The relationship, job, or career has come to an end, and it's time to let it go. "I love this house. I've been here for twenty years. I raised my children here. Now they are all gone, and I've got five bedrooms, and I'm living here alone. I'll always be glad to have lived here, but it's time to sell and find a small apartment in a building with an elevator!"

Another interpretation suggests that the figure pictured is simply continuing his process of cup gathering to complete the set. Where do we suppose the first eight come from, and how did they get there?

Still another casts the figure as searching for the Holy Grail—the true passion of his life, perhaps. The first eight turned out to be only ordinary cups; he is not giving up the search, however, certain that the next cup will be the long-sought object of his desires. A third view is that the "missing cup" lies hidden in the cape of the retreating figure.

Predictably, the interpretation of the Eight of Cups that seems to me to be the most profound is the one that goes within. What do we have when we move feelings into conscious mind, Cups into Hod? Introspection, reflection, an effort to understand our own emotions. The dark mountain is the unconscious, what Jung calls the shadow. We make the journey to this place by the dim, half-light of the moon. And we make it *alone*. We can't take our closest friend; we can't take a spouse, a parent, child, or sibling. We can't even take our therapist! When we enter our own mystery, we return to the experience that is preverbal, the quality of which cannot be captured in the loosely woven net of language and therefore cannot be shared. Whether we make the journey through dream work, meditation, active imagination, or ritual, we must go alone when we enter into our own darkness. And the darkness always brings us to a higher place of self.

Whether we go by pale lunar light (as in lunacy) or in the darkness of eclipse, the clear light of day gives way to the eerie light of the moon, which invites the projections of our own unconscious. The mountain, representing our higher self, is in darkness. We cannot go high without going deep. We cannot skip the painful stages of confronting our own shadow and use the "spiritual" to mask work left undone, truths left masked. As the mountain reveals, the elevation and the darkness are inextricably bound. Mercury, the messenger god and the planet associated with Hod, suggests here the communication between thought (Hod) and feeling (Cups), between conscious intent and unconscious mystery. And Hod, which means "glory" or "splendor," is at its most glorious when properly infused with feeling.

The top of the right and left hips, associated with Netzach and Hod, meet in the solar plexus. This gut-level reality in the chakra system is reflected in both the danger of projection seen in the Seven of Cups and the descent into our own mystery, reflected in the Eight.

Nine of Cups

The Nine of Cups is another card in which there is more than meets the eye. We see a figure sitting with his feet planted far apart, cross-armed, in front of a tall table with nine full cups stacked behind him.

He's wearing a red hat with a red plume and red socks. What a guy! He's got it all! Why shouldn't he be smug and complacent? This is the card of getting into bed with a spoon and the whole carton of ice cream, taking the phone off the hook, turning on your favorite meaningless television rerun, and refusing to be disturbed. It's the card that says, "You know, I've been striving and grappling and groping and growing all month. Time for a break."

The Nine of Cups reminds us to enjoy the good things in life. It's dog heaven. It's recognizing our animal nature: "I just want a hot bath. I don't want to communicate, I don't want to study, and I don't want to learn anything even if I don't have to study to learn it. I just want to kick back." This card is an admission of part of who we are. We need, every once in a while, simply to have a good time. Sometimes we just want to be by ourselves and sometimes, downright selfish.

Another possibility is that the Nine of Cups is a kind of magician. The suggestion is that the table is so high because it is an altar, and the figure's pride is the result of his having successfully conjured the cups upon it.

However, as we look at the card a question eventually occurs to us. Why is that blue tablecloth so long? Many people naturally refer to it as a curtain and not a tablecloth at all! Is something hidden behind it?

At this point we have to remember that the Nine of Cups falls in the sefirah of Yesod, associated with the Moon and the unconscious. Whatever is behind that blue tablecloth is unconscious, hidden from our awareness. The negative of the card, then, has to do with sweeping things under the rug, distracting ourselves with the pleasures of life, and involving ourselves, once again, in denial. Very often when this card turns up, especially if it turns up reversed, we're dealing with addiction. I define addiction as whatever we do, not for its own sake, but for the sake of altering consciousness rather than dealing with it. If we take the position that there is a card for every experience, the Nine of Cups reversed represents using whatever is in the cups—whether it's wine, cocaine, or food—as a distraction from whatever we don't want to face, from whatever is behind the blue curtain to which we have our back. Years ago I did a short reading for a stranger at a psychic fair. When the Nine of Cups emerged upside down, I suggested she find a twelve-step program. She replied with amazement that she had just gone to her first Overeaters Anonymous meeting.

We don't necessarily distract ourselves with something ingestible. We can do it with the telephone, movies, house cleaning, intellectual pursuits, charity work, or professional advancement. The particular choice of distraction isn't important; what is relevant is that we are using one thing to keep from experiencing something else. So when the card is upside down, it's a kind of red flag, in my practice. What am I not facing that I need to be dealing with? What have I swept under the rug and from what am I distracting myself? Workaholics, as the coined word implies, have a lot in common with alcoholics.

A related interpretation has to do with the fact that the figure in the Nine of Cups, while presenting himself as jaunty, is all alone. He has more than enough for many but no one with whom to share it. The crossed arms seem to say, "I don't care," but I for one don't believe him; do you? We have explored the Four of Cups; we recognize the defensive closing off of the channel between the heart and the solar plexus. Perhaps as one friend suggested he is in need of bravado because with all he has—a table so crammed with cups there is room for no more—he's turned his back on everything. If the Suit of Cups represents love, why is his back to it, leaving him, finally, a lonely figure? And why does he pretend to have all the cups when we know there is a tenth? For the answer to that, we would have to look under the blue cloth.

Yesod is associated with the axis between the genitals and the base of the spine connecting our most primitive chakras, those of survival and procreation. It is called "foundation," and like the unconscious, serves as the foundation of our lives. The unconscious, hidden behind the blue "curtain" in the Nine of Cups, will prove the truth of our lives, red cocked hat with matching socks notwithstanding!

Ten of Cups

Finally, we come to Malchut where we find the Ten of Cups, and a very joyful card it is. It is the card of a happy family. In the Ten of Pentacles we also saw a family, but the card seemed cluttered; the pentacles seemed to be interfering with interpersonal relationships. Here we see a happy family, people who are out in nature, in the open. It's not just that they have a great deal, but that they are enjoying what they have. The couple direct their attention to a rainbow filled with cups above a pleasant landscape, through which a stream runs before a nice enough, big enough house. They appreciate all they have received.

What is a rainbow? The rainbow first appears in the Bible after the flood. God creates a rainbow as a pledge to Noah that He will never again destroy the world. So the rainbow is the symbol of peace after the storm, of God's covenant with us for perpetuity.

The couple stand close together, the man's arm around the woman's waist. They are of equal height, suggesting a relationship of parity rather than domination. They are perhaps the couple we saw in the Two, now seasoned, their love matured. They no longer face each other, gazing drunkenly into one another's eyes, but, arms extended to the world at large, share a vision. Looking in the same direction, they see the world in the same way. They have found joy on the earth plane of Malchut within the real confines of family life, not just in some imagined dream of bliss. The children are dancing unselfconsciously. They feel safe and loved and happy. The triumph of the Suit of Cups is the joy and the wonder of feeling in this world, in Malchut, the kingdom, the planet Earth. If a man's home is his castle, the man pictured feels himself master of all he surveys—and so, clearly, does the woman. They are the sovereigns of their lives in the Kingdom of Malchut. Malchut is associated with the soles of the feet; skipping and playing is just the way feet should be used by children! And the mature couple seem to know that the ground on which they stand is holy.

Yet there is further development possible and ultimately necessary, for we find ourselves once again looking at a separation card. The family unit takes love beyond the romantic, broadens its circle, but still those loved are separated from the rest. It is tempting, natural, even good that we protect, love, and sequester those closest to us. For love to be complete, however, it must be inclusive. We are all one: connected or not by blood, we are connected by soul. Later in our study we will discover a card that suggests, as Arthur Miller says, that they "are all our sons." (Feel free to search the cards and find it for yourself! Peeking ahead is not only allowed, it is encouraged!)

CHAPTER 5
Swords: The Edge of Truth

*A*S I SUGGESTED in the chapter on Pentacles, we each have certain Tarot suits with which we are particularly attuned. Anyone who denies that this is the case is not being honest. If we were all in such perfect balance that we related equally well to every suit and every card in the deck, we would have no reason to be on Earth. We are here because we have work to do, and the work, as suggested both by Kabbalah and Tarot, is to get ourselves into balance. Of the suits to which I am particularly attuned, the Suit of Swords comes second, which may seem downright perverse. The Swords are very difficult cards. This is not a suit where people have a good time. However, we learn some of our most valuable lessons through our pain; comfort carries a tendency toward inertia. Most of us committed to personal growth are in sympathy with this suit even if we don't like it very much.

The Suit of Swords, which deals with intellect and determination, is the suit of the truth seeker. It is the suit of awareness and understanding. T. S. Eliot writes, "We had the experience, but we missed the meaning." Here in the Suit of Swords, we are going, by gum or by golly, to get the meaning.

The Suit of Swords represents the willingness to experience whatever it is we need to experience to get to the truth. And the truth, rumor has it, can hurt. The truth will set you free, but as Werner Erhardt adds, "First it will piss you off." Some of us will pursue the truth irrespective of pain, regardless of cost, submitting to confusion and despair, on only a promise of clearer understanding. Conversely, if we are drowning in pain and are thrown a rope, we will not catch hold of it if we know the rope to be a lie.

Because the truth can hurt, in the Suit of Swords we are also dealing with courage. It takes enormous valor to go through the pain that is depicted in these images. As each suit has its way to spirit, the way of Swords is not only the way of intellect, the search for objective truth and clarity. It is also the way of courage.

The Suit of Swords is additionally important for people who are interested in Tarot, because no matter how bright we are, no matter how intuitive we are, how perceptive and deeply feeling, if we haven't got the commitment to look at our own life intrepidly, we will never learn anything from the cards. It's amazing to me how many people come for a consultation after driving long distances just to find me. They put in a lot of energy and happily pay my fee, but really don't want to know. They *think* they want to know, but they really don't. What they truly want is to be supported in a belief system that is not serving them well.

When people literally don't want to see what is "in the cards" and are not ready to take an honest look at themselves, there is absolutely nothing anyone can do. A cardinal example was a self-proclaimed enlightened being. He was working with a yoga master, meditating and doing yoga seven hours a day. He said to me, "You know, I've been divorced three times. Every one of my wives has been a monster. Every one of my wives has mistreated me. In fact, everybody mistreats me. I'm just too good a person, too nice a guy. My own children have chosen to live with their stepmother rather than with me, their own biological father. Not since Job . . . ." When I looked at his cards I was not stunned to find that this was an inaccurate assessment of his situation. The Two of Swords and the Eight of Swords—the only two cards in the Tarot whose figures are blindfolded—were both in prominent positions, while the immature Page of Swords was the card he chose to represent himself.

When we start to read professionally, we must be clear on our purpose. We do not read to be brilliant; we read to be helpful. It is sometimes less valuable to convey everything we see than to communicate what needs to be understood in a way that can be heard. (Remember the Six of Pentacles? We give people only the information they are ready to receive.) So I began gently nudging this gentleman from different angles. "Well, you have three children, and they all decided to live with their stepmother. Any ideas about why that might be?" Or, "Can you think of anything you might have done, in any one of these three marriages, that was not contributory to its success?" But he didn't want to see. As a result, he took a long drive, involved himself emotionally in a consultation, paid me his hard-earned money, and left without learning anything.

A reader can provide the insight, the intuition, and the perception, but only the querent can provide the courage. Dedication to truth, symbolized by the Suit of Swords, was not a part of his nature at that time.

The Suit of Swords, then, is beloved to lovers of truth, to those of us who are ruthless with ourselves in the pursuit of truth. It is just because the truth can hurt that it is represented by the double-edged sword. It can as easily lacerate the wielder as the object of attack.

The Ace of Swords

ACE of SWORDS

The principle of *truth above all* is symbolized in the Ace by the fact that the sword pierces a crown. What this means is that nothing is beyond question, nothing is beyond challenge, nothing is too sacred to be looked at with skepticism in terms of its truth. The Suit of Swords engenders the frame of mind that proclaims, "But the emperor isn't *wearing* any clothes!" There's got to be somebody to say, "No matter how important you are, no matter how powerful you are, no matter how much harm you can do to me personally, if something isn't true, it isn't true. And saying it or acting as if it *is* true doesn't make it so." The Ace of Swords will pierce through any authority to address the truth.

I had a very interesting firsthand experience of this phenomenon when I was working for CBS Cable Cultural Network. It was a marvelous conception. William Paley, who was the chairman and president of CBS at the time, had come up with the idea of a purely cultural network whose programming was ballet, opera, quality theater, and fine films. A marvelous conception that nobody watches because it has been off the air since nine months after its marvelous conception. Why? Because nobody wanted to tell Bill Paley that he'd gotten it wrong! This was *Bill Paley,* the founder and head of CBS! So he was saying things like, "When we take advertisers' money, we won't accept less than a million dollars." That was the minimum commitment an advertiser could make! All of the Senior Executive Vice Presidents, who wanted to remain Senior Executive Vice Presidents, said "Yeah! Yeah! That's the way we'll do it! That's right! That's the way we'll do it!"

When this information filtered down to the sales staff, we reeled back in horror! Because we then had to go out into the real world and try to sell a brand new kind of programming idea without any of the necessary sales tools, but at an enormous price. So I call on an account executive at, say, J. Walter Thompson. I show them the promotional tape and assure them that it's going to be terrific. Now this account executive at J. Walter Thompson doesn't want to make the brilliant media buy of the century. What this account executive wants is to be an account supervisor next year. What he really wants is not to make any mistakes. So he says to me, "Well, how many people watch CBS cable?" And I say, "Ah . . . um . . . nobody knows because we're not measured by Nielsen: But it is in five hundred thousand households," I added brightly. "Yes," he replies, "and mine is one of them. I get it free, and I haven't watched it yet." I was considered a crackerjack salesperson, but even I couldn't follow that up with "Well, how about just a million?"

Within nine months, this brilliant station went bust. There wasn't anybody willing to pierce the crown and say, "Bill, it's not going to work that way. You're in fantasy land. We have to have some research, we have to have a basis on which to tell people what they're getting for their money, how many viewers, how many subscribers. We don't have any data! You may be the head muckity-muck here, but that's not the way it's going to work." If there had been someone to tell the emperor that he wasn't wearing any clothes, we might be enjoying CBS Cable Network today.

There are of course more serious examples. What if there had been people in Germany who had been willing to say, when the concept of the master race was introduced, "This is a load of crap. This is garbage. Who do you think you're kidding?" If there had been people right at the start—Jews, Germans, Poles, Rumanians, Hungarians, French, English—if there had been human beings who were willing to stand up and say, "I don't care who you are. This is just not true," much horror might have been avoided. But people were afraid. When there's great power involved, we're tempted simply to go along. "If that's what they want to be truth, then let it be the truth." It's very dangerous to be surrounded by yes-men. It's very dangerous for all of us, including the crowned one.

Hanging from the crown are both the laurel and the palm: the laurel of victory, but also the palm of peace. We can use intellect, the sword, to win if it comes down to that, but we don't need to. We can use it to negotiate peace. The best use of the intellect is to figure out, not how to win, but how to create a win/win situation so that everybody walks away satisfied.

Now let's take a look at the Ace of Swords a bit more closely. Keter, we recall, is the place where divine energy first enters the Tree. It is called the crown, where God's presence first becomes manifest in the universe. In Keter we find the ace of each suit, and the Ace of Swords, like all the other aces, reveals the hand of God entering into the world, coming out of the heavens through a cloud, shining with a halo of white light, to offer a gift. This time the gift is honesty, clarity, and intellect. It is the gift of mind, the glorious, splendid human mind. We see as well the presence of the little flamelike Yods, the first letter of the Holy Tetragrammaton. They assure us that the gift is a gift of love. As always, they represent the presence of divine energy in the world. And since there are six of these little Yods, we are reminded of Tiferet, the heart place, the number-six sefirah, the place of the sacrificed god. We are reminded of the cost involved in the search for truth.

We see in the background of this card the stark mountains of pure truth. There is nothing by way of foliage to soften or distract us from the truth. Nothing makes that landscape more gentle; it's harsh and cold and unremitting. What we see is unadorned, abstract, objective truth. Here is something we cannot attain by our most powerful intuition nor by our deepest feelings: freedom from subjective experience.

It can be obtained only by intellect. It alone makes possible the manifold, awesome gifts of science.

The sword of intellect carries the power to cut through knotty problems. We may remember the myth of the Gordian knot. In ancient Greece, there was a knot of great size and complex involution that no one seemed able to undo. It was prophesied that whoever could undo the knot would rule the world. Thousands, armed with wit, patience, and strategy, tried in vain until one man came along, drew his sword, and boldly slashed through the knot. He wasn't trapped by the preconception that he had to untie the knot, to pick at the little threads one by one. His name was Alexander the Great.

When we receive the gift of intellect, we have the capacity to cut through illusions; there's more than one way to undo a knot. In Eastern philosophies, the conscious mind is the bringer of *maya,* illusion. In Kabbalah, however, as we recall from our discussion of Hod, the thinking mind is valuable and necessary for balance. The intellect is called "glory" or "splendor," and the Ace of Swords is the only ace in which a crown appears. As the gift of the Ace of Swords comes in through Keter, the place of the crown chakra, intellect can be seen as our crowning glory. As Keter is associated with the entire cosmos, the single standard of truth applies to all equally.

The Two of Swords

We move to the number-two place on the Tree, Chochma, the place of relationships. The Two of Swords is a difficult card, the first of many, and by no means the most difficult of the suit. Why is that? Because relationships don't work very well, as a rule, if we try to figure them out. We may recall the paradigm of the Two of Cups, the greeting that is respectful, courtly, and sweet. Once we start analyzing relationships the simple joy is lost.

What does the Two of Swords represent? We see a figure, generally perceived as female, who sits solidly by the light of the waxing moon on a square stone seat. The seat rests on a pavement at the edge of ruffled waters troubled with rocks before a far-off island. She holds two swords crossed over her chest, and she is blindfolded. How shall we begin to understand this image?

The problems represented by this card are many. First, we are dealing with isolation, in the very sefirah whose energy is relatedness. The figure is consummately solitary. In addition to sitting alone and apart, she has blindfolded herself. Why would someone blindfold herself? Well, we don't know, but if she didn't want it that way, she'd put down the swords, take off the blindfold, and pick up the swords again. We're going to be looking at a figure a little later on who doesn't have that choice. But the Two of Swords could easily take that blindfold off if she chose, so we have to conclude that she likes it the way it is. She has covered her heart chakra with her crossed arms, closing off the feeling place. In short, she's stuck.

There's a lot of stuckness in the Suit of Swords because intellect by itself often leads us into obsessional thinking. We go round and round, over and over, but we don't get anywhere. Does that mean we should throw out intellect? No, it means we should balance and integrate intellect with our other functions of consciousness. While we need emotions to give vitality to our thoughts, we need intellect to keep us from going off the deep end emotionally.

The Two of Swords pictures someone immobilized by a choice she is unable to make. It suggests a time when the mind fails us. We can't figure something out. We're on the horns of a dilemma that leaves us paralyzed. Swords can represent concepts. The dilemma may involve self-image. "On the one hand, I don't want be selfish; on the other hand, I don't want to be a pushover. I can't decide what to do. I think I'll just sit here." Or, "When I say 'no,' I feel guilty; when I say 'yes,' I feel put out, used, and resentful. I'd better not do anything." Or again, "I don't want to be a coward, but I don't want to be foolhardy. I just don't know whether sailing a small craft in this weather is a safe thing to do." We've thought the issues through over and over again, but no clear decision emerges. Chochma, we are reminded, refers to the right lobe of the brain, the intuitive, creative lobe. There is wisdom in putting up our swords, as Shakespeare might say.

The suggestion here is that it may be a very good time to tune into the unconscious, as represented by the moon and waters and scattered rocks. This is not a card that carries the clarity of sunlight, of rational thinking. This is a card that depicts troubled waters—not turbulent, but hardly smooth. There are enough ripples to suggest activity; the unconscious is stirring. Perhaps there is dream life; maybe we can get helpful information from this source. The presence of the moon conveys the hope that some lunar influence will help us out of our dilemma. When this card shows up, we are not to rely entirely on the intellect, but to balance it with intuition and feeling. This is not the time to approach matters logically, but, with our physical eyes covered, to be open to third-eye information.

The primary meaning of the card, however, is that there is something we don't want to see. Why else would we choose the blindfold? But why would we choose not to see? *Because we want to avoid taking action.* If we don't see, we won't be forced to act.

Remembering that the Two of Swords, like the twos of every suit, is associated with Chochma, the place of relationship, we can best understand the image in that context. One way to avoid leaving an unfaithful husband is not to know he is unfaithful. "The wife is the last to know"—I'm sure I've heard that somewhere. Family, friends, and neighbors wonder why there is suddenly the need for so much overtime at the office. His mother-in-law raises an arched brow when her daughter explains why he'll be joining the family only for weekends at the cabin this summer. The denying wife doesn't notice the scent or lipstick on handkerchiefs when she does the laundry, nor that there are now seven, not eight, pairs of jockey shorts when she puts them away. The clues are all there; she has to blindfold herself not to see what, somewhere beyond conscious thinking, she knows. That part of her wants to believe it will blow over and she won't have to face it. If she doesn't want to leave her husband, she won't see anything that will require her to do so.

If you don't want to confront your wife on what everyone else recognizes is a drug problem, you just don't see it. She's tired or overstimulated or tense. Hey, she's an M.D.! These are *prescription* medications. She knows what she's doing!

SWORDS

And I, loving the programming so much at CBS Cable, was surprised when it failed. My secretary was job hunting months before the debacle, but I couldn't see it coming. A job that involved showing tapes of the performing arts, taking people to elegant restaurants, carried an impressive title at a top-notch company, and doubled my previous paycheck? Are you kidding? Gimme that blindfold!

We have stressed repeatedly that every card has both a positive and a negative charge. Now, what can the positive of this card be? Well, as pertains to relationship, agreeing to disagree. And you can bet that when you meet a couple who have been happily married for thirty or forty years, they do a lot of this. The positive meaning of this card is *it's not worth fighting about.*

"You are never going to pick your socks up off the floor, and I'm tired of telling you to put your dirty underwear in the hamper. I'm tired of fighting about it. So you know what? I'll pick up your socks and underwear and put them in the hamper. You're a good man. I love you. It's not worth fighting about."

"You know, I think you're much too attached to your mother. I really don't see why you have to talk to her every day and why you have to see her every weekend, but you're a good wife and I love being married to you. So part of every weekend we'll spend with your mother. It's not worth fighting about."

"You're never going to convert to Judaism. I'm never going to convert to Catholicism. Does that mean we don't want to be together?"

"I'm never going to be a Republican. You're never going to be a Democrat."

"I'm never going to give up Tarot. You're never going to believe there's anything to it. So let's choose what is worth focusing on and what we're just going to let go."

The Two of Swords is a card of keeping the peace. It's a card of not sacrificing a relationship to perfectionistic insistence on unflawed harmony. It's a card of being willing not to "win." *It's a card of not having to be right.* We are, after all, in Chochma, which means "wisdom." That's the positive aspect of the Two of Swords, and there's a lot of wisdom in approaching relationships that way.

If, however, we take that virtue one step further, we are led back into difficulty. There are people who believe in peace at any price—the pleasers. Up until very recently, women were raised to be pleasers in our society. It was very difficult to ask for what we wanted, say what we meant, and insist on our own rights. In fact, many young girls are still being raised in this repressive way. Yet we don't walk away from situations in which we have swallowed our needs and feelings without a big lump in our throat. So this card may well represent people who need to stand up for themselves.

Before we leave the Two of Swords, we must recognize it as another of the separation cards. It is relatively clear why this stuck image is a card of separation, having to do with intellect that is out of balance. Intellect always has the function of separating us from something. As Ram Dass puts it, thinking is always about something; it is never the thing itself, so it is always one step away from the action. In reflecting on our emotions, to cultivate objectivity, we separate ourselves from feeling. In thinking, "I'm meditating," we separate ourselves from the process. That's all it takes to lose the meditative state. Intellect is a power of discernment, definition, delimiting. Unchecked, it separates us even from our own lives, leaving us on the outside of our own experience, looking in.

Three of Swords

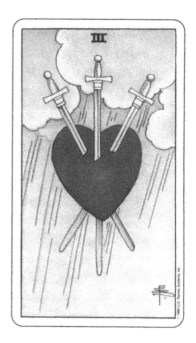

We move next to Binah, the place of Saturn, the constricting influence, and we see the Three of Swords—few people's favorite. When this card turns up in a reading, it's difficult to clap your hands and exclaim, "How delightful! This must be your lucky day!" Yet, as always, the Three is the fulfillment of the suit.

The essence of the Suit of Swords is the pain that comes through facing the truth and engenders growth. Not surprisingly, then, in the place of the supernal mother, where we are born into the world, into this vale of tears, as it were, we come to the quintessential card of the Suit of Swords. What good thing can we say about a card depicting a heart that is not protected by even a rib cage, much less by a chest, much less by clothing, much less by armor, but rather, is totally exposed and pierced by three swords? On the off chance that this image isn't miserable enough, the heart is being rained on. It is not a good day for this heart!

We don't need to dwell on the negative aspects of the card: the Three of Swords can suggest three disasters of any kind—traumas, relationships, accidents, problems with all three of your children, for example. Or they can represent, say, work, family, and health—problems in every area of your life.

What good can we see in this particular image? How can it be viewed as a fulfillment of the Suit of Swords? This question leads us to the ultimate issue about Swords and, arguably, life: What is pain, and what is it for? What are we supposed to do with it? What is the appropriate response to suffering?

We are supposed to take pain into our hearts; that's what we are supposed to do with pain.

Nobody gets out of this world alive. It seems often that we're still reeling from the last blow when we're hit again. We may well remember the figure in the Nine of Cups, distracting himself from the pain swept behind that long blue tablecloth. He'll just have another drink! That doesn't change anything, but taking pain into our heart does.

When pain comes it's time to grieve. But what's fascinating and heartening is that when we stop denying and resisting pain, when we allow pain into our hearts, it doesn't come unaccompanied. Something else comes along with it. In my life, it's been peace and faith and love and hope: a sense of the divine presence. The worst part of pain, we often find, results from resisting it, pushing against it. "It can't be true, I won't let it be true, I don't accept it, I can't stand it, I can't bear it!" If we can somehow release the resistance and say, "This happened. I don't know how I'm going to live through this, but it really has happened," something else is released. Panic, perhaps, the fear of not being able to go on. The grieving is clean, if I may put it that way. The feeling is of a clean wound. The blood flows, the tears flow, nothing festers, it all gets flushed through. It hurts and hurts and hurts and it keeps on hurting. And then it heals.

There's nothing to do with pain except take it into our hearts. We can't get though pain by letting time elapse. We can't lock it in the closet, put it under a blue tablecloth, and figure, "I'll be back in eleven months when it's gone. . . . Oops! There it is, waiting for me!" It's like the dirty laundry, you know, or the dishes in the sink. Time will not get them clean. Sooner or later we've got to do them. Like them, pain is endlessly patient and immovably loyal. It will wait for us. Sooner or later we've got to feel it. Finally, when we feel the pain, when we let it into our hearts, something in us changes. That is what pain is for. That is where transformation comes from. That is where growth comes from. Suddenly we are not as we were before. Having taken in the pain, we do not become bitter, cynical, callous, or hard. We become wise. The Three is the fulfillment of the Suit of Swords because it shows the willingness, the courage, the honesty to experience the pain in our lives.

The Two and Three of Swords reflect the right and left temples respectively, and meet at the place of the third eye in the chakra system. It would be difficult to envision two images more in need of third-eye insight.

Four of Swords

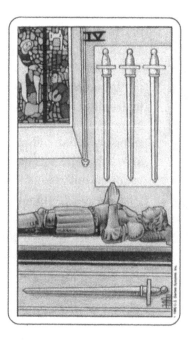

We move next to the place of Chesed, the place on the Tree where God's loving-kindness is manifest—the place of the expansive, generous planet Jupiter. It is the fourth sefirah, and as we can recall from the Four of Pentacles and the Four of Cups, the fours depict a kind of stability. Often, however, the stability lacks dynamism. There is generally a lethargy in the fours. The Four of Swords can certainly be seen in this way, as a card in which not very much is going on. It's not so much a card of death as a card of withdrawal and rest, a card of meditation and prayer. It is a card of removing ourselves from the world so that we can quiet ourselves and deal with our pain. In the painful Suit of Swords, we would expect to find this respite only in Chesed.

The contemporary Buddhist teacher Chogyam Trungpa says that

most people are "forever caught in a traffic jam of discursive thought." Our minds click away all the time; we're figuring things out, analyzing; ideas tumble over and interrupt one another. We lose all sense of ourselves; there is no sense of peace. This is the card of withdrawal from that head space to a place of quiet and serenity.

The Four of Swords shows the sarcophagus of a knight lying in state, his sculpted counterpart in repose beneath a stained-glass window. Three swords hang on the wall beside him, the fourth runs horizontally beneath him. The card has been referred to as the yoga card and certainly reminds us of *sav asana,* or "corpse pose," in which practitioners lie on their back in total stillness, all muscles relaxed, and keep the mind focused and alert in an apparently inert body. If the Four of Swords shows up in a spread in conjunction with other cards of death such as the Ten of Swords, the Tower, or Death, and in a position that suggests the physical realm, actual bodily death can be implied. But more generally by far the card suggests a turning inward.

This interpretation is favored by the position of the three vertical swords. In pointing at the third eye, the heart (or perhaps the throat), and solar plexus, they stimulate the chakras. The fourth sword parallels the entire spine, the central focus of hatha yoga.

In final support of this view, since these are swords, they are concepts, ideas. While this might be the kind of meditation we associate with Buddhism, in which we attempt to still the mind and sense nothing, gently pushing thoughts away, it is even more suggestive of the Jewish tradition of meditation, in which we work with God on whatever comes up for us. Perhaps it is most compatible with the Jungian practice of active imagination. In fact, in the Morgan-Greer deck, instead of the stained-glass window, we find an open window with the four swords floating through it. We have the sense of sustaining a dream, allowing unconscious material to stream into awareness in a free flow, with no interference or control. But whether we regard it as Eastern meditation, dialogue with God, or waking dream, the Four of Swords depicts the willingness to quiet the ordinary mind and access the inner life by closing out the external world. That is certainly a merciful way of dealing with *Three* of Swords experience. The "right hand of God" is clearly evident here.

The subject of the stained-glass window is Jesus healing the sick.

This is not death then, but a healing experience. From a Jungian perspective, each of us has Christ consciousness or the capacity for it within us. From a Kabbalistic point of view, each of us has within us Tiferet, the place of the sacrificial god. Healing can come from that source, the divine light that emanates down the Tree from limitlessness, God's essence, and is the essence of the soul.

There is another important aspect of the Four of Swords to which we may now direct our attention, and that is the difference between action and activity. If someone calls you and asks, "What did you do today?" and you say you had a busy day, you probably don't mean that you spent it meditating. You probably mean "I was running a lot of errands. I visited a sick friend, then I had to pick up the dry cleaning and drop a book off at the library before my doctor's appointment. Later I had a hairdresser's appointment, and then I had to bring some soup to my mother. And of course I always do my charity work on Tuesdays. . . ." That's an action-packed day. It is also a passive day. Rachel Pollack makes the point that true action always changes us. Activity and action may be seen to be in the same dichotomous relationship as ego and soul: the ego can use activity to distract from the soul's purpose, but when the soul takes action, it may appear from the perspective of the ego that we're not doing anything. "Oh, I just had a lazy day. I was reading and meditating." Yet that is not a lazy day; it is just a quiet day. Although the Four of Swords is an image of inactivity, it is a card of taking action in our lives.

Five of Swords

We find ourselves next in Gevurah with the Five of Swords. We have come to expect difficult cards in the number-five position, the place of the great limiter. It is without surprise, then, that we observe the Five of Swords to be the nastiest card in the deck. Under a menacing sky of jagged clouds, before a sea reminiscent of the Two of Swords' disquiet, we see three male figures of widely varying size. Their backs are to us. We cannot see the faces of the two smaller figures, but the smallest has dropped his head in his hands, his shoulders hunched in the suggestion of grief. The largest figure stands holding two swords in his left hand. Two more lie at his feet while he balances the fifth in his right hand, perhaps gathering it up. His hair and mantle blow in a cold wind, and the smirk on his face is spiteful, gloating, vengeful, and truly loathsome! It is the card of taking the last laugh, enjoying power and advantage over others. Who has this terrible energy? *You* do, everyone of you reading this book (and everyone *not* reading it). And so, of course, do I. Every one of us has this dark capacity within us.

Does that mean we all act this way? Absolutely not. Does it mean we all *want* to act this way? I should hope not. Does it mean that sooner or later we all *will* act this way? I don't think so. Does it mean we all *could* act this way? You bet! If we are all one, if we are clones of one another, if that energy that descended into me also descended into you, it is part of the universal energy. It is out there and it is in each of us. That's what makes it so challenging to be a human being. That's what we're doing in Malchut, the material world—bringing ourselves to the kind of awareness that enables us to make the choices by which we improve and evolve. We are here to take responsibility— the ability to respond—seriously, and we cannot do that when we are in a state of denial. First we have to recognize that yes, we're all capable of being genuinely vile.

When we look at the Five of Swords, it is extremely useful to ask, "With which of these three figures do I identify?" The answer will vary with time and circumstance for each of us. For years it never occurred to me that anybody could identify with any but the major figure standing in the foreground. Yet an experienced Tarot teacher amazed me by confessing that it had never occurred to *her* to identify with any but the smallest figure in the far background! If we feel ourselves at the moment to be the victor, gathering up the swords of the conquered with that particularly vicious expression on his face, we have to be aware that we really have it in for somebody—possibly with good reason. We have been treated badly! Someone has abused or betrayed or taken advantage of us. Now finally we have the upper hand, and it feels good! If we identify with the smallest of the three figures who hangs his head in retreat, it means that we are feeling, at that time, demeaned, humiliated, conquered, diminished, and ashamed.

For years I saw this card as imaging an odious victor and two pathetic, vanquished opponents, the depiction of a win/lose situation. What we see when we look more carefully is an odious victor exulting over his success, a vanquished adversary who is defeated and depressed, and someone who is simply walking away. Interestingly, few people identify with the middle figure; few even recognize that the middle figure is different from the small one. Most see only victor and vanquished. But the middle figure does not hang his head, and he walks in a different direction from the smaller one.

This leads us to the real meaning of the Five of Swords. The recognition of the difference between the two smaller figures raises the question, "Do you want to play win/lose? Do you want to be involved in a situation in which someone has to lose in order for you to win?" The middle figure says, "I don't like that game. I'm leaving. I'll find a game with different rules, or I'll create a game that is win/win." The middle figure simply knows how to walk away from a situation in which he neither wants to be humiliated nor to take the advantage.

Let me flesh out this concept by volunteering my Five of Swords experience. I was fired from a job in advertising sales because I was earning too many commissions. When my employer fired me, he simply had his office manager call me one night and say, "Don't come to work tomorrow. Or ever again." There was no explanation, but it soon emerged that I wasn't going to be paid my commissions.

My reactions were interesting. I had fantasies of taking my keys and running them vigorously across the paint job of my former boss's new Mercedes. I had visions of breaking into his office at night and putting chewing gum in the new computer, smashing windows, burning files. Did I do any of that? No. If I had learned that he had been in an automobile wreck and was quadriplegic, would I have been happy? No. But when I learned that he had lost some of the magazines he had been representing and that his income had been vastly reduced, I was delighted!

Yes, I have a vengeful, spiteful side. I don't have to act on it, but I do have to know it's there. And I learned something interesting from this experience. I learned, on a gnostic level, on a level that was genuinely knowing, something I'd understood intellectually all my life. I understood ghetto kids. I understood them because my anger toward this employer extended beyond just him. It extended to all of the bosses in the whole damned advertising industry! I would go to an Ad Club luncheon, look around, and feel hatred in my heart for all those people who were taking advantage of their sales staffs. So I thought to myself, "Oh, poor me! I was taken advantage of . . . once." Ghetto kids have known nothing except disadvantage and mistreatment. Imagine, they're breaking into the cars and houses of people who have never done anything to hurt them! People they have never even met! What a big surprise! Because of my own experience, suddenly I could understand the anger, the self-righteous rage that spills over past its object into whole classes of people.

The experience was valuable for me in another way as well. I have never tended to be shy or self-conscious, but now I was faced with a dilemma: I needed a job; the best place to look for one was at an Ad Club meeting, but how could I show up at the next luncheon? Everybody knew I had been fired. How could I hold up my head? I mustered all my courage and strength, arranged my face, and gamely went to the meeting. At the bar during the social hour before lunch, one luminary of the industry came charging up to me, exclaiming at the top of his lungs, "What *happened?* I heard you were *fired!*" There were three hundred people in the room and every one of them heard him. As heads turned, and I felt myself the center of quintessentially unwanted attention, I had a new grasp of the smallest of the Five of Swords figures. What we least crave in our moments of abject shame is a large audience.

It is obvious that the Five of Swords is a separation card. The nature of the separation, in the case of each of the three figures, is relatively clear. The smallest figure, in wretched disgrace, feels alienated, cut off, shunned from all of humankind. The bully in his momentary triumph experiences the pleasure of his victory only because he is cut off from any sense of compassion. Were he to feel empathy, connectedness to those who suffer at his hand, he would be unable to savor his success. And the middle figure, who has cultivated detachment, has consciously separated himself from the cycle of misery.

What is the positive meaning of the Five of Swords? It's hard to imagine that there could be one. It was uncovered for me by a student who was a painter. When she looked at the savage face of the large figure, she said, "That looks like me! I can feel my face tightening into that expression sometimes." She had done a painting on commission, and being creative, she did not simply reproduce something she had done before. She painted something entirely new. In consequence, the person who had commissioned it did not want it as it was and asked her to change it. Scrunching her face into a wicked smirk my student said, "No. I won't do that! This is my work, and it's good." She returned the money and kept the painting—and her right to work as her creativity dictated.

Let's stop to think of artists who died in poverty: Van Gogh, Mozart, El Greco, Beethoven, Rembrandt—pick a genius! These are people who have reached a certain degree of recognition, no? These are no longer inconsequential names. Yet they died in disgrace and poverty because they were so far ahead of their time that nobody could keep up with them! People liked their early work, and they wanted to keep liking their early work, but genius continues to evolve. "I've done that. Now I'm doing something else." Beethoven's later quartets sound like Bartok, and his earlier symphonies sound like Mozart. Figure out how that happened in one lifetime! However, it can't be done without a certain amount of "I'm going to stick it to you yet." It can't be done without the energy of "I'm going to show you! I'll show you all!"

I have a friend who was a double Olympic gold medalist. His career as a world-class athlete began when his father mortified him at age ten. He was swimming with his friends when his father called to him, "You'd better come in the house now. Your friends can stay and swim if they like, but you're always getting sick." That was the moment when a macho little California kid decided he wasn't going to be the sickly child who couldn't keep up with the others. So he became an Olympic champion.

My favorite example of Five of Swords wicked delight involves the legendary rivalry between Leonardo da Vinci and Michelangelo. They were proud and competitive, and each begrudged the approbation of the other. One day Leonardo was offered a slab of marble, beautiful white alabaster, but peculiar in shape. It was long and extremely narrow. Leonardo refused it, saying no one could carve a statue from marble of such proportions. So Michelangelo carved *David* from it—the long, thin body that has amazed and mesmerized the world for centuries. And I'll bet an expression of joy at his enemy's discomfort lit up Michelangelo's face when Leonardo first saw the carved stone he had rejected as unusable.

The positive meaning of the Five of Swords is being sure of ourselves and ready to protect and defend ourselves, even if it means attacking others, so that our creativity isn't destroyed. In a sense the Five of Swords can be seen as the iconoclastic artist who is true to her inner vision even if it requires the vengeful destruction of those who would undermine her work.

We need everything we've got. We need the high, light energies; we need the rich, dark energies. We need our anger. We need our revenge. If we learn how to use these forces, they can all work for us in creative ways.

Gevurah, as we know, occupies the central position on the Pillar of Severity. It is the most difficult sefirah on the pillar whose vessels are all of a restrictive, "negative" nature. Associated with the warlike planet Mars and the left hand of God, with which He smites us, we are not surprised to come away from Gevurah somewhat bloodied. Yet, once again, it is clear from the Five of Swords why the pillar is called severe and not evil. The experience is chastening but necessary. Finally, it does not destroy us; it frees us. Finding the venomous, gleeful bully within is a prospect only vaguely more appetizing than discovering the subjugated, spineless failure we each harbor as our potential self. Yet only by going through this "dark night of the soul" can we realize the liberated, detached being within, who, marching to the beat of a different drummer, is free. It is this part of each of us that emerges from Gevurah as heroic, strong, and enduring.

Meeting at the throat chakra, the right shoulder of Chesed, and the left of Gevurah invite us to vocalize our experience of the Four and Five of Swords. The former perhaps is a mantra; the latter an anguished sob or a gurgle of satisfaction.

Six of Swords

We move to Tiferet, the number-six sefirah on the Tree, the place of woundedness and sacrifice. Here we see another very difficult card, the Six of Swords. We see a ferryman poling a punt across a river. Besides the ferryman, the boat carries two hunched figures. Six swords pierce its prow. What we see is the making of a sad journey, a difficult passage under difficult circumstances.

The ferryman is usually seen as male. Most people see the hunched, hooded figure as a woman, but there are those (usually men) who see it as a man. Many people don't even notice the little child, almost as if the child is an appendage of the adult. They are making a serious passage of the kind that all of us have to make from time to time.

This is one of the more richly ambiguous cards in the deck. What is the relationship among these people, and what is their relation to the journey? Perhaps the important question is, "Which of these three figures am I?" The hunched, hooded figure is looking down and seems deeply depressed. But the surefooted ferryman straddling the thwarts of his boat is looking up, focused on the opposite shore. This is not an endless journey out on the boundless sea; it is finite, the end is in sight, and the tree-studded shore promises pleasant relief when the passage is completed.

As I have come to see it, this is a card of going through life with a handicap and getting on with it as best we can. The sorrow is that of making our crossing in this world with a disadvantage. Now the handicap can be one of two distinctly different sorts: ones to which we need adapt, and ones of which we should rid ourselves as soon as possible. If this card represents someone who is the subject of physical abuse by a spouse or a lover, and the situation is ongoing and has been passively accepted, that's too bad. If we are codependent with someone who is abusing drugs or alcohol, and we just find a way to live with it, again, too bad.

On the other hand, if we are living with a handicap for which there is no cure, then the Six of Swords becomes a card of bravery and endurance. I did a reading for a very beautiful young woman, well dressed—dressed for success, as it were—and one of the questions she asked me was whether she was ever going to regain the sight in her right eye. She said, "It was my own fault. I was using a screwdriver improperly and it slipped and blinded me." She took the responsibility for what had happened to her. Further, she didn't say, "And therefore I now have no choice but to get into bed for the rest of my life. I can't see." She just treated the handicap as an inconvenience and got on with her life.

We all have handicaps. Some of them are physical, but some of the most damaging handicaps are mental, spiritual, or emotional. When we look at Ray Charles, Stephen Hawking, Toulouse-Lautrec, Stevie Wonder, we know they're a whole lot less handicapped than people who can't feel, can't love, can't relate, can't create, can't involve themselves in the world. *The Six of Swords teaches us how to treat our limitations.*

The Six of Swords can refer to a life circumstance as well as a personal handicap. Sometimes we stay in a bad situation until it becomes a chronic ache, rather than a sharp pain, because we're pressured not to make changes. "There's never been divorce in our family! When you marry, you marry for life. Don't you know anything about loyalty? What do you mean you're not happy?! You stand by your man! You stay with your woman! We're a respectable family! We're part of a community! All you think about is yourself!" There can be a lot of leverage applied to keep us in jobs, even careers, where our lives are severely depressed by the problems we encounter daily. "Everyone in our family has been a doctor! What do you mean you want to be a musician? You'll be a doctor like your father and your grandfather and great-grandfather. We're a proud line of physicians." If we acquiesce to that and become what other people want us to be, our lives can feel like a weighted-down journey with no end in sight.

What does the card mean when it's upside down? Well, that depends. Perhaps you have been dealing with a handicap that you are now ready to release. "You know, friend, you've blackened my eye for the last time. I'm out of here! After twenty years of having my jaw cracked and my ribs broken, I'm through." When we turn the card over, the swords fall out of the boat and the water rushes in, the boat seems to sink, and everything goes into a tailspin of confusion. It takes a lot of courage even to get out of a bad situation. It involves a frightening transition. But in that context, the reversal of the card is positive. It means, "I am no longer willing to submit to mere survival. I'm out of it!"

On the other hand, this card showed up in a reading for a young man who reminded me of Lord Byron. He was perhaps the handsomest man I have ever seen; his face was exquisitely beautiful. He was tall, slender, very bright and articulate, with a terrific sense of humor. He had had polio as a child, and his right arm was withered. His entire life was on hold because of that arm. He was depressed, possibly suicidal. He did not think of himself as someone who was disadvantaged, someone who was somewhat incapacitated, rather inconvenienced. He thought that he *was* a shriveled right arm. The Six of Swords reversed can represent not dealing with a handicap.

Again, although I have great appreciation for the twelve-step programs, and I know that Alanon and Coda are of enormous value to many people, these, like any other program or belief system, can be misused. Often when this card comes up reversed, it represents a middle-aged person who hasn't yet stopped whimpering and whining about some aspect of childhood. We have all had handicapping situations. We all need to address them. We all need to work through them. But we are not to use them as excuses to be less than we can be.

The river in the Six of Swords might be the River Styx, which in Greek mythology separates the land of the living from the land of the dead. The ferryman would then be Charon and the passengers the dead. In the absence of other cards that would support such an interpretation, however, this is generally not a card of death.

The river might also be the River Lethe, the river of forgetfulness. If so, the journey can take us to a place of release from past torment.

We might also think of these three figures as three aspects of one person. If you have a parent who has Alzheimer's disease, you may see the hooded figure as the parent whom you are ferrying over the river of forgetfulness to a place where they can remember nothing. As the child of a dementia victim you may wonder whether the shrouded figure represents you as well. You may also feel yourself to be the small child who still needs that parent, as well as the adult who is now responsible for the parent's safe journey.

The Six of Swords is a sad, difficult, and complicated card, but it is an energy that allows for a lot of growth. The card belongs to Tiferet in that it calls upon us, as sacrificed gods, to evolve past the ego place of self-pity to a loftier perspective. It's certainly a card that goes right to the heart, whether we are born into this life with a major handicap or are heir to one with which we need to live. If we can overcome the wounds of our lives and move forward, despite our handicaps, the sacrifice of ego is in the service of our divinity. The sun of Tiferet shines fully on such a life, the sun of enlightenment and joy.

Seven of Swords

Now we come to the Seven of Swords, the second-nastiest card of the deck! We are dealing with an extremely unpleasant energy here: the sneaky Seven. Oooh! Here is a figure with a rather enigmatic, purposefully ambiguous facial expression. He is prancing off gleefully with swords that quite clearly do not belong to him. In the background, the tents and the flags suggest an encampment; the swords are the swords of his enemies. This is a card of deceit, betrayal, and treachery. Someone is getting away with something that is not rightfully theirs. Who has this deceitful energy, this capacity to be so dishonest? Every one of you reading this book—as does its author and everyone else. No good pointing to the hat as proof that the figure is a foreigner. We would all like to project this unattractive characteristic onto someone else, but Kabbalah and Tarot have taught us better. What any of us has within, each of us has within. We are cut from the same cloth.

It is interesting to recognize the contexts in which this energy can emerge. I did a reading for a woman for whom this card showed up in the immediate future. We couldn't figure out what it could represent. She called me the next morning to say, "Last night my car was broken into, and my radio was ripped off!" When this card shows up, don't be above examining the safety of your physical environment. Be aware of where you park your car, whether your door is locked, and who is in a position to hurt you.

There is dishonesty out in the world. That's all there is to it. There are people who will mislead you, disadvantage you. If you have confided in a friend, you have empowered that friend, and it is important to be very sure the friend is trustworthy. Will she steal your man? Will he go after your woman? Will a confidence be broken, a trust betrayed? We must ask those questions. It's important to look around at the people with whom you work. Is there someone who reports to you who has their eye on your job? I had a snake in my nest at one point. When I was the western advertising manager of *Omni* magazine, I was forced to hire a salesperson because she was a personal friend of the publisher. She was constantly bypassing me and my boss (the national advertising director) and calling the publisher directly at her home, trying to turn every situation to her advantage. So if this card comes up, look at your workplace, your home and ask, "Is there anybody there who can do me harm? Is there somebody who wants my apartment, who's going to call the police complaining that my dogs are barking, even though I don't have any dogs? Who is out there trying to get something away from me that is mine?"

Of course, the other perspective of the card requires asking, "Am I being completely straight, or am I taking advantage of someone? Let me do a little soul searching." Years ago I did a three-card reading at a psychic fair for a woman who was involved with a new man. The third card was the Seven of Swords. I said, "Be careful; this may be somebody who simply wants to use you in some way. Don't be too quick to trust him because he may not have your best interests at heart." Then I added, "But you know, it is also important to recognize that it may be you who has the impulse to take advantage of him. Are you being fair?" At this point she burst out laughing and said, "That's exactly what it is! I don't really like him that much, but he's paying my bills and putting me through school." So yes, we all have the capacity to exploit others. Having the capacity does not mean that we act on it, but we have to be aware of our temptations.

Suppose for a moment that you have just found a wallet in the street. You open it up and there are a thousand dollars in hundred dollar bills in the wallet. If there is an identification card of any kind, I assume that you will return it. If there isn't an identification card, I assume you will keep the money. Now, are you hoping that there is or is not an identification card in the wallet?

We would all like a little something for nothing; that's just human nature. We like freebies. "A two-for-one sale. Oh, great! Can't pass that up!" There's nothing wrong with the impulse, but we have to be careful not to use it improperly.

There are, naturally, positive meanings to the Seven of Swords. It can be understood as a card of disarming our enemies. The figure, after all, is not turning the swords against his adversaries; he's just prancing off with them. A kind of playful, dancing, mischievous energy colors this card, reminding us of why it is in Netzach, the place of high energy flow. Imagine being in the presence of someone who's really angry with you. With a little charm, with a little humor, you may be able to disarm them. To take the swords away is to take the charge out of the situation. We can defuse anger by making people laugh.

Even if the play is not entirely aboveboard, it may be relatively innocuous. The figure may represent somebody who says something slightly embarrassing to you in front of other people, but you all wind up having a good laugh. Or it can suggest somebody who is simply tactless, who makes a joke about your weight or complexion or debts or affections without understanding how much what they say can hurt.

A profound meaning of the Seven of Swords was pointed out to me by a client who said, "You know, this represents the mindless attitude of people who don't care about or see the big picture." There are people who just have to have faster cars even if they do pollute the atmosphere. Their only concern is prestige. The same can be said about people who persist in using aerosol cans. They think that for their personal convenience it's worth depleting the ozone layer. To avoid the bother of recycling glass, aluminum, and plastic, they just throw it away. But as the national parks newspapers ask, "When you throw something away, did you ever wonder where 'away' is?"

I don't much like to hike, but since everybody I know loves to hike, I sometimes take hikes. The allure is to find yourself in scenes of such extravagant beauty that your effort is rewarded, regardless of how hard it is to get there. And what do we find after laboriously attaining these gorgeous vistas? Trash! Soda cans, beer bottles, fast-food wrappers, junk-food containers, and cigarette boxes. Who are these people who love nature enough to hike into it but not enough to protect it? Who are these people who support the Sierra Club and praise Native American ways, but use Styrofoam, which has a half-life of a billion years or so? Do the oil companies consider the consequences of their lack of preparedness for emergency measures in case of a spill? Why is it that until a child gets hit at a dangerous intersection we can't get a politician to put in a traffic light? Until a disease reaches epidemic proportions, we can't get public health bureaucracies to supply inoculation against it?

There is a mentality that cannot grasp the evil that can result from carelessness, from mindlessness, even when there is no wrongful intent. Yet when we are of this mind-set, we are not evil, malicious people. We're just not clued in. We just aren't paying attention. We think that what we do is harmless or fun, and we don't realize that we carry dangerous weapons. But it's interesting to note that in the Seven of Swords, the swords are being carried by the blades. There's a good chance that the capering figure will slice himself to ribbons. Sooner or later our irresponsible actions catch up with us.

When the Seven of Swords is upside down, it has a related but different meaning: participating in our own victimization. If rightside up means being taken advantage of, reversed may mean enabling someone to take advantage of you. There are people who are perpetual innocents, who seem to be congenitally unable to hold trust in abeyance until they get to know a person. They meet someone; they have a good feeling about them, trust them, and are taken advantage of over and over again.

A good friend of mine is an angel who, I suspect, literally descended from heaven. And who was living with her? You'll never guess. Her daughter's ex-boyfriend. Her daughter wouldn't talk to him anymore, so he moved in with his girlfriend's mother. Excuse me? She *allowed* it! He didn't pay any rent but did run up three-hundred-dollar phone bills calling Hawaii. He emptied the refrigerator, and when he got annoyed, he put his fist through the wall. She finally insisted that he leave. Good? Within twenty-four hours, in moved another "friend" who wasn't paying any rent, who was carrying tuberculosis and refused to be tested for it, and who was infecting the neighborhood. Of course, she needed to be taken care of all the time because she was so sick! When my friend decided she didn't want to put up with such treatment anymore, people stopped exploiting her. They no longer could. So if the Seven of Swords turns up for you reversed, ask yourself whether you are putting yourself in jeopardy. Whether it's borrowing money or clothes and not returning them, crashing in your house for three months at a time without contributing toward rent or food, or smashing up your car and taking no responsibility, someone may be using you in ways that you allow or enable.

There is another meaning of the Seven of Swords reversed that must be addressed. Sometimes the card in this position can suggest someone who never trusts. Childhood abandonment or severe abuse can leave a person prone to permanent suspicion. Repeatedly broken promises and continual disappointments can engender a systemic wariness of life. I know a man who to this day never plans anything but operates purely spontaneously. When he was a five-year-old, his parents would manipulate him into doing chores, keeping quiet, and being "good" with promises of a trip to the circus on Saturday, the zoo on Sunday, a baseball game on the last day of kindergarten. The parents assumed he would forget by the weekend. Instead, he has remembered all his life that "you can't trust anybody."

There is no such thing as establishing a track record for such people. Twenty years of loyal, honorable behavior in a relationship does not guarantee loyal, honorable behavior now. "People change," they seem to say as they size you up. "Conditions change. I don't know who you are today." Some may even suspect years of sound behavior as a ruse, a way to trick them into letting their guard down. Some may believe that selfishness or deceit has simply remained undiscovered. There is no way to prove conclusively that you have never been, and never will be unfaithful, or that abandonment is not your mode of dealing with difficulty and stealing is not one of your vices. Some people, especially in certain macho street cultures, take pride in never trusting anyone. They believe it makes them savvy, tough, nobody's fool.

People can go through a temporary Seven-of-Swords-reversed phase after a painful disappointment. If a relationship ends badly, involving lies, it is only natural to react warily for a while. But people to whom you need prove yourself on every occasion, who are as prone to suspicion after years of friendship as on first acquaintance, need to work with this card. So when the Seven of Swords appears reversed, we must ask ourselves, "Why is it so hard for me to keep the jury out for a while before I trust somebody? I don't have to trust on sight. If I have a good feeling toward someone, it probably means that I'm a loving person, not that the person is trustworthy." Or conversely, "Why am I never fully open to anyone? Who damaged that part of my spirit?

If I believe in no one, it probably means I'm too suspicious, not that I have never met anyone honorable and solid."

Mark Kampe, a friend and colleague, has come up with a particularly rich insight regarding the Seven of Swords and its place in Netzach. If Kabbalah is indeed a study in balance, the playfulness and fervor of Netzach can be understood as relieving the potentially immobilizing power of intellect carried by Swords. This perspective becomes immediately persuasive in relation to the succeeding image. The prankster, with lateral thinking, has come up with a creative solution to an embattled situation: it will be hard for the enemy to attack with five of their seven swords gone; with a little luck, they'll fight among themselves over who shall wield the remaining two.

Eight of Swords

We move next to the Eight of Swords, which is in Hod, the place of intellect. Since we have the suit of intellect in the place of intellect, we see exactly what we would expect when intellect is totally out of balance. As Ram Dass says, mischievously misquoting Descartes, "I think, therefore I am . . . confused." There is a place for thinking, but it will lead to confusion if it is cut off from the other functions of consciousness. At that point we begin to obsess and despair, because we think if we can't figure out the solution to a problem, that means there isn't one. What crust! What arrogance! "I can't figure it out; therefore, there's no solution." As I once read, "Nobody knows enough to be a pessimist." There's always the wild card. There's always what we can't foresee.

When Andrew Lloyd Webber was asked to write the music for *Phantom of the Opera,* he refused. He hadn't read the story, but he "knew" what it was about and he didn't want to be bothered. Why did he change his mind? Because he happened (coincidence being God's way of remaining anonymous, as they say in *The Course in Miracles*) to be walking past a used-book store, and he happened to see an old paperback of *The Phantom of the Opera* selling for twenty-five cents. He thought, "For twenty-five cents, I'll see what it says." That's why we've all been treated to his extraordinary score. We don't know enough to be pessimists. When we think we do, we find ourselves blindfolded and trapped.

The Eight of Swords depicts a woman in a red gown, blindfolded and bound, standing on marshy ground amid eight swords. She is alone; behind her at a distance is a castle on a hill. When we look at the card, we may see at first a figure surrounded by swords. Yet this is not the case. This card is the Eight of Swords: there are three swords on one side of her and five on the other. That exhausts the eight. That means that no swords can be at her back. She's *not* surrounded.

The Eight of Swords is the card of preconception, the natural result of Swords in Hod. Hod, we recall, is the final sefirah on the Pillar of Severity. Hod means "splendor" and "glory." It is associated with the wonders of consciousness, the dazzling quickness of Mercury, the brilliance of the human intellect. It is in Hod that our capacity for objective, analytical thought originates. Science, law, and all technical thinking are generated from this energy center. It is, however, a sefirah that is off balance in and of itself. It does not fall to the central pillar, but to the left-hand pillar of the Tree. In the Suit of Swords, the needed balance is not supplied. Because Swords, too, carry the energy of intellect and mind, the inherent problem of Hod is exacerbated. Hod provides the needed structure and containment for the energy of Netzach, but the Suit of Swords brings to Hod not energy, but more ideational form. Isolated from emotion, intuition, and groundedness, our thoughts become cyclical and obsessive. We go round and round within the closed system of our own preconceptions.

Now preconceptions are very dangerous, because unlike assumptions we can't question them. How can we question what is *preconceptual,* what we can't even articulate as a position we hold? Funny example: A woman in one of my classes called to ask whether she could bring along her cousin that night. I agreed, but when they arrived, I reeled back in shock! The woman arrived with her cousin all right, but her cousin was a *man!*

Now, I know what *cousin* means. I know how you get to be someone's cousin. But it never occurred to me that a cousin could be a man because when I picture a cousin, I picture *my* cousins, and they're all women. If this were an assumption, it would obviously be ridiculous. But because it was a *pre*conception, it never occurred to me to question it.

I've got a better example. You have to take my word that the story is true, because it strains credibility. One of my friends has been married for twenty years to an internationally known geneticist whose lab made a major breakthrough in recombinant DNA research. He is invited to speak all over the world and gets huge honoraria for his speaking engagements. One day my friend went into the kitchen, opened the trash pail and found, sitting atop the garbage, a check made out to her husband for fifty thousand dollars. *In the trash.* How could this happen? Well, in her family of origin, her mother—in deference to *her* husband, a busy doctor—always slit open the envelopes before leaving the mail on his desk. In her husband's family of origin, a slit-open envelope meant, "This mail has already been processed; look at it only if you wish." So for twenty years, she'd been slitting open envelopes with huge checks in them, he'd been seeing the slit-open envelopes— and throwing them away. It never came to anyone's attention because she paid all the bills and made all the deposits to their checking and savings accounts. She wasn't expecting the checks, and he didn't know they weren't being deposited. If they had been dealing with assumptions, she might have said, "I assume you'd like me to open the mail for you." Then he would have said, "That would be great," or "No, I'll take care of it." But they were dealing with preconceptions.

That's the danger of preconceptions. We don't know that we have them, much less what they are. We're all full of preconceptions. Unless something draws our attention to them, they can exercise an enormous force over our lives that we would never allow if we were aware of them and could question them. If you want to discover your preconceptions, get married. If you are a woman, is there a less-than-conscious expectation that you never need to check the oil in your car? If you are a man, is there a subconscious anticipation that your wife will take the day off when your child has a stomachache? John Bradshaw tells about the difficulties holidays introduce: In his family, presents were torn open rapidly and simultaneously on Christmas Eve. In his wife's family, presents were opened on Christmas morning one by one, with all eyes on the person unwrapping the gift; the ribbon and paper were carefully saved. How many Christmases were filled with vague irritation, disappointment, and hurt feelings before there was a discussion about what each held to be "the only way" to enjoy Christmas?

The figure in the Eight of Swords has a number of options. While it's true that she's blindfolded and that her arms are bound behind her, to say that she's trapped is never to have seen a martial arts movie. If her legs and feet are free, she is not trapped. She can edge her way through the marsh, albeit slowly and with difficulty. Or she can make an about-face and head back toward the castle. There's nothing to prevent her turning around, making the *t'shuvah* (the return). Often precisely what we need when we're involved in preconceptions is the capacity to make a one-hundred-and-eighty-degree turn and just go the other way.

The Eight of Swords has a political and sociological interpretation as well. It says that one way in which people have always been kept down or kept victims or kept in bondage is by isolation. This card addresses the need to break seclusion. The figure needs help. It's why the twelve-step programs work so well. So part of the meaning of the card is that if you think you're totally alone in your misery and help-lessness, find a support group. You're not the only person who's ever been violent under the influence of alcohol or drugs. You're not the only person who has gained fifty pounds because you can't control your appetite. You're not the only person who's ever been promiscu-ous because you can release anxiety only through sexual contact. Find a support group. Don't allow yourself to be solitary. This interpreta-tion is supported by the fact that we are not dealing here with the Two of Swords. Until someone unties this figure's hands, there is no way she can remove her blindfold. The image of the Eight of Swords re-minds us that companionship and contact are essential. We are pack animals. We are meant to be gregarious. We are not meant to be alone.

I remember the year I was working full time in a new demanding sales position and raising a child alone. Either the house wasn't clean, or I was leaving work early, or my kid wasn't getting enough attention, or the dogs weren't getting exercised and brushed. I was the bread winner, housekeeper, and sole parent. I did the marketing; I kept clean laundry in the drawers and hot, balanced meals on the table. I showed up for work on time every day and bore the pressure of making sales and earning commissions. I'm the one who sewed badges on the Girl Scout uniform and took the dogs to the vet. But sometimes my daughter went five days without a shampoo, and the punitive voice of shame would demand, *What kind of mother are you?* I went around with a nagging feeling of guilt and worthlessness all the time. It wasn't anything I articulated to myself, because if I had analyzed it, I would have said, "Hey! I'm one person and I' ve got two full-time jobs here! I'm trying to be a great mother *and* a professional success. I'm not doing so badly."

Gloria Steinem has said, "The purpose of the women's movement is to show that the personal is political." Is losing your job a personal problem? If you're going to have a baby, it can affect your job security unless, of course, you're a man. A man who is going to have a baby doesn't have to go through pregnancy and delivery. He doesn't have to struggle with the option of breast feeding. When he shows up for work the very next morning after the baby has been born he hands out cigars. That's a political problem, not a personal one. More than half the people on this earth are women. That's something that should be taken into account in our social structure, and in fact, in Scandinavia it is.

Often what we experience as personal is general, if not universal. We need other people to give us a new perspective on our situation, and, by so doing, reveal the preconceptions that make us feel stuck, trapped, and immobilized when we are not.

The final meaning of the Eight of Swords is having the courage and faith to move forward even when we can't see where we're going and even when we feel helpless. Many people see this woman as stopped dead in her tracks, just plain stuck. But some people see that she's edging her way forward, doing the best she can under the worst possible circumstances. Perhaps she has come a long way just to arrive where we now see her; perhaps, deprived of clear thought, intuition has guided her to the place from which she can thread her way between the swords.

We all feel this way immediately after divorce, death, or other traumatic change. We feel this way in the first weeks out of a care unit, where we have detoxed from drugs or alcohol. Our lives are now entirely different—and scary. Can we make it, clean and sober? We don't know how we're going to get through the next day, but we know it's going to be one step at a time. Some even see in the Eight of Swords a certain serenity, a resignation of personal will to a greater will, a certainty that when the time is right help will arrive.

Netzach, associated with the top of the right hip, and Hod, associated with the top of the left hip, meet at the solar plexus. The prancing figure of the Seven of Swords is perhaps the very one to cut free the lady in the Eight, and trick her out of her preconceptions. In the chakra of solidity, the marsh may become easier to traverse.

Nine of Swords

The Nine of Swords is a very difficult card, one of enormous pain. It is arguably the most painful card in the Minor Arcana. We see a ghostly white figure sitting bolt upright in bed in the dead of night, head in hands, entirely alone. Men invariably see this figure as male, and women invariably see it as female. What most people see, in fact, is a photograph of themselves, which has somehow been stolen out of their night-table drawer, for the purpose of reproduction in the Tarot deck. Everyone gets to feel at some time or other the pain portrayed here. As a nine the card falls of course to Yesod, the place of the unconscious. Yesod is where material too painful for us to deal with on a rational level is lodged. It is where our nightmares come from, where, by the light of the moon which belongs to it, our perceptions grow shadowy and distorted.

Some of us don't have nightmares, but wake up feeling awful and don't know why. There have been mornings when I've thought to myself, "I've been awake for ten seconds. What could I have done in ten seconds to justify feeling this rotten? I haven't had *time* to screw up yet!" (I'll bet I'm not the only person who's had that experience.) The Nine of Swords represents whatever lurks in the darkness of the unconscious with which we can't deal on a conscious level. This is a dark card; no light illumines or softens its black background.

It is interesting to consider the Nine of Swords in relation to the Three of the suit. The Nine is a card of nightmare, anxiety, depression, and despair. Nine after all is the trinity of trinities, the three of threes. The Three of Swords depicts the necessity of taking pain into our heart so it can work the transformation for which it was given to us. But what happens if we don't allow ourselves to feel the pain? If we sweep it under the rug? It comes back and back and back, at three times its original strength. If we don't process it when it comes, it just hangs around in the unconscious, festering and growing. We have exchanged lancing pain for chronic depression and melancholy as a way of life. But if we're able to say, "Oh God, that hurts, that hurts, oh, that hurts, I can't stand it!" yet stay with it, we are very unlikely, nine months or years down the road, to be subject to the insomnia, nightmare, terrified awakening, or desolation depicted by the Nine of Swords.

Also of interest is that the swords in the Nine of Swords are not in position to menace the figure in the card. The suggestion is that, the pain being experienced is pain for someone else. Maybe you love someone who is very sick, perhaps in critical condition, or someone who is involved in self-destructive behavior. The cause of our grief and despair is someone other than ourself.

There is a further extension of this meaning to a kind of cosmic proportion, what the Germans call *weltschmerz,* "world-sorrow." Supporting this interpretation is the quilt: the red roses of passionate feeling are interspersed with the signs of the zodiac. These latter suggest that the pain is universal in scope. No matter which sign we are born under, we will share in this experience. It's not just that I am still in love with someone who doesn't want me anymore, it's that *this happens all the time.* What a world, peopled with heartbroken lovers! It's not just that I'm worried to death about my father's health. It's that everybody's father eventually dies. *Everybody's!* How can we stand it? How can we bear pain that is so great?

The Nine of Swords also carries a sense of our own mortality. The bed on which the figure sits looks hard and narrow like a coffin. Into its wooden side is carved the image of a satyr chasing a nymph that Keats writes about in his "Ode on a Grecian Urn." Keats says, basically, "How lucky you are! You will never catch her! She will always be young and fresh and consummately desirable. You will always be excruciatingly alive with passion. You'll never have a chance to be disillusioned or simply bored. You'll never reach a point where you're satisfied and, past satisfied, satiated and tired of it. You'll always be at that pinnacle moment of ecstatic yearning." Certainly that's not our experience of life. In reality, we project our dream of perfection onto an object of desire. While we may experience the intense feelings portrayed, they possess us only fleetingly. Instead, if we're lucky, we get to know our love object as a person and eventually feel the letdown of recognizing their limitations and flaws. Then we've got to get down to the hard work of loving that person as a human being. But the euphoric peak moment, that magical, exquisite zenith of desire, is gone forever. That in itself is a loss beyond expression.

We come to awareness of the ineluctable limitations of mortality in many ways. Imagine what it's like to be a ballet dancer or a great athlete and to be old at twenty-eight—to know you've had it, you've bought it, you're past it at twenty-eight! What is the rest of your life going to feel like? There are people who never recover from that experience. Every country in the world is full of people dragging around their past glory: the former captain of the high school football team who wasn't good enough to play professionally but could never accept an ordinary job because he had been a hero. His life was over at eighteen, when he graduated from high school. Perhaps you are a scientist who, at sixty, recognizes that his research will never break new ground. Perhaps you are a woman who realizes at forty-eight that you will never have a child. You will never dive the Great Barrier Reef or fly over the Serengeti Plain or see Naples. The sorrow in the Nine of Swords is universal: it is the sorrow over what we have always longed for and now know we will never have; over what we have most prized that has been lost to us, never to return.

For years I closed my lectures on the Nine of Swords by saying, "There is, of course, a positive meaning to this card, but I have yet to discover it." One evening an astrologer came up to the podium beaming and helped me out of my quandary. She pointed out that the zodiacal signs on the quilt were there to remind us that "this too shall pass!" As the planets pass through the different signs, we can absolutely count on shifts and changes. The universe will not leave us stuck in our despair. The axis between the base of the spine and genitals carries our most primitive, basic, and deeply held experiences, but what is buried in Yesod *can* be moved into consciousness, where we can work with it.

Ten of Swords

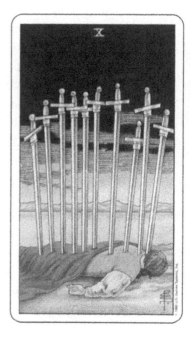

As difficult as the Ten of Swords is, it is a quite different matter from the Nine, in that the good news is immediately obvious. And the good news is that there is no Eleven of Swords! This is as bad as it's going to get. We have finally hit bottom! It can't get any worse!

The Ten of Swords is an enchanting image of a figure lying face down in the mud in the dark of night with ten swords piercing his back, from neck to buttocks. (In the Royal Fez deck, the swords continue down into the thigh!) The Nine of Swords falls in Yesod, the place of the unconscious, the place of nightmares and fears, depression and those larger-than-life mysteries that come out of our darkness. The Ten of Swords appears in Malchut, the end of a process, a culmination in the world, on Earth. Something ends, but we don't end. Like the sap of the Tree, we remain mobile.

When we work Kabbalistically, we work not only down but up the Tree, as well. We have reached the point at which our only choice is a *t'shuvah,* a return, a turning toward God. Having gone as far as we can go, we're ready to move back up the Tree. Things have got to get better.

The relation between the Nine of Swords and the Ten of Swords is subtle and complex. This may read like a joke, but I think a lot of people suffer from never reaching the Ten of Swords place. Let me tell you what I mean. I once arrived at an AA meeting at the same time as an extraordinarily good-looking, athletic young man who came bolting in off his bicycle. He was charming, articulate, and overflowing with good health and good spirits. He had come from a large family get-together. He said, "My family is Irish, and they drink. That's what they do. They think it's part of being Irish. They drink until they pass out. That's what our family gatherings have always been like. We all get together, the aunts and the uncles and the cousins, and we play cards and we drink and we eat and we drink, and then we pass out. Last year I hit bottom. I knew I couldn't do this anymore. And boy, am I lucky, because I see my uncles sitting around, and they're forty-eight years old, and they don't hit bottom. If they get sober now, they'll still be forty-eight! I look at them and think to myself, 'I'm so lucky to have done this and be on track again. I could have hung around, drinking for another twenty or thirty years. I've got my whole life ahead of me to be sober.'" Those uncles are still at the Nine of Swords place, finding ways to hold their lives together just well enough to keep from having to change. He was lucky to reach the Ten of Swords place, to *have* to make an end of that self-destructiveness at twenty.

Some people absolutely have to push things to the limit. I knew a very brilliant young man who had graduated from Harvard in Scandinavian languages. He was of Scandinavian descent, and he had been awarded a Fulbright scholarship to Stockholm University, but when I met him he was a drunk living in a shack in Malibu. He couldn't afford gas for his car. He could barely afford food. I remember his carefully measuring out a small portion of luncheon meat—that mysterious stuff of an unnatural color that you wouldn't want to eat even if it were fresh. He was living rent free as a "custodian." He was brilliant and charming and drunk and desperate.

The last time I spoke with him, he was teaching Scandinavian languages at a major university and working on his Ph.D. I asked him what had happened to turn him around. He said, "One night, I drove home drunk, and I woke up in the morning to find that I had parked my car a thirty-second of an inch from the tree in the front yard." He had been one thirty-second of an inch away from killing himself. I guess he thought that was close enough. He really didn't have to get any closer. He saw the car but he couldn't remember driving it there. He couldn't remember parking it. But seeing where it was, he thought, "Time for a change!"

Whether it's in terms of humiliation or degradation or physical abuse, some people have to hit bottom before they can see the writing on the wall. Until it comes to a point of clear choice—live or die—they will not make the change. So the Ten of Swords is a "good" card in that it finally puts an end to something that simply has to come to an end. And it can only happen in Malchut, on the planet Earth. We can't reach that point intellectually in Hod, or passionately in Netzach, or anywhere else on the Tree. Malchut is associated with the soles of the feet; finally, we must walk our talk. We must *experience* where we "know" we are. Only then does the golden sun rise, promising a new day and the opportunity to get back on our feet again, as the horizon in the Ten of Swords suggests.

The Ten of Swords reversed can be a serious problem, because it very often represents the end of a relationship, a job situation, an addiction pattern, or whatever, but refusing to admit or accept it. Resisting the awareness. Being in denial. "It's *not* over. I *won't* let go. I *can't* change. It's not that *bad.*"

On the other hand, the reversal can have positive interpretations. It can mean that things truly *aren't* that bad. It's the end of something, but nothing essential to our lives. We can handle it. Another positive interpretation is that the worst is over, and the swords are about to fall out. The law of gravity eases them out. In that case, the querent is faced with the challenge: "All right, these swords have fallen out of my back. I'm in a resting place now. But I'm the one who got myself into that situation. How am I going to make sure that a year from now I don't find myself in the same place?" It's critically important when the card is reversed to see accurately what the problem has been and what changes we must make to keep it from recurring. Otherwise, we may replace our debt to Visa with a debt to MasterCard, or alcohol with cocaine.

A final observation of great significance was suggested, once again, by Mark Kampe. Appropriately enough it was made at his father Tom's memorial service, where Mark and I first met. He pointed out that the visible hand of the moribund figure falls into a configuration of blessing, reminiscent of that which we see in the Hierophant (or High Priest) of the Major Arcana. With the ring and small finger crossing over the palm, held down by the thumb, and the index and third fingers open, the suggestion is that part of the holy mystery shall be revealed, while part of the mystery of death shall remain hidden. (You may recall that we have explored this symbol of benediction in relation to the standing figure of the Six of Pentacles.) In the Ten of Swords the great mystery is death—and, as the yellow sky of a newly dawning day implies, rebirth. Whether the death is literal or symbolic, physical, emotional, or even spiritual, our understanding of the transformation is partial at best. Only as we make our return to life can we come to understand the full nature of the death we have undergone.

With this observation, we leave our exploration of the Suit of Swords. Rare is the reader who does so with regret.

CHAPTER 6

Wands: Life More Abundant

*L*ET'S LOOK BACK for a moment at our work so far. Having compared the values of balance and integration in Kabbalah and Tarot, we contemplated the Suit of Pentacles, associated with Jung's sensate function and with the element of earth. Its way to spirit is that of appreciation and service; its flaw is accumulation, forgetting that there is always a star in the coin. We examined the Suit of Cups, associated with the feeling function, in Jungian terminology, and the element of water, whose way to spirit is love and whose flaw is passivity or surrendering to dark, negative emotions. And we have explored the Suit of Swords, associated with air and Jung's thinking function, whose way to spirit is courage and the pursuit of truth, and whose flaw is harsh criticism and the despair that ensues when we cut the intellect off from our other functions of consciousness.

If we take a good hard look at the world and just think things through, it becomes clear that we're not going to get out of this one alive! Thinking does not engender hope, because we can't prove that there's anything beyond our material experience. Throughout the ages, brilliant minds, philosophers and saints have tried to prove God's existence. Saint Anselm, Saint Thomas Aquinas, but also Spinoza, a Jew, wrote such "proofs." All attempts failed, of course—because for every argument there was a counterargument. The "proofs" all depended on the acceptance of their premises, which were often precisely what were in doubt. But at the Simon Wiesenthal Center during Holocaust Remembrance Week, a rabbi said something very beautiful. He said, "There are no proofs of the existence of God, only witnesses." Fortunately, we do have among us witnesses whose lives are a testimony to divine energy permeating the world. What more convincing proof of God's existence could we have than Mother Teresa? So it is not our rational faculty that leads us to apprehend the presence of God in the world, of life beyond life, of life beyond the body. It is something else.

Each suit needs to be balanced by and integrated with the others. We have seen, for example, that Pentacles, the suit of earth, action, service, and appreciation, need the deep feelings of Cups to keep from experiencing the world as merely a collection of material objects. The Suit of Cups needs Pentacles, so that emotions find useful expression. Cups also need Swords so that, in the face of passionate feeling, we are still able to take a giant step to the side and say, "I'd better think this through. Is this the objective truth of the matter? Or am I being overly sensitive, capricious, overreactive, or whatever?"

The Suit of Wands is associated with the Jungian function of consciousness called intuition, and intuition is really quite miraculous. It is a way of knowing that has nothing to do with reason and very little to do with perception. It is *knowing without having learned.* Something has come to mind that is totally new. It is not the result of study or of inductive or deductive processes. If we had scoured our brains, all our ideas, and our entire conceptual framework, we would never have come up with what has suddenly come to us in a flash. What we experience is a miraculous entry into consciousness of something that seems to come from somewhere else. All at once we just *know!*

It seems appropriate to me that the element of Wands should be fire, with its quickness, suddenness, and dissimilarity to its source. You begin with a match and a matchbook, and all of a sudden—in a flash—you have a flame, which looks nothing at all like either the match or the matchbook. There's no way to figure out how you can get fire from these two inert little pieces of cardboard. That's the way intuition flashes into consciousness.

The Suit of Wands represents as well life energy of all forms, what Freud called *libido.* It is the animal energy that drives life, the vital force that we feel surging up within us. And although those two—intuition and libido—may strike us as totally different from one another, they really are related, as suggested by the word *sublimation.* Sublimation clearly means "to make sublime." So if we take that basic life energy and express it, not in its most primitive way, not in terms of frank physical sexuality, we can elevate it to a point of artistic expression. By moving the energy to that creative place, we make it sublime.

We must remember an important lesson of Kabbalah: the Tree of Life—the universe, each of us—is a closed system. There is no way to get rid of anything. Nothing ever goes away. Energy can be transformed but it does not disappear. We saw an example of this in relation to the Five of Cups. Grief can be experienced until it transforms us into a readiness to turn our lives around, to see the two full cups, the bridge, and the house. Or it can be transferred to the unconscious, behind the "curtain" of the Nine of Cups. But neither grief nor sexual energy nor anything else simply goes away when we ignore it.

This is a secret that religious orders have known for thousands of years: the life force, the energy that creates life, doesn't go away if we don't discharge it sexually. It moves into other areas, which is why celibacy has been central to so many religious traditions. If you are a monk or a nun in the Catholic Church, the sexual energy you hold back can, if you choose, be redirected or transformed, elevated to a higher level of expression. Lovemaking leaves us with a serenity and sense of well-being that does not tend to motivate passionate work. The tension that builds in abstinence demands an outlet, making us more aggressive in our pursuit of truth and creative endeavor.

Now of course in the Western tradition, we run into the contamination of puritanism: guilt, shame, and all of that garbage. But the notion behind abstinence is that there is powerful energy here. It is one of the reasons why virgins have been prized in so many societies. There is a sense is of magical power that has not been diffused or dissipated. In the Eastern tradition, Buddhist monks remain celibate for just that reason. The yogic discipline of awakening kundalini through meditation is based on the same principle. The choice seems to be between physical and spiritual climax. It's the same energy. So the restraint of sexual energy from immediate expression has long been recognized as powerful; it was not Freud's discovery.

The Suit of Wands represents such energy on both ends of the spectrum and all points between. Again, just as we don't talk about higher and lower energies on the Tree of Life, we don't talk about lower and higher on the spectrum of sexual energy. Our sexuality is less than sublime only when it is split off from other functions of consciousness: the leisurely sensuality of Pentacles, the tenderness of Cups, and, ideally, the approval of Swords. If it is wedded to the spiritual, emotional, and mental realms, sexual energy in its most basic and direct manifestation can be sublime. Fire obviously remains the element best associated with this aspect of Wands. We see this even in our choice of language. We speak of the "igniting of passion," the "flame of desire." The suddenness and quickness of "burning desire" bespeaks its fiery nature.

The way to spirit for the Suit of Wands is inspiration. This justifies the association many make between Wands and the element of air. (Fire is then attributed to the Suit of Swords, whose steel is tempered by fire. If the steel survives successive heating and freezing, fire and ice, it becomes a true sword. This is an apt metaphor for the torment of the soul we saw depicted in that suit. If the soul survives its trials, the result is its own metamorphosis.) Adam was formed from clay, but not created until God breathed life into him. There is a reason why "inspiration" is obviously related to "respiration," and the word for breath and the word for soul in Hebrew share the same root. This makes breathing a pretty exciting pastime, when we think about it. It's as if, when we inhale, we're filled with the breath of God, filled with life. That's what animates and drives our existence.

Whenever we inhale, whenever we take in breath, we interact with the universe; we receive something. Whenever we release breath, we offer something. This wisdom is not exclusive to mystical Judaism. In the Eastern traditions, the student of meditation is directed to focus attention on the breath. In the yogic practice of *nadi sudi,* we inhale for half as long as we exhale as an expression of our desire to give back to the universe twice what we take from it. This awareness, like all spiritual truth, crosses cultures and religious backgrounds.

The way to spirit for Wands is inspiration—intuitive knowing, sudden understanding that we cannot explain or justify. It is the way of liveliness and the fullness of life—of the life force itself. However, Wands, like every other suit, has its flaw. In the case of Wands, it is "air-headedness"—impetuosity with no follow-through, impulsiveness without plan, passion without vision or discipline, quick starts that go nowhere and find no completion. We have seen how the other suits need each other. Now we can see how Wands are not sufficient unto themselves. A flame that climbs ever higher and burns ever brighter eventually burns itself out. So the fire of Wands needs Pentacles because Pentacles are earth—fuel. Pentacles ground Wands so they can accomplish their dreams. Fire also needs air for combustion; we smother a fire if we deprive it of air. So Wands need Swords, too—the clarity of mind to envision the whole and the determination to sustain effort.

If I had a nickel for everyone who said to me, "Someday I'm going to write a book," I could pay off my mortgage. This is because the idea of writing a book is fun and exciting, and sitting down to write a book is something else entirely. Everybody knows someone who has either a garage or an attic filled with unfinished projects. "Well, what I *really* wanted to be . . . .", "What I've always *wanted* to do . . . ." So you go out and buy an expensive set of drums and you set them up, and you find that having them does not make you Ringo Starr. After a while the drums wind up in the garage, because what you really wanted was to be was a terrific figure skater. So you buy the best ice skates you can afford, and then you go around the rink and fall a couple of times. You look at all the elegant, athletic skaters who have been at it for years, and then the ice skates wind up in the garage, because it's too hard to stay with skating, and you're not really in good shape. Then what you *really* want is to be a writer, so you get a word processor and sooner or later that winds up in the garage because you find out that the word processor doesn't write the book; you've got to sit down with the word processor and keep it company and do a little thinking. After that come the tropical fish. How many people do you know who have vast tropical fish tanks? Who could resist those gorgeous, brilliantly colored fish? But nobody mentioned cleaning the tank. So it gets really gross and the fish die.

Funny story: A friend of mine who had a tank of fish said to her roommate, "I feel so guilty! I haven't changed the water for those fish in so long they're barely moving." The roommate replied, "Maybe they're stuck." So the fish tank winds up in the garage, too. In short, we need to integrate Wands with the other suits to balance our functions of consciousness.

When we look at the Suit of Wands, we see that the images have become extremely simple. In every case, if we look at the card and then look away, we can easily hold the picture in our minds—unlike the Ten of Pentacles, for example. Why? Because we approach each suit with the function of consciousness that the suit represents. In other words, we approach Pentacles, the sensate function, with our own sensate function. We approach Pentacles with perception. Cups relate to feelings. The question to ask of a card in that suit is, "How does it make me feel?" Swords carry our thinking; we analyze Swords cards. But since we associate Wands with intuition, what is most important about these cards is what clicks for us when we look at them. What we can best ask ourselves is, "What is my inkling about this card? What comes through for me?" For this purpose, structurally simple images are best; detail would be extraneous distraction.

Ace of Wands

As always we begin in Keter, where divine energy first enters the Tree, first enters the universe. We see once again the huge hand that can only be the hand of God, emerging from the heavens, through a cloud, shining in a halo of white light, offering a gift. The gift this time is a rod, or wand. Before a pleasant landscape, God offers us the life force and the power of intuition. Keter is the crown, and perhaps more than in any other suit, intuition seems to come to us as a delicate explosion through the crown chakra. The most interesting aspect of this image, arguably, is that not all of the leaves are attached to the tree. When I looked at my first Waite deck, I thought the card was flawed. When I looked at my second Waite deck, I thought, "Wait a minute . . ." My third Ace of Wands made it clear that every deck had this "misprint," so I allowed my intuition to respond to the image exactly as printed.

Clearly these are not dead, falling leaves. They're not yellow or brown dried-up leaves that have reached the end of life. These are plump green leaves that are virtually exploding off the bough because they're so full of sap! They're full of life! This is the life force at its most powerful, an explosion of leaves off the wand that God is offering. When Jesus said, "I come to bring you life more abundant," I believe that this is what he meant. He wasn't talking about more years to watch reruns of sitcoms; more years in the same old rut isn't life more abundant. That's just doin' more time on planet Earth. He meant more cluck for your buck! More life for our life, vitality, the feeling of being quiveringly alive every minute that we're here.

The Buddhists talk about life's yearning for manifestation, the yearning to *be* in the world. The life force has an intrinsic need to funnel its way into living things. Dylan Thomas writes, "The force that through the green fuse drives the flower drives my green age." This is what the miraculous image of the Ace of Wands portrays—God gives to us the same life force as the sap that thrusts the flower through the sepals of the bud.

We can recognize in these ebullient leaves the little Yods, the first letter of the Holy Tetragrammaton, the unpronounceable description of the God that has no name, the *Yod He Vav He*. As always the Yods are the presence of divine energy in the world. It is interesting to note that there is only one ace that has no Yods: the Ace of Pentacles. In the Ace of Swords they masquerade as flames, in the Ace of Cups as drops of water, in the Ace of Wands as leaves. Why are there no Yods in the Ace of Pentacles? As Stephan Hoeller suggests, the pentacle itself is a representation of God's presence in the manifest world. So the Ace of Pentacles alone doesn't need Yods. But the Yods in the Ace of Wands hold so much *juice* that there's no way to contain it, and they fly out into the air.

At this point, we must address directly a subject we have discussed more generally, and that is that the Wands carry explicit sexual energy; in particular, phallic energy. (For the faint of heart and overly delicate, be forewarned: this is the X-rated chapter, and my only hope for marketing it through "adult" bookstores.)

The suits of the Tarot fall into two categories: female and male. Pentacles suggest pregnant bellies, Cups are symbols of the receptive female sexual vessel. Swords and Wands, on the other hand, are more or less classic phallic symbols, images of male sexuality. This is clear in the aces of these suits, especially the Ace of Wands, the cardinal image of virility. The way in which the wand is held brings to mind a certain African tribe that attributes the entire creation—all the stars of the universe—to an act of onanism by a single male god. (Keter, we recall, is associated with the vast nebulae of the entire cosmos.)

The Ace of Wands is a wonderful card for undertaking any new venture, because its energy, better than any other, can break through the obstacles of inertia.

Two and Three of Wands

Because of their obvious similarity, we will depart from the usual format of this book and examine the Two and the Three of Wands together. Aren't they somehow redundant? In each case, there is a single figure. In each case male. Each stands perfectly still, each with his face averted, and in each case he looks out over a body of water. Each holds a wand. Why do we need both of these cards?

To understand why we need both images in the Tarot, we must remember that we are dealing with Wands, and therefore with intuition. The question is not how much alike the cards are *perceived* to be, but what *sense* we have of them. We get a totally different sense of the personality types of these two figures, of what energies are being expressed. The Three of Wands makes us feel peaceful, carries an aura of great serenity; the Two of Wands carries one of impatience and urgency. So beginning with that, let us look at the images more closely.

In the Two, we see a gentleman who is dressed in patrician garb; we might gather that he is a nobleman. It seems to me that he is standing on his own balustrade or the turret of his own castle, looking out over the sea. He holds a wand in one hand—the life force, energy, inspiration, intuition—and in the other he holds a globe of the world, suggesting the material plane. His crest is made up of the red roses of desire and the white lilies of pure thought. The stark mountains in the background suggest objective clarity.

This card is often referred to as The Lord of Balance. This is someone who has done his spiritual work as well as his worldly work. He feels passionately, but he thinks clearly. He has done all that is in his power; what is left is to await his reward. But perhaps he looks out over the ocean as if to say, "Well, universe, I've been doing all the work here. What are you now going to offer me? When does my ship come in?" Or perhaps he is reflecting dispassionately on someone who has just sailed away. Is it his offspring, perhaps, whom he has prepared both spiritually and materially for independence? Yet now that the children have struck off on their own, he muses, wonders, questions their readiness.

The figure in the Three stands dressed in garb that suggests a more ancient time. A student likened the figure to Joseph in his coat of many colors. The robe and headband can also suggest the time of ancient Greece. In the Rider version of Waite's designs he stands in the golden glow of sunset or sunrise. He looks out over a river on which we see three boats. What does the card mean? How is it different from the Two?

If we look at the figure in the Two of Wands, we see that he can't stand in that position very long. How heavy is a globe of the world? How long can you stand with your arm crooked, holding one? Now look at the Three. Which position would you rather be in if you had to remain standing for an hour? There is a suggestion of impatience and urgency in the Two.

Whereas the figure in the Two is surrounded by worldly riches, the figure in the Three is out in nature without any belongings. The mountains of objective truth have receded into the background and appear much smaller than they do in the Two. Analytical judgment is of diminished importance. The key differences emerge, however, when we examine the ways in which the two figures hold their wands. The figure in the Two holds a wand that is perched precariously on top of a stone wall, as if to balance it, to keep it from falling over. The wand held in the Three is planted, or at least embedded in the earth, and the figure leans on it. He is not supporting it, he's gaining support from it. He's resting on it. He is grounded; his body language shows him to be comfortable. He's there for the duration.

Finally, we see in the Two of Wands a figure in profile, whereas the figure in the Three stands with his back to us. What here is at issue is faith and trust—how we really feel about our intuition. In standing with his back to us, he is vulnerable to attack, to someone sneaking up on him, but the Three's figure is not worried about that. He trusts that if there were something amiss he would sense it. He would some-how know it. Two of his wands are simply planted in the ground be-hind him, where he can't keep track of them. Suppose somebody steals up and makes off with them? But no one can; he trusts in himself to know if any danger approaches.

The Two of Wands, on the other hand, represents someone who does not trust his intuition as much as he *thinks* he does. The moun-tains of objective truth loom large and near; the figure is challenging and checking up on his intuition. The wands of his intuition are not grounded, so he cannot trust them to hold steady without conscious help. This is why, in holding one wand, he supports it rather than be-ing supported by it. As if this message were not clear enough, his sec-ond wand is bolted to the wall! He's actually got it bolted to the wall! This is a man who has to be in charge, has to control everything, and can leave nothing to chance. And while he's not exactly looking at us, he's positioned so that he can easily glance over his shoulder. He does not have the faith in his intuition that he would like to think he does.

For our intuition to serve us, we must be willing to submit to it, but the figure in the Two attempts to govern it. Rather than relying on his intuition, he has decided that he is entitled to some result or re-ward, and he expects the universe to deliver it right then, while he stands holding a heavy globe. We are reminded of the facetious prayer, "God, grant me patience—and I mean right now!" The card may well mean, "You will get what you have earned, what you deserve, but not necessarily on command."

This card turned up many times for me during the two-year pe-riod between my leaving advertising sales and finding my current work. I had provided for myself financially, making it possible to forgo a bi-weekly check. I had searched my soul, prayed, meditated, cajoled, and finally walking on the beach, railed at the heavens and ranted at the sea, "Why can't I find my true work in the world?" I found it—but not just then.

Let us ask next what the difference is between the ocean and a river? The ocean represents something "out there," separate from ourselves, from which we await something. The river is a metaphor for each of our lives (we have examined the "river of life" in earlier discussions). It's an interesting and appropriate metaphor, first, because like a river, we change all the time. While the river is always "the river," the water in it is never the same. We can return to a river, whether it's the Missouri, the Nile, or the Colorado, not having seen it for seven years, and be in no doubt that it is the same river. Similarly, every seven years, every cell of our bodies is replaced, but people continue to recognize us when we meet them on the street. It is not as if after three years people notice that we look a little strange; after five years, they aren't quite sure whether or not they know us; and after seven, pass us as if we are strangers. We remain the same even though particulars change. Our experiences flow through, as do our feelings, our thoughts, and our deeds, and yet there is the consistency of who we are. *We* are always the same, the capital *I* as opposed to the lower-case *I* of our lives. We, in our essence, are always the same. The river, then, is the symbol of constancy in the face of change.

Let us return now to the Three. In the Rider deck, the color that permeates the rendering is gold. The color of the water and the color of the sky are exactly the same. In the Universal Waite deck, they are of similar hue. This suggests the Kabbalistic truth that the soul and the God-stuff from which it emanated are one essence. It comes from the Ein, through the Ein Sof and Ein Sof Ohr, into the Tree. Whether one is in this body or another body or no body, it's the same essence. It's all golden light. That's what we are: golden light. Only the vessel changes from the rarefied medium of the sky to the denser but more dazzling medium of the water. The colors in the Two of Wands are more divisive. Individuation is much clearer. We can see where one thing lets off and something else begins. But there's a lovely blending and melding in the Three.

The peacefulness with which the figure in the Three looks out over the river of his life, on which float three boats—three relationships, jobs, opportunities, careers, goals, whatever—says, "There are three boats here. I wonder if one of them is the ship that will come in for me?" There is no urgency. There is no attempt to push the river. The figure has learned to go with the flow. He knows that if any of these boats has his initials on it, it will come into port without his doing anything further. He also knows that if it doesn't, he can't get it into his harbor with a gettin'-it-into-the-harbor machine! What is meant to be will be, and what is not meant to be will not be, no matter how much we want it.

The river can also be seen not as a single incarnation but as the soul's journey, in which case each boat would represent a life on earth. The Three of Wands symbolizes the capacity for detachment and the achievement of spiritual perspective on life and its events. Always and ever we remain golden light.

Beginning with a comparison of the Two and the Three is instructive. If we start with our perceptions, we see the cards' similarities. If we begin with our intuition, we may begin to understand their differences.

Since we are dealing with Chochma and Binah, we're dealing respectively with relationship and completion. As we mentioned in our discussion of Pentacles, the suits are not equally comfortable in every sefirah. The Suit of Pentacles, having to do with earth, shows increasingly positive cards as it nears Malchut, the kingdom, while the Two is uneasy and off balance. The Suit of Wands, which is fiery, naturally moves up and therefore is at its happiest high on the Tree. (This point will become even clearer when we examine the Nine and Ten of the suit.)

The Two of Wands, then, falling in Chochma, is a card of balance. Chochma means "wisdom" and refers to relationship; the Two at its best reflects the wisdom of establishing a balanced relationship between our spiritual and our earthly natures. The card suggests encompassing the full range of existence, as Chochma, associated with all twelve signs of the zodiac, implies balanced fullness. The successful executive whose inner life is a void has become a cliché in our society. Just as tragic, however, are those whose disrespect for the mundane results in noble intentions whose effects are disastrous. My heart sinks when a "new age" querent announces in the course of a reading, "If I'm on my true path, the money will come to me. The universe will provide." From a spiritual perspective, that statement is absolutely true. The universe *will* provide, but what? *What* will it provide? What the universe provides may not be what we want! Mick Jagger's reassurance that "you get what you need" is cold comfort for someone envisioning a universe that provides what they *want.* The streets of every major city are littered with the broken dreams and broken bodies of failed lives, spirituality notwithstanding. When clients talk with me about leaving an unfulfilling job to strike out on their own as healers or psychics, I cannot encourage them to do so before they have provided for their material needs.

In the third sefirah, Binah, the supernal mother, we see the understanding of the eternal feminine, the trinity that brings opposites—time and eternity, perhaps, in the Three of Wands—into a newly created union. The Three, as always, is the fulfillment of the suit. In Wands, it is trust in our intuition, in our own life force, in our connectedness with God energy. Binah has brought forth the child of perfect faith, who knows intuitively that we belong on this earth and are exactly where we are supposed to be. How many lives, how many lifetimes of Saturnian restriction and discipline, are required to arrive at this place of peace?

The right temple of Chochma and the left of Binah come together at the third eye. The profoundly evocative images of the Two and Three of Wands may more fully reveal their mysteries if given the benefit of this powerful and mysterious chakra.

Four of Wands

In the Four of Wands we come to an interesting expression of Chesed, God's manifestation as loving-kindness and mercy. We see the overflowing bounty of Jupiter, the largest and most expansive of planets. Two figures rush forth from what is clearly a harvest celebration taking place at the castle in the background. Arms raised high above their heads, hands filled with abundance from the earth, they hasten toward a canopy that is laden with fruits, gourds, and vegetables—a harvest canopy.

This canopy is an important symbol in the Jewish religion, in which there is a harvest festival called *Sukkhot.* For this holiday, people traditionally build a *sukkhah* (the singular of *sukkhot*), an arrangement similar to the one pictured, in which they take their meals, sleep, and spend their days. This is fascinating in terms of the Suit of Wands! Why? Because most of us would feel terribly vulnerable living outdoors under a flimsy canopy, spending the night exposed to unseen dangers without any walls or locks to protect us. Sleeping in the sukkhah is the acknowledgment of our trust in God, not just to bring forth fruit from the earth, but to provide for all our needs, including protection. As a point of interest, our own Thanksgiving traces its roots to this ancient celebration. More significantly for our work, Rabbi Ted Falcon teaches that the true sukkhot are not the ones we construct "out there" of branches and fruits, but the sukkhot we make of ourselves. If we recognize our gifts with kavanah, if we make them kadosh, we come to trust the *Adonai* (Lord) and the *Elohenu* (Creator). When we trust in God and the God within—our life force and our psychic knowing—then we are free to be in the world without walls, without protection, open, welcoming to the stranger, and laden with gifts to share.

Additionally, Jewish people get married under a canopy like this, which is called a *chupa*. It's nice to see how a marriage can easily be conceived of as a harvest. We don't marry easily. It takes a lot of hard work before we reach the altar. We have to work on the relationship and we have to work on ourselves. We learn to believe in our own intuition as well as in the other person. Before the harvest of the wedding, there is a lot of sowing, cultivating, nurturing, and pruning of the relationship. The Four of Wands is a fitting symbol of a wedding and a useful perspective on marriage.

Now I do want to say a word or two about marriage. When we talk about marriage, the most important thing is not the governmental writ saying that a relationship is legal. It's not the marriage license that makes it a harvest. It is the bonding. And this bonding, obviously, can take place on any level between any two people. Marriage is an interesting metaphor. A friend of mine had had a troubled relationship with

156

her mother, who died while the young woman was pregnant and before they had a chance to resolve their conflicts. To my friend, this was the final insult. "You've never given me what I need, and now, when I really need you, you die!" (We often feel anger at being abandoned when people die, but most of us can't admit it, because it's not rational, let alone nice.) Not wanting to have or wear anything of her mother's, she gave an aunt all of her mother's jewelry. After several years she asked her aunt if she would return one piece—the wedding ring. She was ready to forgive and accept her mother. Shakespeare writes, "Let me not to the marriage of true minds admit impediments." What my friend did in wearing her mother's wedding ring was marry her mother in the very real sense of bonding with her. The fact that they were the same sex didn't matter, the fact that they were mother and daughter didn't matter, and the division between life and death didn't matter. It was a true marriage. It was the bridge that crossed the divide between the kingdom of life and the kingdom of life everlasting.

The two figures at the center of the Four of Wands are clearly androgynous. They are intentionally drawn to make their gender ambiguous and have been perceived as two women, a man and a woman, and two men. They are rejoicing, gifts from their harvest held overhead, and racing out from the small gathering—to do what? To become a cornucopia, bring their riches out into the world. We are reminded of the difference between the *Yetzer Ha-tov* (impulse toward good) and the *Yetzer Ha-rah* (evil impulse). God creates us as beings whose essence is to receive but not to retain. In the Four of Pentacles we saw an image of the Yetzer Ha-rah, receiving the bounty of Chesed and hoarding it. Here we see an image of the Yetzer Ha-tov, of people who have received the harvest and now want to share their wealth. It is obvious from comparing these pictures wherein our happiness lies.

It is important to recognize that the only thing we can properly do with Wand energy is bring it out into the world. When we are inspired, when we receive light, we are meant to impart it, express it, make it of use to others. When we look at some of the other cards, we'll see the trouble that results when we hold back Wand energy.

Before leaving the Four of Wands, there is a final detail to which we may profitably direct our attention—a small bridge in the background that some readers, I hope, will recognize. We saw it first in the Five of Cups, but at that point the figure wasn't even aware of it, being overcome with the heartache of loss. The presence of the same little bridge in the Four of Wands promises that it is possible, if we go through our pain, to come to a place of harvest, bonding, and celebration.

Five of Wands

Here we are, back in Gevurah. Everybody's stomach falls an inch, in anxious anticipation. We know by now that, from our usual perspective of ego consciousness, nothing "good" is going to come to us in Gevurah. The fives are always difficult. The fifth sefirah is the place of judgment, the place of severity. As the central sefirah, it is called "severity" and is the most dread-full, awe-full place on the Pillar of Severity. So we know that we are going to experience the dark side of life. What we need always to do in Gevurah is remember that what is a problem on the ego level is exactly what the soul has been craving: the kind of challenge that enables us to grow and change, the kind of confrontation in which we have an opportunity to stretch and transcend. It is the purpose of our being incarnate on this earth.

Once again we have an image of strife. This time, it's conflict, pure and simple. We see five figures armed with heavy rods of wood, apparently doing battle with one another. To begin with the literal, if this card shows up, look around at your life and see if there is someone who is trying to hit you "upside the head"! (But ask whether there's someone you're trying to knock around, too!) Certainly this is a situation that we experience in families all the time, a perfect picture of sibling rivalry. It's also something we experience very often in the workplace, in personal relationships, and sadly, in society in general.

The image of the Five of Wands reminds us of humankind's natural tendency toward dissent and divisiveness. We perceive differences as threatening and use them as an excuse for disdain, antagonism, and even hatred and violence. This is obvious in any large city where racial and ethnic diversity is pronounced and makes targeting of an "enemy" easy. It may even seem inevitable that people of such different cultures as Chasidic Jews and African-Americans should clash when living in the same section of Brooklyn. Yet the actual source of the conflict is not the degree of difference between the cultures but our bent to perceive and maximize differences.

The farther we are from people, the more homogeneous they appear. In America, we talk about "the Arab states," "Great Britain," or even "Germany." When we think in terms of the sweeping differences between, say, Native Americans and Caucasians, we wonder what problems could occur in these seemingly monolithic societies. Yet conflicts among Arab states contribute heavily to the crises in the Middle East; the English are derisive of the Welsh, and the Bavarians are happy to distinguish themselves from the Prussians—and vice versa! No more serious conflict exists than that between Northern Ireland and Ireland itself, but even in England, the "rugged" men of Yorkshire despise the soft-living gentlefolk who live in London. And in Holland, that forward-looking bastion of tolerance, the people of Amsterdam make fun of those "Hague people"! At worst, the single figure with the vertical wand is besieged by the other four figures, and we see persecution of the minority, whether it be a group or an individual.

Of course the Five of Wands has positive meanings. There are those who see this card, not as combative or competitive, but as cooperative. More than one person has perceived it as figures involved in an Amish barn raising. (My perception of their faces makes it hard for me to interpret the card that way.) Alternately, not all competition is destructive. If we look at the card carefully, we see that the figures are not swinging their rods at one another. They are not trying to *hurt* each other.

If we begin with the assumption that there is a card for it, what would the card be for the NBA, say, if not the Five of Wands? We do see combatants dressed similarly, their tunics differing only in color. And all the figures seem to be youths of roughly the same age. Are they competitors in uniform like the men in their multicolored tank-tops and shorts, lined up for the Olympic 440?

The Five of Wands can represent any spirit of competition that results in progress and improvement, whether in sports, science, technology, or industry. If General Motors' motivation is to outsell Ford, we all wind up with better cars. Further, anyone who believes that researchers work back-breaking hours in labs with no thought of the Nobel Prize, a contract with a pharmaceutical company, or being the *first* to solve a problem has had no firsthand experience with scientists.

If the Five of Wands means conflict, but not of a mortal nature, we should be puzzled. How does this card warrant the number five with its associations of karmic rectitude? How does the fiery, bloody planet Mars work through this image? How does Gevurah, the great limiter, find expression here? To find the answer, as always we must look within. In so doing we come to some of the most challenging, important, difficult concepts of the entire Suit of Wands.

First, regarding our prejudices and hatreds, we need to recognize and own what within ourselves we project onto another individual or group against whom we wage battle. If I am in conflict with someone who I feel is lazy and irresponsible, to what degree do I wish I had the courage to express that ease-loving, carefree part of myself? If the object of my hatred is cunning, manipulative, successful, and rich, am I jealous of that capacity to milk and control life? What part of me would like to be the show-off in red silk, dancing in the center of the floor? What part of me would like to take any car I covet, even if it means stealing, and lose myself in the high of cocaine, able to shrug off the consequences?

Second, as Wands represents libido, the Five can suggest sexual conflict. It could mean guilt at expressing sexuality, difficulty in accepting the feelings themselves, or confusion about sexual identity. The most obvious of the concerns can revolve around being gay or straight, but there are subtler confusions. If I am taller than my boyfriend, like to help him work on his car, and can take him in an arm wrestle, does that make me less of a woman? If I tint my hair, like to wear purple, and prefer symphony to soccer, does that make me less of a man? If I am mesmerized by the grace of a woman in my sorority, does that mean that I want to make love to her and am too repressed to know it?

Finally, because Wands represents intuition, the Five of Wands depicts chaos of the intuitive function. This is a most painful condition, but one in which we all find ourselves, sooner or later.

For example, I'm in a work situation. My boss, the person to whom I report, says to me, "You're not doing it, Isabel. You're just not doing it. You're going through the motions, you're doing an adequate job, you're producing, but that's not why I hired you. There's no energy in your work, there's no excitement, there's no creativity. I expect more of you. I need more from you. I need you to get really involved in this project." And my reaction is, "I'm out of here! I don't need this pressure in my life. This woman wants more from me than she has any right to expect. I'm not here to make her look good, I'm just here to do my job. She's already admitted I'm doing it well. So what does she want from me? I have other interests, you know. She doesn't own my life!" Is that the voice of my intuition? Is that the Elohim, the God within, the God that has filtered all the way down through the Tree of Life from the place of the One? Or am I really saying, "Listen, I've reached this stage of my life without committing myself to anything, and I'm certainly not going to start now!" Which is the *truth?*

Suppose someone says to me, "Let's get together over the weekend." I say, "Great!" Monday night he doesn't call me. Tuesday night he doesn't call me. Wednesday night I'm starting to get ticked off. He doesn't call me. By Thursday night when I don't hear from him, I'm fuming! Friday at four o'clock, he calls and says, "So what time do you want me to pick you up?" I think to myself, "*Excuse* me! Was I supposed to keep my whole weekend open, waiting to find out when *you,* Your Majesty, were going to find time for me? Am I supposed to be at your beck and call?" I reply, "I'm terribly sorry, but I've made plans for this evening and the rest of the weekend. I'm not going to be available. We'll have to plan something more definite in the future."

Now if I do that, am I saying, "I'm here too!" Is my intuition saying to me, "You don't have to be treated that way! You don't have to be pushed around. You don't have to be a pawn to somebody else's whim. Stand up for yourself!" Is my true intuition telling me, "Take charge of your life, woman!" Or is it that I like to be in total control in all my relationships? Is it that I have to be the one who says when and how things work? "I expect to know on *Monday* when you're picking me up on Friday!" Am I really saying, "I'm a control junkie. I have avoided being flexible all of my life, and I'm certainly not going to start trusting the moment now! We'll do it my way or not at all!"

Suppose I develop a relationship with a man, but after seven months I'm just not getting what I want from it. A little voice inside my head says *"Get out now!* There's the door; run, do not walk. Leave. This is never going to work." Is that the voice of my true intuition? Or is it that old tape that says, "Sweetheart! Darling! If it's not perfect, it's not good enough for my Isabel! Why should you have to work at anything?"

How do we raise our children? What are reasonable expectations? When my daughter was eight or nine, friends of hers who were frequent dinner guests and often spent the night with us would repeatedly telephone and ask for her without so much as acknowledging me. "Hello, Andrea," I would say. "I recognized your voice! How are you? How is school?" I would call my daughter to the phone, wondering what sort of parents would bring up a child without any notion of good manners . . . until I heard my daughter call to speak to Andrea. Is it reasonable to expect a child to behave politely when it is out of vogue among her peer group? If so, does failure of courtesy warrant disapproval? Punishment? When are we overreacting? One voice in my head told me that she had pressures and stresses that were best honored by allowing her the space of self-discovery. Another voice insisted that my responsibility as a parent included requiring behavior that would ultimately serve her well, whether she liked it or not, and that leniency in order to avoid unpleasantness was abnegation of that responsibility. Which was true? (Would that this were my greatest dilemma in child rearing!)

As if our problems aren't bad enough, we have the added distress of not knowing whether we are lying to ourselves, and the brighter and more reflective we are, the greater the confusions. I had a friend, a very brilliant woman, who taught psychology. She was involved for a long time with a guy who I think most people would agree treated her like dirt. He never took her anywhere, but on a Thursday night at eleven o'clock, he'd call up and say, "I feel like coming over, OK?" That didn't seem much like a relationship to me. He never introduced her to his friends, and he never wanted to do anything with her, except come over at eleven o'clock at night for a few hours. And she, a brilliant Ph.D., would say, "This poor suffering soul is so closed off, he's incapable of trusting, of loving. If I'm not available to him, his life will be totally isolated. So of course I tell him he can come." What?

We're all capable of self-deception. In the Five of Wands place, we don't know when we're deceiving ourselves and when we're not. We don't know whether the voice we're hearing is the voice of true intuition or the voice of what a client of mine, a lawyer, calls "the jury."

Everybody has a voice, everybody has a say in what decision she should make. Maybe you have seen a program on TV called "To Tell the Truth." Someone is described by occupation, and each of three people try, by answering questions, to persuade a panel of judges that they are really that person—really the lion tamer. The punch line is "Will the real lion tamer please stand up?" The Five of Wands can convey the torment of wanting to be guided by our true intuition but hearing only the clatter inside our heads so that we don't know what to do. When we see this card we wish we could ask, "Will the voice of my real intuition please stand up?" It *is* a card difficult enough to appear in Gevurah.

What we need to remember always is that the Tree of Life is a perfectly balanced and symmetrical figure. If, when we look at the sefirot on the Pillar of Severity, we think we would be better off without them, we have to think again. If we found a way to eliminate this left-hand pillar, the Tree would lose its balance. It would fall over. It would no longer be the Tree of Life.

The Four of Wands is associated with the right shoulder of Chesed; the Five of Wands with the left shoulder of Gevurah. These meet as always at the throat chakra. It strikes me that the vocalization appropriate to the former would be song; to the latter, introspective argument guided by intuition.

Six of Wands

We move from the hell of not knowing whether we're crazy or clear to Tiferet, the place of the heart, the place of the sacrificed god, of Christ consciousness, of the Messiah, the Bodhisattva, the wounded healer.

Here we have the most complex image of the entire Suit of Wands. What we see is a figure riding a white horse, crowned with a victory wreath. There is another wreath on the wand he carries, and he is accompanied by various followers on foot. The Six of Wands is generally perceived as a victorious return from some battle, venture, or undertaking. In fact, the card is *called* "victory." There's even something about it that feels triumphant. When the card turns up, the most immediate and often most accurate meaning is that the querent will succeed at whatever he is setting out to accomplish.

However, never happy to leave well enough alone, let us look at the Six of Wands a little more closely. We must now recognize that one of these wreaths, the one mounted on the wand, looks like a funeral wreath. So a deeper interpretation of the card is that sometimes triumph depends on a kind of death; that sometimes for us to succeed, we have to allow a part of ourselves to die. What has to die? That depends on who we are. Maybe it's our pride. Maybe it's our insecurity. Maybe it's our compulsiveness. Maybe it's our stubbornness. Maybe it's our doubt. Sometimes it's an entire belief system. It can be a way of approaching people—shyness, cockiness, bossiness, an unwillingness to express our feelings, passive-aggression, active-aggression, whatever. This card informs us that to succeed as human beings, something within us has to die.

Because Tiferet is the place where all the high, light energies from the top of the Tree and all the rich dark energies from the lower portion of the Tree meet, it is the most human place on the Tree. It is the sefirah that affords us the opportunity of our full humanity. What has to die is ego, because finally our success as human beings depends on it.

I referred earlier to the principle that the soul and the ego are consummate adversaries. The ego has specific needs and desires which can rule our lives entirely. It's very demanding, it's very persuasive, and it's very loud! The ego makes a lot of noise! But for us to achieve our highest good, it's absolutely necessary to allow the ego to die. When the aggressive father, champion athlete, and successful businessman can put aside the ego expectations he had on the day he passed out cigars, he can experience the joys of parenting a frail, sensitive son, a shy daughter with a physical deformity, or a mentally retarded child. The fulfillment of nurturing with love, free from ego gratification, is greater than any triumph the ego can provide. The bright sun of Tiferet radiates its light and warmth upon us when ego is eclipsed by soul.

We are not our bodies, and we are not our personalities. What we are—the golden, flowing river of the Three of Wands—goes through many incarnations. So it's appropriate that in the place of the sacrificial god, the ego be allowed to die.

Of course, that's just what Christ did. Jesus was not able simply to look down from heaven and figuratively pat people on the head, saying, "There, there, it's going to be all right." He had to get down into it. He had to be literally willing to make the sacrifice; that was what made the Resurrection possible. The ego consciousness has to die. The body has to die. The personality has to die. If Tiferet is the place of death and resurrection, then it makes a lot of sense that true victory in life depends upon sacrificing the control of ego and opening to inspiration and faith.

Other meanings of the Six of Wands are darker. One of the first things we notice once we are focused on ego is the disgruntled faces of the hero's retinue. Are they resentful that he gets to ride while they must walk? The Six of Wands can represent someone who has succeeded at the expense of his subordinates. We all know of executives who pass on creative challenges, difficult problems, and arduous assignments to their staff. They give them the praise of lip service but do not acknowledge their efforts to management, instead taking all credit for themselves.

Most interesting in our exploration of the Six of Wands is the peculiar way the blanket covers the white horse. Would you put a blanket on a horse covering his legs so that he trips? Covering his tail (if you get my meaning)? While this way of draping a horse was common *ceremonial* practice during the Middle Ages, we are clearly not witnessing the pageantry of a joust in this card. Some other explanation is required. Further, even in medieval times a horse would not have been covered in such voluminous folds in which it could easily become entangled. What is this image is telling us?

We asked of the Nine of Cups, "What's behind that long blue tablecloth?" Now perhaps we want to ask the same question about the green horse blanket. What *is* under that blanket? It looks as if something is being hidden. From a slightly different perspective, it looks almost as if that white horse head might be part of a costume. There might be a couple of people crouching under the green blanket. Perhaps it isn't a real horse at all.

Rabbi Levi Meyer has interpreted the story of Jacob and his wives in a fascinating way that is relevant to our current discussion. Jacob, you will remember, served Laban seven years in order to marry his younger daughter, Rachel, who was "beautiful and well favored" (Genesis 29:17). But Laban tricked Jacob, providing Leah, his older daughter, as the veiled bride and requiring that Jacob work seven more years for Rachel, his promised wife. What has this to do with the Six of Wands? The name Laban means "white." The message is the same. Beware of anyone who rides a white horse. Suspect those who present themselves as "pure." There is certain to be something hidden. Do not trust those who appear to be without blemish; there will always be more to them than meets the eye.

The most important question then is, "If the victory we are looking at is victory on the earth plane, what has been the cost?" Have we risen on the backs and shoulders and heads of the very people to whom we owe the most? Is that why these people look so angry? Tiferet, associated with the heart and heart chakra, is the place of our deepest compassion. If to achieve success, the rider has had to hide his real motives and sweep his treatment of others under the horse blanket, his victory is Pyrrhic, for it has been at the cost of his own soul.

Seven of Wands

Now we move to Netzach, "victory," the sefirah charged with Venusian passion, and we see the Seven of Wands, a card of high energy. Here is a lone figure who stands on a little hill holding a wand with which he seems to be warding off six approaching wands. He has elevated himself to a position that he is not about to let anyone take from him. He is prepared to fight to maintain what is rightfully his. The small mound, on close examination, looks like an entire landscape. When we stand up for ourselves, especially in matters of principle, we feel as if we are Colossus, astride hill and dale.

This is clearly a combative card. Often it represents lawsuits. Furthermore, the figure is clearly outnumbered and in a position of defense. A woman I read for some years ago comes to mind. She had a small cosmetics company and had come up with a product she felt had marketing potential beyond her means. She submitted it to a large, internationally successful cosmetic manufacturer, where it was allegedly rejected. Shortly thereafter the product was manufactured by this firm without any compensation to her. She took the company to court with her one lawyer to confront their six—or more likely six *teams* of lawyers. The only question then was who could afford to sustain the legal battle longer, who had more money. The world being what it is, she lost her case—but she was willing to fight for her rights, unwilling to concede what she had achieved without doing battle.

I'm very fond of the Seven of Wands. This is the confrontational, powerful animus figure. Sometimes I get lucky, and there's someone who will fight for me out there in the cold, hard world. More usually, it's something within me that protects my poor little anima! None of us can make it without a certain degree of feistiness or we become victims, collaborating with those who would take advantage of us.

This is the figure who says, "You can't push me around just because I'm _____!" Fill in the blank: small, uneducated, weak, old, female, whatever. "I will not relinquish what I have rightfully earned, what I am entitled to."

This is an especially important card for an artist. Innovations in art are never received with any great enthusiasm, *because they're new*. They're not what people are used to, not what people expect. I like to think about Hieronymus Bosch, an artist of the fifteenth century. While everybody else was painting beautiful, sweet pictures of the Madonna and Child, Bosch was depicting absolutely hideous, grotesque monsters and demons. Such dark images are, of course, part of everybody's psyche. It wasn't until four hundred years later that the German expressionists addressed this as a legitimate area for artistic expression. So you can imagine how delighted everyone was at the sight of a bizarre creature defecating coins, when everyone around Bosch was painting halos. Yet Bosch is now recognized as one of the great geniuses of the art world. Outnumbered does not necessarily mean wrong.

Arguably, the most interesting aspect of the Seven of Wands is that the figure wears one boot and one shoe. Why? I wondered about this for years until the meaning came through. This is the card that says, "I have the right to my eccentricities as long as they don't hurt anybody." As Alan Watts puts it so eloquently: "Everyone is entitled to his own weird." If I'm doing something that strikes you as very peculiar—*back off.* Back way the hell off. It's not your business, and I have a big stick here to encourage you not to mind it.

It's terribly sad to see how much needless suffering there is in life when people don't have the courage to stand up for their right to be exactly as they are. The paradigmatic example of this is the cross-dresser, a man who not only loves but feels compelled to wear women's clothing. Sometimes there is a further compulsion, or at least desire to go out into the streets so attired. Now whom does that hurt? It's simply an idiosyncrasy. And yet instead of taking an assertive "Back off!" position, most of these poor souls who aren't hurting *anybody* are overwhelmed with shame, self-loathing, and guilt. For what?! For nothing.

So this is the card that urges you to have the courage not only of your convictions but of your "abnormalities." "You know, this is what I do. I sleep until three in the afternoon. That's what I do. And then I get up and I write music until five in the morning. That's my schedule. I have breakfast at about five in the afternoon; I eat lunch at midnight. That's me. Any problem with that? Back off! You don't like it? Back way off! Just back way the hell off."

"Yeah, I spend all of my money on tropical fish, and I eat peanut-butter sandwiches. You think that's stupid? Who asked you? You think that's a pretty strange way to live? Keep your opinion to yourself! Go to a restaurant and eat a steak. I'm going to sit here and watch my fish."

"I happen to wear one boot and one shoe. I also like ketchup on my tuna-and-banana sandwich. That's the way I do it. Next you'll be telling me my socks should match. Why? Just *back off!* That's the way I am. I don't hurt anybody—but you could be an exception to that rule if you don't get out of my face."

There is a benign interpretation to the Seven of Wands. The same blessed soul who perceives the Five of Wands as a barn raising, a cooperative effort, sees the figure in this card as planting the wands in the ground. Few of us have seen planting proceed in this fashion, but it's conceivable that six of the wands have already been shoved into the ground and that with the seventh, the farmer's work will be complete. Others see the figure as unnecessarily defensive: they maintain that the six approaching wands may present no threat, may simply be "visiting." But I see the Seven of Wands as the wonderful card of standing up for ourselves or for the eccentricities of those whom we love. I see the passionate, Venusian energy of Netzach.

Eight of Wands

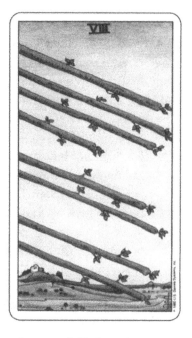

Returning to Hod, we arrive at the place of intellect, mercurial quickness, "splendor," and "glory." Here we encounter the Eight of Wands, a strange-looking card, the second of only two Minor Arcana in which there are no human figures. The card simply shows eight wands shooting through the air. So what we have here is a virtual explosion of vital energy.

As I mentioned in relation to the Ace of Wands, this is the X-rated chapter of our study, so I will forge ahead boldly and remind the reader that, as wands carry libidinous energy, they can be specifically sexual in their symbolism. Combining this with my conviction that for every life experience there is a card, if there is a card for sexual climax, it would have to be the Eight of Wands. The phallic nature of the card encourages this interpretation. At the opposite end of the same spectrum of libidinous energy is the intuitive counterpart to orgasm, which is Epiphany—the sudden realization of Jesus' hosts, at the supper at Emmaus, that they were in the presence of God, the resurrected Christ, never before seen by ordinary mortals. So the Eight of Wands can also be a climax of intuitive energy, an explosive "Eureka!" experience.

The Eight of Wands is clearly a very positive card. New information rushes to us as a gift, without our having to learn it. When the card is rightside up, the wands promise to become grounded, thereby avoiding the major pitfall of Wands. This is because the sheer exuberance of Wands is balanced, given form, by the mental influence of

Mercury; Hod allows for planning. A river runs through the pleasant landscape toward which the wands fly. As the river in Tarot is always the river of life, we are assured that our very lives will be altered by the wands' arrival.

When the card is upside down, there is a danger that, of all these eight wonderful inspirations, intuitions, ideas that have come bursting into consciousness, none of them will find expression. They are all going to float up into the air and dissipate. Better to choose one of them and bring it to completion, we are warned.

There is, however, a positive interpretation of the card reversed: that the sky's no limit for this person's creativity and intuition.

There is also a negative to having the card upright. Depending on where you're standing, if you get hit by eight wands flying through the air, it can be very painful. We all know that an explosion of intuition can hurt. If I have been lying to myself all my life, for example, about my relationship with my kid sister, a sudden realization of the truth will not be pleasant. I tell the world, and I say to myself, "My sister and I are so close. We have an incredible relationship. I call her every day. She and her family come for dinner twice a week, and I always send her home with leftovers so she won't have to cook. Whenever she's sick, I move in to take care of her, and I usually baby-sit for her on Saturday night. Last week she was having friends for dinner, so I bought her a new outfit. I cooked the main course and made the dessert and helped her clean the house—she was so nervous! I told her to just leave the dishes, that I'd be back to do them in the morning. My kid sister is my best friend!" One day my sister refuses to pick me up, the one time my car breaks down on the highway. When it occurs to me in a sudden awareness that my sister is a taker who never extends herself for me, I'm going to be emotionally black and blue. Sometimes an intuitive explosion delivers a lamentable truth.

The Seven of Wands, at the top of the right hip associated with Netzach, joins the Eight of Wands, the top of the left hip associated with Hod, at the solar plexus. In the chakra system, this grounding place offers a stabilizing influence to the figure in the Seven, who is prone to fly off the handle or err on the side of touchiness. It brings the wands of the Eight to a solid resting place, a place of completion, or, if the card is reversed, supplies the firm springboard to launch them beyond the realm of dreams.

Nine of Wands

At Yesod, the foundation, we find the Nine of Wands, the second most complicated card of the suit. We see a figure standing guard over eight wands, holding the ninth, his body language suggesting great stress. His head is bandaged; he has not yet recovered from the last blow and is tensed for the next. He is a burly fellow, his brawn repre-

senting moral fortitude. The Nine of Wands is a great favorite of mine, for the same reason I am so fond of the Seven. In fact, the two make kind of a before-and-after pair. In the Nine we see someone who has the loyalty, strength of character, and the endurance to stand by what he believes in, to protect what he values.

The negative of the card has to do with stubbornness. It may be that, if I'm getting beaten up all the time, it's because I'm clinging out of habit or rigidity to things I should let go. The example that follows is—trust me—absolutely true: A woman I knew many years ago was returning from a drive one Sunday with her husband and two sons. They were listening to a classical music station, and Mrs. Always Right commented that she always enjoyed hearing Brahms' First Symphony. Her husband said that he too enjoyed Brahms' First, but that at the moment they were hearing Beethoven's Eighth. Mrs. Always Right said she was certain it was Brahms' First, and maintained her position in the face of both sons' agreement with their father. Before the symphony or argument came to a close, the family arrived at home where they decided to settle the question in the simplest way. Mrs. Always Right slipped Beethoven's Eighth Symphony from its record jacket and put it on the family stereo. To no one's surprise but her own, she heard the music they had just been listening to in the car. Stiffening slightly, Mrs. Always Right announced, "This record has been mislabeled!" Sometimes our strength can be better spent challenging our own position than defending it.

Another negative meaning carried by the Nine of Wands is remaining defensive when the need has passed. A tremendous amount of energy is being expended on protecting ourselves against the anticipated next blow. But what if we have already experienced the *last* blow? What if no further blows will follow?

This is a wonderful card for the general who is still fighting the last war. I had firsthand experience of this energy in an amusing way one evening some years ago. I am a person so rich in faults that inventing additional ones for me is unnecessary and extravagant. Paying even casual attention will reveal a wealth of real ones. On the evening in question, I was out to dinner with a man I'd known socially for eight or nine months. He had chosen a Spanish restaurant whose flamenco floor show was clearly at odds with the chosen route of the waiters. We enjoyed a sherry, watched the dancers, and grew increasingly famished. By 9:30, with no aroma of food promising relief, I was ravenous. It was then that I lost my head. *I ordered a second sherry!* My date was suddenly transformed into a captain of the Spanish Inquisition. Did I cook much with wine? Drink much at home? Alone? Although we had been out together dozens of times, and he had never seen me tiddly, much less drunk, he was unhinged by my ordering two drinks before dinner instead of one. Why? Because the reason he had divorced his wife was that she was an alcoholic. So he was tensed, just waiting for the next woman he liked to have a drinking problem.

Another sorrowful meaning of the Nine of Wands has to do with its relating to sexual energy, as all Wands cards do. I have found in my practice that this card very often turns up for someone who has been sexually abused as a child. The figure can be seen as someone whose sexuality has been wounded. The complexity of this abuse is obviously exacerbated when it involves incest. The victim is then confronted with the dilemma of adjusting to the torment of abuse or acknowledging the abomination and its perpetrator for what they are. As any psychologist will tell us, the latter choice is never made. So dependent are we as children that any treatment by a parent is less terrifying than being orphaned.

Imagine, or better, remember being five years old. We can't reach the light switch, we can't read a storybook or a clock face, we can't tell a dime from a nickel ("dinkle" was my daughter's guess), and buttons seem to have even less to do with buttonholes than the shape of our socks have to do with the shape of our toes. Left shoes seem to gravitate to right feet; shoelaces require the dexterity of a violin virtuoso, and "lost" means around the corner or seven houses down the street. We don't have the words for most of what we feel, but being taken care of is what we need most, even if we *can't* say it.

Children consistently feel guilty and shamed by their abuse; believing themselves responsible gives them some sense of power or choice, even if it intensifies their pain. And it is less threatening to believe themselves deserving of abuse than to believe a parent, on whom they are totally dependent, to be untrustworthy and cruel. The figure in the Nine of Wands can be seen as defending the very source of his suffering, even as he stiffens against it. By extension of meaning, the abuse may be physically violent or verbally undermining, but the possibility of sexual abuse is always present with the appearance of this card, particularly if it is reversed.

Finally, if we return to the notion of Wands as carrying intuition, the Nine of Wands can represent comparable damage to the child's magical, creative, psychic function. In patriarchal societies, we tend to be rewarded and congratulated for quantifiable success—mastery of the alphabet, correct answers to arithmetical problems, good marks in school. Our fantasies, imaginings, inklings, and artistic expressions are more likely to be dismissed as foolish and pointless, or even as naughty lies. In that case the card represents protecting intuition in the face of past assaults that we have every reason to suspect will continue.

Here we see the first separation card of the Suit of Wands, and the meaning, though complex, is clear. We have been separated from our own intuition and therefore from ourselves. No wonder we are suspicious, watchful, and uneasy. If we have been convinced that we can't trust our intuition, where are we to turn? If we have been convinced that we don't know what we *know,* what can we trust? If we see and sense animosity between parents, sexuality between an older sister and her boyfriend, or anxiety about a brother's health or a father's employment, we *know.* To be reassured that we are only imagining things, or accused of making up stories, looking for trouble, or stirring up nonsense puts our trust in our deepest selves at odds with our faith in the people on whom we are most dependent. Separated from his own intuition, the figure in the Nine of Wands regards his own wands with suspicion.

It is clear that the image of the Nine of Wands is an appropriate one for Yesod, the foundation, and the vagaries of moonlight. What the various interpretations of the card share is their grounding in unconscious issues. What we manifest in Malchut will depend on how we deal with these issues in Yesod; our extroverted behavior is indeed based on how we process our childhood wounds.

Ten of Wands

Looking at the Ten of Wands, we can see clearly that the Wands have become increasingly burdened as they move down to Malchut. Here is a figure carrying ten wands before him, bent with the effort and unable to see past his bundle to his destination—perhaps the house at the back of the card. We observe here the reverse effect from the one we saw in the Two of Pentacles. Pentacles, being earthy, are off balance in Chochma, in the rarefied realm of emanation. Conversely, the fieriness of Wands makes them uncomfortable in the kingdom where energy must be solid.

The Ten of Wands is a simple card. Insofar as Wands represent intuitive, creative energy, they require a mode of expression. The energies of Wands must be integrated with other suits to make this expression possible. Without it, they become an unwelcome weight.

It is not the proper use of intuition to let it accumulate. We are meant to make use of it, bring it to harvest. When that doesn't happen, when the creative process is dammed up, it becomes an encumbrance. Wands need the powerful feeling of Cups to motivate follow-through, the rigors of Swords to organize inklings into thoughts, and the earthiness of Pentacles to bring them into the material world. When we fall short of the courage or clarity to bring our creativity into full manifestation, inspiration becomes a burden. We would just as soon not have it at all.

174

Perhaps the most common presenting problem of my clientele is, "I know I'm supposed to be doing something else—I have all these feelings that I can't express, but I know they're important. How can I find out what I should be doing with them?" The Ten of Wands is the card for having received much, psychically and spiritually, being affluent in gifts for which we have not yet found direction. The pain of this search is very great; John Milton refers to his poetry as "that one talent, which is death to hide." Holding back our generative capabilities is indeed a kind of death to the psyche.

Specifically, the Ten of Wands represents the writer's block that keeps us staring at a blank page, the stage fright that keeps a talented performer in the wings, and so forth. But we must remember, as always when dealing with Wands, that they also carry explicitly sexual energy. If the Eight suggests sexual climax, the Ten must convey celibacy, the holding back of libido. When the card is reversed, there can be the suggestion of sexual frustration, either in celibacy or in unsatisfactory relations.

Wands, the suit of fire, embody the most rarefied of our energies. Their natural tendency is to reach higher, climb to loftier realms. In fact, after years of working uneasily with the Ten of Wands, I realized what was tweaking at my own intuition, which led to a clearer understanding of the card. What was troubling me was the body language of the figure, the angle of his body as he carries his load. I defy any reader to lift, let alone carry, a heavy load in this way. It is, I then realized, just how you would carry an armful of helium balloons! The figure is not lifting the wands, *he is holding them down*. The difficulty consists in holding back what is, by nature, meant to fly.

Wands need to be balanced by the grounding effect of Pentacles and are not themselves easy at the more mundane sefirot of the Kabbalistic Tree. Here in Malchut, the Earth itself, the problem of the Ten is expressed and exacerbated by its being a separation card. Malchut is associated with the soles of the feet, and the figure is indeed on the move, pushing forward on his own two feet. However, he is separated from his own creative expression. We see in him someone who literally can't see the forest for the trees. Getting to the house, not dropping a single wand, seems more important to him than allowing his intuition to fly, trusting his creative thrust to carry them aloft, making manifest his inspiration.

With this examination of Wands, we conclude our discussion of the suits of the Minor Arcana and their relation to the pillars and the sefirot of the Kabbalistic Tree. Our study in balance and integration will continue as we consider the court cards of all four suits, conceiving of the Tree in terms of its olams.

CHAPTER 7

Court Cards: Our Many Selves

*I*N EXPLORING the numbered cards of the Minor Arcana, we have related each to its respective sefirah on the Tree of Life, weaving our way among its pillars.

In examining the court cards, we approach the Tree in terms of its horizontal divisions, its four olams or realms. Three of these are described by three sefirot each, which form triangles. The first, composed of Keter, Chochma, and Binah, forms an upward-pointing triangle called a fire triangle, since it is the nature of fire to move up. The second, composed of Chesed, Gevurah, and Tiferet, forms a downward-pointing triangle, a water triangle, since water moves down, seeking its own level. The third, composed of Netzach, Hod, and Yesod, also forms a downward- pointing water triangle. The final olam, as you may recall, consists of the single sefirah of Malchut that, being the earth plane, of course represents the "element" of earth.

There are those who would like to say that either the second or third triangle must be an air triangle, and it is certainly tempting to take this position. Air is the fourth "element"; completion and symmetry seem to demand its presence. There is only one problem with adopting this view, and that is that there is no justification for it. Air does not always move down! The position—as I see it—is therefore reductionistic.

What we are left with then is the question, "How can the Tree of

Life, microcosm of the macrocosm, have no olam of air?" I have no answer to that question, but I do have a perspective on questions themselves that is shared by Zen and Chasidic traditions.

A devoted and driven seeker of truth travels for many months to the house of a great master, one who reputedly has *The Answer*. When he finally arrives, he is denied an audience and subjected to jeers of the many who have preceded him, knowing that the master has kept his solitude unbroken for twenty years. But our hero is not to be deterred. He waits until everyone has fallen asleep and steals into the master's chamber.

The master looks up and demands, "What do you want?" "I have a most important question," replies the seeker. "Tell me, Master, what is truth?" The master's response is a slap across the face! Stunned and hurt, the petitioner cries, "Master, my question is sincere and selfless! Why did you strike me?" The master's response is a second slap, after which the seeker is pushed out of the chamber, the door resoundingly slammed behind him.

At this point the young stranger finds a bar, but his attempts to console himself with brew fail so obviously that a town elder approaches him to question the source of his distress. Upon hearing the young man's plight, he begins to pace, tugging at his beard and musing. Suddenly his eyes light up in delight and his wise old face crinkles into a smile of understanding. "It is clear that the master slapped your face the first time to teach you something very important: that questions are better than answers. It was his way of saying, 'That is a good question! How can you be such a fool as to believe you need an answer to it?' Now I realize why he slapped you a second time. It was to teach you something even more important. He was showing you that there is never any connection between a question and an answer!"

This parable itself leaves us with a question. Certainly on a literal level there usually *is* a relationship between what is asked and what is answered. The first hard knock we have to accept, however, is that while answers are more *gratifying* than questions (at least on an immediate basis), questions are more *valuable*. Questions open lines of thought, discussion, and possibility, while answers close them off. Exploration depends on questions; answers spell the death of imagination, hypothesis, and wonder: as long as we "knew" that Earth was the center of the universe, astronomy as a science was shut down.

The second blow we need to accept is that when we go beyond the mundane "What time is it?" order of questioning to questions that genuinely open our minds, the answers that come to us may bear little logical connection to the original inquiry. Instead, we are led to areas of reflection, memory, and speculation beyond our mental awareness at the time the question was posed.

Reductionistic thinking would attribute air to one of the olams of the Kabbalistic Tree to tie things up neatly and provide an answer. The question "How can the 'element' of air not be represented along with fire, water, and earth on the Tree of Life?" leaves us uncomfortable and bewildered. Given this choice, I would opt to stay with discomfort, leaving the matter open for future discovery. More on this subject follows shortly.

The topmost of the olams, Atzilut, is the realm of emanation. It is into this realm that the divine essence, God energy, has radiated from the *Ein* (the One) through the *Ein Sof* (limitlessness) to the *Ein Sof Ohr* (limitless light) and into the Tree itself at Keter, the first sefirah of this supernal triangle.

The second of these triangles, the first downward-pointing triangle, is Beriah, the world of creation. The third olam, the second downward-pointing triangle, is Yetzirah, the universe of formation. Clearly, as we move down the Tree, the olams grow more specific and manifest. Finally we arrive at Assiyah, the olam that is composed of the single sefirah of Malchut, the realm of action.

What are the correspondences between these four olams and the four court cards? Traditionally, the olam of emanation, Atzilut, belongs to the kings, because the kings are the most highly evolved of the court cards. They are the final expression of the energy of their suit and so claim the loftiest realm of the Tree for themselves. To the realm of Beriah, creation, is assigned the queens. To the realm of Yetzirah, formation, the knights are assigned. So far this system works. Creation is what we women do; we bring the babies into the world. And young men set out to make their mark in the world, give form to chaos and change the formation of things—governments, belief systems, and so on. In Assiyah, the olam of action, we have the pages, the least developed of the court cards, falling to the earthiest of the worlds.

The system delineated has much to commend it, yet the more I thought about it, the less satisfactory it seemed. The reasons were three, the first being simply visual. The aces of each suit depict an oversized hand, which can be only the hand of God, coming out of the heavens through a cloud, offering a gift. Which of the court cards appear to have just received these gifts? *Look at the cards.* There is something in the demeanor and the posture of the pages that powerfully suggests to me just having received something brand new.

The second question I raise in relation to the traditional system is that Malchut is called "the kingdom." Sounds like a good place for kings to me! Where could the king belong if not in the kingdom, and who but the king could rule there?

My most crucial concern with the system, however, is that the work of the world needs to be done, not by the youngest and least experienced of the court cards, but by the wisest and most fully developed. If the first nine sefirot can be thought of as the gestation period, anything that does not reach Malchut, anything that does not reach manifestation, is stillborn. Who can say what has been lost when a baby is stillborn? It might have been the next Mozart, John Kennedy, or Gandhi. All we know is that here in the world nothing has been accomplished, nobody benefits, nothing has been expressed. *If the king is the fulfillment of the suit, he belongs in the olam that is the fulfillment of the Tree.*

For these reasons I believe that development moves down the Tree from the pages to the kings. For years, I was tempted to keep the queens in Beriah and the knights in Yetzirah because it felt intuitively correct. This of course leads to an interesting problem: the normal court card progression of page, knight, queen, king is disrupted. The sequence with which I was left was page, queen, knight, king. Even though this system intuitively seemed more fitting, I was tempted to throw it out on the grounds that it couldn't be right.

As I have already suggested, however, I am of the tradition that holds a good question to be more valuable than a good answer—and certainly preferable to an unsatisfactory answer based on rigid or simplistic thinking. So I left open the question, "How can the natural progression of the court cards be disturbed if they are being properly assigned to the olams of the Tree?"

Recently, this question was answered to my satisfaction. The suggestion was made that the queens could easily belong to the universe of formation and the knights to the universe of creation. If we stay with the paradigm of birth, it can be perceived that *creation* occurs at the moment of *conception*. The knights on horseback represent the movement of the sperm to the ova. The queens can then be seen to reside in the realm of formation where, over a nine-month period, they give form to the potential of the egg, making a baby from a single fertilized cell. For those of us comfortable with that scheme, the natural order of the court cards is then restored: page, knight, queen, and king, moving from Atzilut to Assiyah.

A teacher or book can suggest a direction for the student of Tarot, but finally each reader—man or woman—is the High Priestess of this study. Your own intuition is your own highest authority and can never be overridden. What follows is my own highly opinionated, intensely felt, not necessarily correct, and perhaps at times alienating view of who these court cards are and what they mean. My biases will become very clear, and ideally yours will as well.

Before you read any further, I suggest the following as a useful exercise: Take all of the court cards, spread them out in front of you, and look at the array of humankind represented. Ask yourself, "If I could choose only one of these sixteen cards for a friend, which would I choose and why? If I had to choose one of these cards as a business partner, who would it be? If I could have had any mother I wanted, which of these queens would I have chosen for my mother? Which figure would I avoid at all costs as being totally irresponsible and someone whose word wouldn't mean anything at all to me?"

Think about the things that are important to you in your friends and family in your values. Ask yourself, "Who's representing what here? Who's got the best sense of humor? Who's the most charming? Who's the most serious? Is there anybody here who looks a little depressed? Who's the most combative, competitive? Who's the most remote? Who would have made the worst father?" It will be amazing, if you spend time with the cards, what will come through for you! That's a promise.

A final suggestion: when you find cards with which you sense an immediate rapport, put them away and work with the other ones! The ones that elicit a feeling of connection are talking to you loud and clear without much attention. Working with the cards you don't especially take to or understand will yield the richest benefits.

The Pages

Let us begin in Atzilut, the realm of emanation, where the pages receive their gifts from the aces. The pages are the children or adolescents of the Tarot. They have all the virtues of youth—openness, energy, lack of preconception, optimism, faith, enthusiasm, innocence, and idealism. They are, unfortunately, totally lacking in the gifts of age—experience and wisdom. They are more passionate than informed.

Still, we need this childlike quality throughout our lives. Once again, if we approach the cards from a Jungian perspective, we each, man or woman, have all of these youthful archetypes within us. There has been a lot of talk about "the inner child" in recent years, but we have more than one inner child. We have a joyful child, a fearful child, a curious child, a budding adolescent, and a rebellious adolescent among the many inside us. We will see four of them in the pages alone. When one of these cards turns up for us, it very often stands for someone who carries this energy in our lives, but it always represents a part of ourselves that is being activated at the time.

Page of Pentacles

The Page of Pentacles, to my mind, is the most spiritual card in the deck. He stands out in nature under a golden sky; a pentacle like a magical rainbow bubble, upon which he has totally fixed his attention, floats just above his hands. He is mesmerized by the gift of the palpable, emanating from the Ein Sof Ohr, the unlimited light, into Atzilut. In his demeanor the Page expresses appropriate awe of the manifest: genuine reverence that there should be such a thing as the physical world. God could have chosen simply to imagine the universe but instead chose to create it. What generosity! How wonderful! His ap-

PAGE of PENTACLES

preciation of the physical world is understandable; as we know, both pages and Pentacles are associated with Jung's sensate function.

It's clear to me that the Page is fully aware of the star within the coin, of the God energy animating the outer form. Why else does he not grasp the pentacle? He could grab it merely by extending his elbows!

Let me mention in this context that it is revealing to trace certain symbols through a suit of court cards. In the case of Pentacles, watch the different ways in which the figures hold their pentacles. In Swords, follow the birds. In Wands, pay attention to the salamanders; in Cups, the relationship of the figures to water.

The Page of Pentacles is someone who senses the miraculous in the ordinary, or should we say, knows there is no such thing as the ordinary. He does not need to be in a temple, church, or cathedral to experience the kadosh quality, the blessed quality of the world itself. He can see it in a leaf, in the eyes of another person; he can feel it in the fur of an animal. He can hear it in the wind or in birdsong, even in the whirring of a well-run machine, yet he is especially affinitized to the natural world where we find him. He experiences the presence of God in the wilderness, on a beach as he watches a sunset, in the arms of love. The card represents someone who has cultivated the attitude of kavanah, holy intention, so that everything is experienced as blessed.

We must remember that each suit and each of its cards has a flaw as well as a strength. The flaw in the Page of Pentacles is the danger of falling in love with money, power, prestige, status, influence, accomplishment—anything in the material world. It's interesting that in the Knapp-Hall deck, the pages are called slaves. The pages have just received power from the divine hand of God, and they may be amazed, impressed, delighted, or confused by it, but they clearly can become slaves to it. We can all remember being teenagers and our first experience behind the wheel, our first dab of perfume, or our first venture at the stove. In the Knapp-Hall deck, the Slave of Pentacles is in a prison cell, chained to a wall. He looks through the bars of his cell out into freedom and light and up into the sun, which is, of course, a pentacle. He has made that pentacle his glory, the light of his life, and therefore is a slave to it, even a prisoner of it.

How do we know which interpretation to put on the card when it shows up in a reading? We don't; that's what makes the game so interesting. That's why there will never be computerized Tarot and why I urge you to pay attention to your own responses. It depends on what other cards are in the spread and the sense you have about the person for whom you are reading. It depends on your intuition at the moment.

Page of Cups

We move next to the Page of Cups, who gets my vote, hands down, for the most charming court card. He is absolutely irresistible. He looks to be about sixteen or seventeen years old. I used to teach students of that age, and there's something about those young boys, when they're just coming into their own—a jauntiness, a cockiness, a budding macho—that is entirely appealing. They have begun to shave, their voices have dropped, they are building muscle, and they have discovered a use for the comb. They've stopped wearing checks with plaids, and if their shirttails are out, it is by intention. It is just too endearing for words.

The Page of Cups is ostentatiously well dressed. He's in pink tights and an aqua tunic with pink tulips. What a guy! He wears a wonderful Elizabethan cocked hat and stands with his hand on one hip. He's playful, imaginative, full of fun and surprises, and he has no expectations about life. He's ready for whatever comes. He raises a cup to his lips to drink, and a fish jumps out. As Dylan Thomas says of Captain Katt in *Under Milkwood,* "He drinks the fish."

There's no sense of horror. There's no sense of disgust. There's no terror of evil, no "How has this unholy abnormality come about?" Instead, "Hey! Neato! Look at that!" is what the expression on his face conveys. "What a great universe! Anything can happen!"

You know, childhood is an age when anything *is* possible. When my daughter was about two and a half or three years old, we had a goldfish bowl with two fish in it. As she was watching them, one of them swam near an angle of the bowl causing a mirror effect through light refraction. "Look mommy," she said. "Now there are three fish!" That was OK with her. No explanation was required. That's the charm of the Page of Cups. He takes life ever so lightly. He's self-confident and just loves being alive and being a young man. The world is his oyster. He's spontaneous and impulsive and ready for anything.

The Page of Cups has another set of associations arising from his belonging to the suit of emotions. The fish is an emissary from the unconscious, a creature that surfaces to consciousness from the deep, dark, mysterious waters. When this messenger emerges—a dream, an irrational response, an uncalled-for feeling—the Page does not turn away from it. He does not ignore it. He engages the visitor, looking it squarely in the eye. He is prepared to look at whatever material from the unconscious presents itself for his attention. Where does he find such courage?

Unfortunately, the answer is "inexperience." Feelings emanating into Atzilut from the godhead are a gift and, having been newly received, are as yet unknown. The Page has no idea of what John Bradshaw calls "the dark side of love—abandonment, death of the beloved, jealousy, and insecurity." We need only remember our own first love to understand his vulnerability and the lack of experience, the innocence that permits it. Unlike the other court cards of his suit, the Page stands on what appears to be a stage. Some readers, having attuned themselves to the concept, will have already recognized the Page of Cups as a separation card. It is the last we will find, being the only separation card of the sixteen court cards. If water represents emotion, the Page is one step away from the action. It's as if he is playing or playacting. In either case, he has not yet experienced the bitterness of love or the darker elements of his own unconscious. So he is in touch with and honest about his emotions, but doesn't yet know himself or what he is capable of doing or feeling. His willingness to confront the fish, however, whenever and wherever it happens to emerge, will deepen and mature his self-knowledge.

The Page of Cups, for all these reasons, is the card of the performing artist—anyone who enjoys the limelight and being center stage, from stand-up comic to lead singer in a band, from tightrope walker to Shakespearean actor, from diva to party cutup with his string of jokes, card tricks, and wild dance steps.

Page of Swords

We move next to the terrifying image of the Page of Swords. Giving a sword to a page is a little like giving a loaded handgun to a fourteen-year-old. By definition he is not mature enough, developed enough, experienced enough to handle it responsibly. Freud said that no one ever overcomes the trauma of having been a child. This experience of helplessness, weakness, and dependency is exacerbated by constantly having our will overruled. What we all have as adolescents is a residue of anger. It is in this state of being that we receive the sword, floating into Atzilut, the olam of emanation, from God's own being.

The Page of Swords is scary because his weapon is intellect, Swords representing intellect and will. He is articulate and very sure of himself, and he knows just how to wound. Any parent who has raised a bright teenager will resonate to the following experience.

My own daughter was an excellent Page of Swords. When she was about twelve years old, she made a reasonable request: Could she go to a rock concert? She had two reassuring pieces of information for me: first, the friend who was driving had received his license a full week ago; and second, since she had both a history test and math test the next day, she would be home by four in the morning. Even though I knew that a rock concert was a perfectly safe environment, one where there would never be any, say, drugs or alcohol, I said no. Her eyes flashing like the steel edge of a sword, she cried, "You don't care if I have no friends!" Then came the Page of Swords zinger: "You don't care what's the last thing I think at night before I go to sleep!" She did not get to go to the rock concert, but I surmised her last thoughts before she fell asleep. I, on the other hand, didn't sleep at all. So the incident wasn't a total loss for her.

We don't get any brighter from the time we're born—we just get a little more articulate. The Page of Swords has had just enough experience to really know how to use his intellect and words to cause pain. He does not yet have enough experience, however, to know how deep the wounds he inflicts are. I have a brother who is four years younger than I. When we were eight and four, I was a source of constant frustration for him. Although I too was a child, my mastery was worlds away from his: I could tie my shoelaces, cross the street, read, spell, jump rope, and tell time. To add insult to injury, I was a well-behaved child and a good student. I was also strong enough to push him out of my room when he became too irritating to bear. One day in the middle of a fight, he cried, "I hate you!" There was no mistaking his sincerity, and I, startled and hurt, began to cry. My brother's response to my tears was a classic Page of Swords reaction: *delight!* His little face lit up with pure joy. It was that easy to win? That's all there was to it? "I hate you," and the invincible monster, whose bedtime was *hours* after his, crumpled? His hatred was real, but it was the hatred of a four-year-old. He couldn't know how it would be felt by someone who was eight.

The Page of Swords is extremely volatile. As I have suggested, it's interesting to track the birds in the court cards of this suit; in the Page they are in a kind of wild flurry. His hair is tossed by the wind; the clouds and trees are blowing wildly. Look at the ground he's standing on—it looks like water, like it can shift under his feet. Look at the difference between the ground on which he stands and the ground of the Page of Pentacles.

The entire card is explosive. In it we see more will than experience, more power than judgment. There seems to be an ineffectual flailing about, a generalized rage that puts any random passerby at risk. There is an additional element of danger because the sword is, of course, double-edged. The Page is as likely as anyone else to fall victim to his irresponsible attacks. In his inexperience, he is likely to harm himself with the lacerations of guilt, remorse, and self-recrimination.

However, there is a most positive side to the Page of Swords. Here is the young Sir Galahad, son of Lancelot—of all King Arthur's knights, the purest of spirit. He is the consummate idealist who will risk his life for what he believes, something that more experienced, older people are much less likely to do. In 1964, when three boys (two of them white) went down to Mississippi on a Freedom March and were killed for acting on their principles, they were manifesting Page of Swords energy. Some would say that it wasn't the white boys' battle to fight. But it *was* their battle because it involved injustice. One of the most engaging qualities of young people, teenagers, is that they can be appealed to in terms of idealism. Sometimes those who seem the most bitter and jaded are the most vulnerable. Because they want so much to have something to believe in and haven't found it, they create defenses against further disillusion. Yet the passion for right of the Page of Swords burns brightly within them.

Page of Wands

For many years, the Page of Wands was the most enigmatic card in the deck for me. I had a problem with a page who has received the

PAGE of WANDS.

gift of intuition from the hand of God and clearly doesn't know what to do with it. The young man pictured is measuring, challenging his wand, demanding that it prove itself. Yet the last thing we want to do with intuition is to scrutinize it! What we need to do is release ourselves to it, turn ourselves over to it, trust it. But of course, he's only the page. He's just received this gift. It has just emanated into Atzilut from the Ein Sof Ohr. He doesn't know how to use it yet.

What I came to realize was that I had difficulty with the Page of Wands because that is exactly what I tended to do with my own intuition. I was raised in a family, a culture, in which we were congratulated for accomplishing things that were objectively quantifiable: getting good grades, keeping our rooms neat, being reliable, remembering peoples' birthdays. Mine is a family of lawyers. If you don't know what you are talking about, if you can't prove it logically or scientifically, do us all a favor and keep your mouth shut. In our society nobody is very interested in our clairvoyant experiences.

"Oh, stop being silly," we're told as children. "Go do your math homework. Go learn your spelling words." I grew up, as have so many of us, with an overdependence on my Swords function and no trust at all in my Wands.

When my daughter was four, before she "found out" that you can't read people's minds, she sat at the table finishing her toast. I, my back to her, had begun washing the breakfast dishes. The running water drowned out the sound of the morning news. But I wasn't listening to the radio, really. I was thinking about a trusted friend who had let me down. "What a chum," I thought of myself. Imagine my reaction when I heard a little voice behind me pipe, "Mommy, what does *chum* mean?" If I had verbalized my thought—which I hadn't—I'd have had to scream it for her to hear me over the sound of the radio and the running water, with my back to her! She didn't hear it from me, but eventually somewhere along the line she "learned" like the rest of us that "you can't read people's minds." So now she hears like an "adult" only the audible.

I've come to like and understand the Page of Wands better as I've become more comfortable with my own intuition. I've also followed my own advice about working with the Tarot cards with which we connect least well dynamically.

There is a desert landscape in the Page of Wands that runs throughout the court cards of the suit. It reminds us that Wands needs water, that we are left in an arid terrain if all we have are flashes of intuition. But the three pyramids in the background suggest magic—the secret of mummification that went to its grave with the demise of the Egyptian empire. Pyramids symbolize mysteries and secrets that we cannot comprehend but may nevertheless *apprehend* and are therefore appropriate to the Suit of Wands. They refer to the union of opposites through the creative endeavor we associate with the number three. Each face of a pyramid is a triangle composed of three sides and three angles. Having three pyramids, the Page of Wands is filled with the same transformative potential that we have seen in the threes of the pip cards.

There is an additional symbol of magic in the Page of Wands, a symbol we see throughout the court cards of the Suit: the salamander. In medieval times people believed that salamanders were born of fire. This is because salamanders, when they leave the water, crawl into dead, rotting logs whose dampness keeps their amphibious skin from drying out. When wayfarers, stopping for the night, used these dead logs to build a fire, the predictable seemed miraculous: emerging from the flames as fast as their little orange feet could carry them would scramble flame-colored salamanders! So it was believed that salamanders were born of fire and therefore magical. The Page of Wands is the magical child.

The Page of Wands is also the natural student of life, willing to return to ground zero, to start from the beginning, to say, "Maybe I've got it all wrong! Maybe all the things I've learned have really not been true for *me*. How were my identity, character, and self-awareness forged? Let me raise the ultimate question: *How much of my life reflects my life force, my intuition, my life energy, and how much of it manifests internalized ideas derived from others?* Am I simply living out somebody else's script? The Page of Wands represents the readiness to go back in time to the formulation of our values and start again, this time *beginning with our own intuition.*

Again, since Wands is the suit of libido, the Page of Wands represents the time in an adolescent's life, male or female, when sexuality first stirs. We can see the confusion and mystery that the wand carries. The Page seems to be asking, "What is this? And what am I supposed to do with it?"

In closing, a personal note. The figure of the Page reminds me of the statue of David, not the one by Michelangelo, but the less-famous one by Donatello. David, elbows akimbo, having just slain Goliath, stands naked except for a jaunty feathered hat. The Page's feathered hat thus brings to mind the David and Goliath story. What I now see in the Page of Wands is that intuition, in our society, is the David of our functions of consciousness. Yet our dwarfed intuition *can* slay the Goliath of the bullying conscious mind. Linear thinking, logic, scientific method, technology, quantifiable proof, though we live under their domination, cannot defeat us if we honor our intimations and attend to our dreams.

With the Page of Wands we graduate from adolescence and are ready to move on to the Tarot's—and our own—next stage of development.

The Knights

As we travel down the Kabbalistic Tree from Atzilut, the realm of emanation, we leave behind the pages and, with them, childhood and adolescence. The gifts have been received. Now what are we going to do with them? It is time for us to move into Beriah, the world of creation, and in so doing, we become knights.

Of the sixteen court cards, the knights alone are depicted on horseback. They are the ones who are going somewhere! The knights appear as representatives of our psyches whenever we make significant changes in our lives. The knights can of course represent more superficial movement—a change of residence, a move across the country or to a foreign land, a change of job or career, departure from or entry into a relationship. As always, however, our fundamental interest is in changes to the psyche—the ways in which we bring to consciousness material heretofore lost in our own shadow. In so doing we create ourselves anew. There is no more heroic process, none in which we are more genuinely cocreators with the divine. It is through this journey that the self, as well as all art, emerges. For undertakings of this magnitude, only the creative force of Beriah can support us.

The Knight of Pentacles

The Knight of Pentacles sits on a black, heavily muscled horse, sensual, sleek, and powerful. Look at his body language, how relaxed he is astride the massive beast. The horse, an earth animal, is a symbol of the Knight's physicality. Comfortable on his horse, he is at ease in his own body.

The Knight of Pentacles has a solid, trustworthy, steady nature. There is no question of endurance. His powerful steed is up to any journey, but he is in no hurry. Effective and dependable, he has taken the time to position himself on a hill, commanding a view of the entire landscape. Rather

KNIGHT of PENTACLES

than setting out in a direction that could turn out to be wrong, he does not begrudge the time required to set a strategy and prepare for his journey. When he sets out on his way, there will be no wasted motion (not like some other knights I could mention—and will).

Abraham Lincoln once said, "If I had eight hours to chop down a tree, I'd spend six of them sharpening my axe." *Preparation.* The Knight of Pentacles takes the time to do things right. When I worked in advertising sales, there was a sign in the office that read, "Why is there never time to do things right, but always time to do them over?" This is someone who is going to do it right the first time. When he's ready to take action he will accomplish his goal with no wasted effort.

In addition, the Knight of Pentacles gets my vote for the sexiest card in the deck. He holds his pentacle as a gift, an offering. The offering is the gift of himself. He seems to be saying, "I offer myself to you, body and soul." Here is someone who is capable of really turning themselves over to their partner in lovemaking; someone who holds nothing back, who, not needing to be in control, is capable of complete surrender.

In the red bridle of the Knight's black muscular horse, a rich, exciting sensuality is suggested. Some people see a cluster of grapes falling from the helmet of the Knight. Others see it as a plume; still others see a shock of leaves. Whatever it is, it is a symbol of male genitalia, adding to the explicitly sensate nature of the card. What I like best, perhaps, about the Knight of Pentacles as a lover is his patience. This is someone who says, "This horse will go as far and as fast you like. But I'm not taking off at a gallop. I wait at your will, beloved. I am here for you, but I'm not pushing you or pressuring you or manipulating you. When you are ready to receive me, I will be here." This must surely be among the most attractive and pleasing things that a lover can communicate.

The negative aspect of the Knight of Pentacles is that he may not get off the dime. You could grow old waiting for this man to move— especially when the card is reversed. He's just not picking up on the clues. He is being invited to approach, but he deliberates too long, hangs back, not knowing when to advance. In terms of accomplishment this card can represent someone who is so perfectionistic that plans are never executed. Perfectionism flowers into procrastination. Paralysis is its acrid fruit. At his best, however, the Knight of Pentacles sets out to create change in the world, patiently drawing on the creative forces of Beriah.

Knight of Cups

We move next to the Knight of Cups, who gets my vote as the most romantic court card. Again, look at the body language. How straight he sits in his saddle! He sets the highest standard for himself; only his best will do. Look at the gracious arch of his horse's neck, pure glistening white in the sun. This is the Grail Knight, the knight in search of the cup from which Jesus drank at the last supper and which caught his blood when his side was pierced at the crucifixion. On the Knight's armor and helmet are the wings of Mercury, the messenger god. He's moving at a walk. Why? Because when you're doing your life's work, when you're seeking your Holy Grail, when you're finding your dream, you don't have to hurry up and get it over with so you can get on with something more important! The water in this card is a gentle, slow-moving stream. The Knight, setting out on his journey, already knows that you "can't push the river," that the stream will swell in its own time to become the river of his life. When you are going at godspeed, there's no urgency, no rush. What is important is to do the best you possibly can.

This is a Cups card, a feeling card. The Knight pursues his venture with his whole heart. The fish, a curiosity for the Page, examined at a distance, has now become a part of the Knight's armor—and a part of himself. He integrates the stuff of his unconscious into his ego; his self has begun to emerge. He will need the wisdom and power the fish bring him from their oceanic depths. There is a mountain, steep and treacherous, that the Knight may have to scale as he follows his destined path. This is everybody's knight in shining armor. He's setting out in the world to make things right.

The Knight of Pentacles and the Knight of Cups have certain similarities. They'll both bring you flowers. The difference is that the Knight of Cups will bring you flowers because *you* are so beautiful. The Knight of Pentacles will bring you flowers because *they* are so beautiful.

The problem with the Knight of Cups is that he's just too good to be true. He will surely break your heart either because you discover that he has clay feet or because there's no way you can live up to his expectations. No one can be as unflawed as he seems to be or manifest the perfection he's looking for. Beware of a light so pure it claims to cast no shadow. Sooner or later you or he will betray the humanity his image belies—a petty observation, a selfish motive, an impatient response, a cruel or vengeful delight. The disillusionment can even be triggered by clumsiness on the dance floor, inelegant table manners, or an occasionally poor complexion! Still, this is fundamentally a most appealing knight. His quest for a sweeter world, in which ideals are revered as the motivating force of action, requires all the creative dynamic energy Beriah can provide.

Knight of Swords

As we move to the Knight of Swords, those of you who have followed my drift will not be astonished to learn that I love him! There are those who see him as an aggressive knight. I do not. I see him as the rescuing knight.

Here is someone who has set out at a gallop; his horse flies flat out across the ground. Look at the birds. They are being blown helter-skelter in a great wind. The wind tears at the Knight's plume and cape and at the horse's mane. It threatens the trees and rips clouds jagged with its violent force, *and it is the knight who creates the wind!* Yet the birds on the knight's armor and the birds and butterflies on his horse suggest a gentler flight and perhaps a higher purpose.

The negatives of the Knight of Swords are fairly obvious. First, he is going so quickly that if he comes unexpectedly to the edge of a cliff, he won't have time to stop! He'll just zoom right over. Certainly, especially when the card is reversed, he can be violent. He can be a bully. Additionally, as one student sensitively observed, he lacks compassionate awareness. "I don't like the way he's treating his horse.

Look at the eye; he's frightening and hurting it. That's no way to treat an animal."

On the other hand, if I, like Rapunzel, were imprisoned in a tower, this is the knight I'd want to come after me! He is a fiery, determined knight, and I think he's going to get what he's after, don't you? He certainly looks like he means business! Naturally the Knight of Swords is the most willful of the court cards; knights and Swords are both characterized by determination and the thinking function of Jung. I wouldn't want to be waiting for the Knight of Pentacles, as wonderful as he is. Until he got a move on, I could die of old age in a tower or dungeon. The Knight of Cups would stop at every shrine along the way and get sidetracked by every good deed he could perform—while I waited in the dungeon. Under the circumstances, I'd put my money on the Knight of Swords.

KNIGHT of SWORDS .

However, as many of us have found, knights in shining armor are fewer and farther between than they used to be and much harder to locate. So on the many occasions when we do not get lucky, it is best to look for the Knight of Swords where we can always find him—within ourselves. Never mind the American Express card, this is the card I do not leave home without! I have worked in the business world, and I know from experience that there are any number of people who will happily, smilingly, run over your face with cleats on if you let them. The Knight of Swords carries the warrior energy, and by God we all need it, man, woman, and child. This is the card that says, "Not me you don't. Check out my spurs and don't even *think* about it—for your own protection!" This is the card that says, "I make an absolutely graceless victim. If you intend to shaft me do not expect me to participate. I just have no flair for it. I will stand up for myself; I will defend myself. You will not take advantage of me, and if you try, you may well live to wish you hadn't."

As we have noted, the Knight of Pentacles and the Knight of Cups have marked resemblances. These become more obvious in relation to their mutual differences from the Knight of Swords. Pentacles and Cups, remember, are the feminine suits; Swords and Wands carry phallic energy. The former, then, are knights with a highly developed anima (female side); hence their gentle, soft aspect. Whenever we look at the male court cards in the Suits of Pentacles and Cups, we see men whose energy is female in tone. Conversely, when we look at the queens in the Suits of Swords and Wands, we see women with a highly developed animus (or male side).

Sometimes when the need is for sudden and dramatic change, creative energy comes in an assertive burst. Thus the creative force of Beriah empowers the Knight of Swords.

Knight of Wands

We move now to the Knight of Wands. Flakiest card in the deck. (I hope I'm making some of you really angry. If I haven't succeeded yet, keep reading.) First of all, he's absurd looking. His legs are too long for the horse he rides. He never bothered to figure it out. He didn't give it any thought. He just jumped on the closest horse, and it turned out to be too small for him. He doesn't cut a very dashing figure.

Look at the expression on his face. Now look at how fast he's going. It's clear that he's moving much too fast for how uncertain he is of where he's going. This is someone who repeatedly loses money in the

KNIGHT of WANDS.

stock market because somebody calls with a tip, and he has a hunch that he should go for it. It will never occur to him to read a prospectus or earnings report. Research is just "not his thing." He starts a variety of projects, all of which have one thing in common: they are undercapitalized. "I'm going to open this club, and I don't care if it costs me my last dime because it's going to be a great club!" Then there's an unexpected expense, like a sixty-cent phone call, and the guy can't handle it, so the club never opens. But he never learns. He just keeps flying off half-cocked.

In terms of relationship, permit me to wax personal for a moment. Here's the scenario: I go to a party on a Friday night and see someone across a crowded room. There is an audible intuitive click; we gravitate toward each other and spend the whole evening finishing one another's sentences. It seems that we are old souls who have known each other in a previous life. We leave the party and go down to the beach, walk hand-in-hand and talk until, watching the sun come up, we realize that there's no point in saying "good night" because it's morning! So we go to a beachfront cafe for breakfast, and there's this continual mystical interchange that I can't believe. It's so wonderful we just spend most of Saturday together, blowing each other's minds, fingers entwined like tendrils, lips brushing in the most delicate of kisses. Finally we part, and he says, "I'll call you as soon as I wake up!" And I never hear from him again.

I wish I could say it happened only once. (Is it me?) Who are these men, who, after the rapture, never call? Who are these women who, after the enchantment, won't take your calls? "I may not know where I'm going, but I'm going to get there fast!" And off he charges, holding his wand.

The Knight of Wands, on whom I have been dumping, does have his virtues. The pyramids are smaller and have receded slightly into the background, but he does ride through realms of magic. Further, like the Page, the Knight's tunic is covered with magical salamanders. Perhaps this is why he is easily the best risk taker in the deck. (And I won't tell you why it took me so long to appreciate that.) Sometimes you can't gather information. Either there's no information to gather or no time to check it out. You either have to go with an idea, an impulse, a feeling, or not.

A friend phones and says, "There's a limited partnership and three condos are still available. I'll tell you a little about the track record of the partners, but the guy's waiting for my call back right now. I'm buying in. Yes or no?"

Your doorbell rings and you're polishing the car or into the fifth load of laundry and you hear, "We're leaving for Mexico; do you want to get in the car or not?" And you either make the trip or finish the laundry. You've got to decide.

The reason that the Knight of Wands is such a good risk taker is that he has a strong intuitive sense of himself. He knows that if he winds up someplace he doesn't want to be, he can simply get back on his horse, turn around, and go somewhere else.

The whole notion of "mistakes" is highly suspect. From an ego perspective, yes, we all make mistakes. Getting hooked on drugs, flunking out of college, stealing something—these are mistakes. At the soul level, however, from a higher level of consciousness, there are no mistakes. There are only learning experiences. The strength of the Knight of Wands is that he knows *he* is not his "mistakes." He can afford to take risks because he can afford to make mistakes. And he can afford to make "mistakes" because he doesn't get himself confused with them. If a relationship or business venture or career turns out to be a disaster, he can say, "Well, that wasn't it," get back on his horse and leave the so-called mistake behind him.

If you aren't making mistakes, you aren't taking enough chances.

If you aren't making mistakes, life is passing you by.

The creative thrust required for risk taking can come only from Beriah. When the Knight of Wands wins, he wins big. Still, when someone comes to me for a reading wearing what John Bradshaw calls "the codependent flush," if the Knight of Wands shows up, I say, "Batten down the hatches. Wear your ankle weights, keep your eyes open, and proceed with extreme caution!"

The Queens

The gifts from God that emanated into the Tree of Life in Atzilut, where they were received by the pages, were passed on to Beriah. Here the knights put in motion the creative processes now ready to come to rest in the female vessel of the queens. These God-given energies will be given form in Yetzirah, the olam of formation.

Queen of Pentacles

Nowhere is the process of formation more obvious than in the Queen of Pentacles. She is a queen, but her throne, on which we see the earthy goat heads of Capricorn, isn't in a castle or a palace. It is out on the good earth, the nurturing earth from which she draws her strength. She sits in an open field under a bower of roses. We see mountains, wildflowers, a stream, rich soil, leaves, and grasses. She is in touch with all aspects of nature. Because she is in touch with the natural world of God's creation, she is also in touch with her own inner nature, the great lustiness of her sensuality. She is in touch with her motherliness; children are carved into her throne. She is at home with her femaleness, with the harmonious way in which she relates to the earth. She is the Earth Mother.

The Queen of Pentacles is also the most melancholy of the court cards. The key to her melancholy can be found in the lower right hand corner of the card: a little brown hare. The hare is there to remind us of the brevity of life. Hares reach reproductive maturity in a matter of months. They are creatures of prey; most do not survive, but old age comes quickly if it comes at all. (I almost made the mistake of buying a bunny one Easter because he was lop-eared and cute. Afraid that he would be lonely, I asked whether I should get two. The pet-store owner said, "If you get two males they'll fight and hurt each other." I asked, "How about a male and a female?" She said, "If you get a male and a female, by next Easter you will have a thousand rabbits." Pass.)

The hare is not the only suggestion of the ephemeral quality of life. The season is autumn. The last roses are in full flower; the harvest of fruits and gourds on the Queen's throne and the rich chestnut and russet browns of the earth all suggest fall. The Queen of Pentacles, therefore, as loving, nurturing, tender, and sensual as she is, is the only queen who can grow old, because she is the only queen who exists in the manifest world. She is the queen of time.

On her lap the Queen gently holds a pentacle. She gazes at it intently. Here we have the consummate mother holding the creation to which she has given form. It could be a baby, a flesh-and-blood infant, or perhaps her own pregnant belly. But it needn't be a child of her body; it could be rather a child of her intellect and spirit—a painting, a poem, a concerto—any creative spark to which her nurturing has given form and thereby brought to actualization. As always, the Jungian perspective reminds us that *the most valuable life to which we give form is our own.* The being the Queen of Pentacles brings into the world is herself, her conscious self.

The Queen of Pentacles, then, sits with some melancholy and much reflectiveness, gazing at her pentacle, the life to which, through Yetzirah, she has given form. Of course she looks into her pentacle as if into a crystal ball, but she looks as much at the past as at the future. Kabbalistically, we talk about the Nine Gates. As we go through life, gates shut behind us, and once a gate has shut, we can't reopen it. We either go through that gate at the appropriate time of our life or we lose the chance forever. The Queen of Pentacles seems to ask, "Where am I now? What still lies before me? What lies behind me that has passed me by, or that I once had but will never have again?"

Is there a mother alive who, with the benefit of hindsight, does not recall some aspect of her childrearing that she wishes she'd handled differently?

"If only I hadn't pressured him about school so much."

"Why didn't I make more time to read to her?"

"If I had been less suspicious, maybe he would have been more trustworthy. He felt he had nothing to lose."

"I thought I was doing the right thing when I insisted she eat every vegetable on her plate. Now she eats only half-packages of potato chips."

If a querent has lost a child, the Queen of Pentacles can represent sorrow too profound ever to be entirely overcome. The tender way in which she holds the pentacle in her comforting lap and the consuming focus of her gaze suggest that her child and her loss flood her consciousness at times and remain in her consciousness always.

If the Queen of Pentacles turns up for a woman, it may indicate her wish to become pregnant; if she is in her thirties, she may be nervously listening to the ticking of her biological clock. If the card is reversed, she may not have an appropriate candidate for fatherhood. Or her mate may not want children, or there may be physical difficulties. Perhaps she has trouble conceiving or carrying a baby to full term. Pentacles are associated with the earth plane; for the Queen to bring forth her progeny, she cannot be reversed—for reversal symbolizes being out of harmony with Yetzirah, the realm of formation.

Queen of Cups

QUEEN of CUPS.

The Queen of Cups is the most intensely emotional of cards because she is both a queen and a Cup, and both carry the feeling function. She is a queen I always wanted to love—I felt the queen of feelings must be wonderful—but for a time, somehow I couldn't. What put me off was the expression on her face. She peers with tremendous intensity at a covered chalice, as if she would drill holes in it with her laser gaze. I see in that look jealousy, resentment, suspicion, fury, or something equally dark. The way she would pry the secret from this closed cup is somehow menacing.

Gradually, I came to recognize what is remarkable in this queen. Her throne is at the edge of the sea, and the waters of the unconscious swirl around her, into her very gown, so it is impossible to say where her gown leaves off and the waters begin. What we have in the Queen of Cups is a seer, a psychic, someone in touch with the great mystery, the great creative energy of waters. All life, we know, came from the sea, and so we associate creativity with water. Each of us floated in amniotic fluid for the first nine months of life, as we were taking form. The formative waters of Yetzirah bring us from the single cell of creative union to the complex beings we become.

The wonders of the Queen of Cups do not end here, however. Although perched on an apparently precarious, tiny peninsula, the Queen needn't fear. Her throne is on firm ground. She is balanced. She has not tumbled into the waters of the unconscious but has culled their treasures and grounded them. Notice the brightly colored stones that surround the Queen's throne. She has retrieved these riches from the sea, tumbled them until they are smooth and polished, given form to the raw gifts plucked from the waters—dream images, meditational visions, passions, and inklings. Robert Louis Stevenson used to talk about his "dream people." He used to say that *he* never wrote his stories but that in sleep his "dream people" provided them. It is this readiness and ability to tap into the great mystery of the unconscious, and give form to its contents, that the Queen of Cups represents. Childlike creatures similar to mermaids adorn her throne. Are these children of the sea perhaps the creations of her unconscious rather than of her body?

It is fascinating to see that the handles of the chalice are angels with enormous wings, but it is equally instructive to note that the angels are black. When we release ourselves to the unconscious—and thereby to our creativity—we are subject to the dangers of the darker elements of our psyches. Yet this is the only way to avail ourselves of the brilliance and blessedness of our brightest angels. The Queen of Cups is here to remind us that not all emotions are sweet.

Let us now return our attention to the covered chalice itself. What I have come to understand from listening to creative people, whether they are craftsmen, therapists, stand-up comics, painters, dancers, or whatever, is that after they produce their finest work, they never know how they did it. The composer's notes barely graze his pen. It is as if he is literally inspired.

One of my favorite stories concerns Laurence Olivier, who once gave a performance at London's Royal Theatre that brought the crowd to its feet. The applause continued for twenty minutes. When a cast member saw him in his dressing room after the performance, Olivier was pacing back and forth, visibly in torment. His fellow actor said, "Larry, why are you so unhappy? You couldn't have had a greater triumph!" Olivier replied, "I know! And I don't know how I did it!"

Robert Browning once said of a line in one of his poems, "When I wrote this line, only God and I knew what it meant. Now only God knows what it means."

What the chalice conceals is the final secret, not to be grasped by the ordinary mind. It is a mystery not only to others but to ourselves, except when, in dream or trance, we see with the eyes beyond our eyes. When we return to everyday consciousness, the veil again descends, closing off the chalice, leaving us dumb and bewildered. The

Queen of Cups, volcanic with untempered feeling, rages against this moment! At her darkest, she is unstable, subject to fits of possessiveness, jealousy, and rage. If she loves, she would suck the very soul out of a man, unable to tolerate any boundary, even the separateness of individuation. Yet at her best, no one loves as fully as she, or as passionately. And it is through her that the formative energy of Yetzirah converts glimpses of the mystery into art. Who can blame the artist for wanting to will the muse into her presence? Without insistent yearning there would be no creative act.

When the Queen of Cups is reversed, another possible interpretation presents itself. Holding the chalice in her right hand leaves her left hand virtually free. Rather than trying to bore through the cover with her eyes, why doesn't she remove it? Why doesn't she lift the lid and simply look inside? The answer, I believe, lies in the darkness of the angels. To lift the cover is to open Pandora's box, the box that, according to Greek myth, held all the misery, pestilence, and horrors of the world. In opening the box, Pandora unwittingly turned them all loose; they torment humankind to this day. Yet also from the box where it had been imprisoned with its dark companions, in all its grace and loveliness, flew hope.

Pandora's box—or the covered chalice—represents our own unconscious. Evil and danger lurk within, but also our greatest brightness. When the card is reversed, the Queen, again out of harmony with Yetzirah, is unwilling to risk the darkness. Her passionate desire to give form to her creativity is overcome by her fear of what lies within. She is afraid to confront parts of herself she may find morally or societally unacceptable. So although she is able to tap into her great generative gifts, she remains peering impotently at an obstacle she could easily overcome, frustrating the expression of her best self, her inner mystery locked away from any possibility of formation.

Queen of Swords

Queen of Swords? My best buddy. If I had to choose one friend from all the court cards, I would choose the Queen of Swords. I'd probably have more fun with the Page of Cups, but I would choose the Queen of Swords anyway. If this lady tells you she's going to do something, you can start talking about it in the past tense. This is an entirely solid, reliable person.

Here is something new for the Swords court cards: for the first time we see an entire sword. The Page and the Knight have truncated swords. The Queen and the King have swords which are fully visible. Swords are associated with intellect and will. The less developed of the court cards, the Page and the Knight, carry the energy of determination and willfulness, while the Queen and the King, being more highly evolved, carry the love of truth and intellectual acumen.

What has happened to the birds? Only a single bird braves the sky. And we see something else very interesting—the Queen sits totally above the clouds. If we recall the Seven of Cups (the silhouetted figure in an apprehensive posture with his head in the clouds) we become aware that the Queen of Swords presents us with an opposing image. In the Seven we saw some-

QUEEN of SWORDS.

one involved in projection, a subjective reality of his own making, his head literally in the clouds. The Queen, with her head above the clouds, enjoys the clarity of objectivity.

The Queen's sword is held in a perfectly vertical position. This is not a sword poised for action. It is a sword of judgment, suggesting impartiality, justice, and accurate analysis. What is this aggregate of symbols—the vertical sword, the single bird, the head above the clouds—telling us? The Queen of Swords has a single focus: she wants the truth.

I wouldn't mess with this mama no matter who I was! Her imperious gesture says to all, "You may approach. Yes, you may speak." The vertical sword says, "You will get a fair hearing, but always remember that I hold a blade of steel. Spare me your twaddle!"

The key to this card may be found in a brilliant interpretation by Rachel Pollack and resides in the funny little tassel that hangs from the Queen's left wrist. If we think back to the Eight of Swords, we recall a figure whose arms are tied behind her back, who feels trapped, isolated, helpless, and victimized. She's not having a good day. What Rachel Pollack suggests is that the tassel is the remnant of the ties that bound her.

What we see, then, is the image of a woman who has used her pain to become wise—not bitter, cynical, hard, or cruel. She has metamorphosed her pain into power. The proper use of pain, we have learned from the Three of Swords, is to take it into our heart. Having done this, she has learned what she needed to learn from it. She has freed herself from it and emerges, phoenixlike, with strength, confidence, and authority. She is a woman who knows her own worth. Through that experience, through freeing herself, she has become the queen of her own life. Not just the bird, but the butterflies on her throne and crown are the symbols of her soul taking flight.

How do we temper steel to make a sword? We heat it and freeze it and heat it and freeze it until it either cracks and becomes trash to be discarded or grows strong enough for us to depend on when we need it most. That is the reward of the Queen of Swords. Finally in the court cards of the Suit of Swords we see an image of tranquility.

The negative of the Queen of Swords is harsh criticism. She is not a nurturing mother. She sets extremely, perhaps unrealistically, high standards and is exacting and possibly intolerant, particularly when the card is reversed. The child on her throne is just a head. Pure intellect. It will be evaluated for its mental prowess alone. The Queen's double-edged sword cuts no slack for herself or anyone else. She can make mincemeat of an effort, a gift, a relationship, slicing it to bits, analyzing it to death. She can be rigid beyond reason, forgetting the spirit behind the letter of any law. At her worst, Swords symbolizing intellect and mind, her verbal abuse can cut deeper than a knife. Whoever said "Sticks and stones can break my bones but names can never harm me" got it backward. The truth is, sticks and stones can break only our bones—and bones can heal.

The Queen of Swords begins her slow trek to royalty as we all do—as the pupa of the Eight of Swords, swaddled in the cocoon of preconception and immobilized by a sense of her own helplessness. Through the form-giving love of Yetzirah, she is transformed into a butterfly, serene and free.

Queen of Wands

The Queen of Wands. Actually, if I had a friend like the Queen of Wands, I wouldn't sleep nights. Look at her! This is a totally amoral person! She sits on her throne in a position that would give any reader's grandmother fits! It isn't ladylike! If I may paraphrase a Hollywood line, "She isn't looking for Mr. Right. She's looking for Mr. Right Now."

As I have mentioned, pentacles and cups suggest female energy, while swords and wands suggest male energy. It's very interesting to see how these energies play off against one another. In traditional terms, the Queen of Pentacles and the Queen of Cups are clearly the two most feminine queens, while the Queen of Swords and the Queen of Wands are masculine in their tone. In the case of the Queen of Swords, masculinity comes across as strength. The Queen of Wands carries a kind of sexuality generally associated with the male rather than the female and likely to be called promiscuous in women.

There is an open invitation here that does not seem to be terribly discriminating. On the throne of the Queen of Wands are the maned heads of lions. There are lions on the screen behind her throne, and another on the clasp of her cloak. This is the fiery male power of Leo. What we do not find is any sign of children. Sitting with her legs spread in frank sexual invitation, she apparently doesn't care about "right" and "wrong." She doesn't care about "nice" and "not nice." Another woman's husband can satisfy her needs as well as an "eligible" man.

The Queen of Wands cares about only one thing: she cares about power. And she is a very powerful queen; this is clear and understandable. Libidinous energy is extraordinarily powerful, and she draws on it fully. Because she's totally open to the life force, she can tap into it at all points on the spectrum.

The scepter of the Queen of Wands is the sunflower. We see sunflowers on her throne as well. Now, the sunflower is a very important emblem here, because it is capable of tracking the path of the sun across the heavens. We don't know how it does that. As children we're taught that the sunflower always keeps its face turned toward the sun. But the sunflower doesn't have a face—or eyes to watch with, or muscles to turn with. It doesn't have a neck. And yet by some magical power it stays attuned to the sun. What does this mean? It means not losing touch with cosmic energy, solar energy in particular, which in every society is male. The Queen of Wands doesn't care by what magic she taps into this power.

The Queen of Wands' black cat, always a symbol of black magic, is a dead giveaway. Magic is magic. It's all the same to her. Black or white, it's the magic that interests her. She has as well the signature three pyramids of the Wand court cards to intensify her powers. What she cares about is the charge, the power, having the energy flow through her. (I'll bet that unhappy-looking, scrawny little black cat would prefer to belong to the Queen of Pentacles, who would remember to feed her once in a while!)

Because I don't like the Queen of Wands, she obliges me by turning up in my readings when an adulteress is needed. (If you love her, she will not show up for you as the adulteress. Maybe the Queen of Cups will, or the Queen of Pentacles, reversed.) Since I have always felt that the Queen of Wands is ruthless and amoral, she fills that function for me.

However, I have come to recognize that I not only have Queen of Wands energy within me, but that I like it! This is the fiery warrior queen. This is the Amazon, the defiant, queenly force that says, "I can't do it because I'm *what?* You can do it because you're a man, but I can't because I'm *what?* You've got to be kidding! I can do anything you can do—probably faster, better, and with less help!" She is then apt to remind you that Ginger Rogers did everything the far more famous Fred Astaire did, but in high heels and backward.

Additionally, the Queen of Wands is extraordinarily creative, as a result of continuous contact with solar rays. The position in which she sits need not be interpreted as sexually inviting. It is the most common birthing position for women all over the world. (In few societies do women lie down between white linen sheets to give birth. Most women sit in a birthing chair or squat.) Of course the birthing position represents not only the physical birth of a child but also bringing forth all the creations of one's being. Perhaps she is bringing forth creativity itself into the world. To bring her child to maturation, the Queen of Wands depends on the gift of formation from Yetzirah.

The Kings

The kings carry the most highly evolved energy of their suits. They need this high degree of development, for they find themselves in the olam of Assiyah, the realm of action. This universe, you will remember, is occupied by the single vessel of Malchut, the kingdom. Here in the world which corresponds to Earth, they must reign with wisdom and justice; the action taken in Assiyah has consequences that for most of us, most of the time, are the most real.

As I have mentioned, the court cards as well as the suits represent Jung's four functions of consciousness. To the kings are assigned the intuitive function. This means that each king carries the intuitive aspect of his suit, indispensable to those in power. Kabbalistically we are taught "as above, so below." Only the kings can take on the responsibility of implementing this equation.

King of Pentacles

Of the four kings, there are two who just love being king, and there are two who would prefer to be somewhere else. The King of Pentacles is one who obviously loves it. He is the king of the material world. He has wealth, power, prestige, fame; he is surrounded by luxury. What a great place to be king! In the King of Pentacles alone, of all the Tarot kings, the trappings of kingship are spelled out: the castle, the land, the protective wall. As the Pentacle King, he is sensual, earthy, and solid. His throne bears the bull heads of Taurus—he is at home on this earth. His throne is in a garden, and his robe

KING of PENTACLES

and his garden seem to be one. In the same way that the Queen of Cups' gown merges with the waters at her feet, the King of Pentacles' robe blends gracefully into his vineyard. (Those who don't like the King of Pentacles say, "He is so mired down in his throne, he couldn't get out of it with a getting-out-of-your-throne machine.") We are reminded of the ancient notion of the king and his land being one. Shakespeare refers to the King of Denmark *as* "Denmark." When the land sickens it is only the sacrifice of the king that can restore it. When the king is tainted, the land is subject to famine and plague—an idea we can trace back to Oedipus, at least. With flowers adorning his crown, the King of Pentacles is clearly a man who loves nature and is at one with it.

Let us look at the way the King holds his pentacle. He doesn't worship it, offer it, or reflect on it. His hand simply rests on it. He takes it for granted. It is his. Abundance is his birthright. Why wouldn't it be there? He's easy with wealth. (Can you remember the only other figure in the suit whose hand rests on a pentacle in just that way?)

The King of Pentacles is not afraid of his royal responsibilities. He welcomes them. They go with the territory. His body language conveys how comfortable he is on his throne. He has claimed the success he set out to achieve.

Finally, the King of Pentacles has a kindly demeanor. The expression on his face is pleasant. His eyes are lowered; he's not challenging or confrontational. He's relaxed, benevolent, and at home in the world. Yet in keeping with his practical nature, he wears the armor of the warrior. If challenged, he is willing and able to defend his kingdom.

However, like every card in the Tarot, the King of Pentacles has negative aspects. He can be too earthbound, immersed in the material to the exclusion of other considerations. His enjoyment of the world can pull him off balance—he can be a gourmand (as opposed to a gourmet). He can be a libertine, excess driving him past sensuality to womanizing. He can be lascivious. He is capable of grossness, especially if the card is reversed. Yet at his best he has the power, the common sense, and the easygoing disposition to rule the kingdom well and to take action that is practical in the olam of action.

King of Cups

The King of Cups is a very different kind of king. He sits on a stone throne that floats on a raging sea. The waters roll and roil; two boats in the background look as if they're about to capsize, and a fish leaps out of the water. He seems unaware of the cup he holds, and the expression on his face seems to say, "Who, me?" This is a card of tremendous emotional intensity that is not being consciously processed.

Yet although he is in denial, his body language gives him away. Look at his feet. He looks as if he'd like to make a break for it if the slightest opportunity presents itself! He is not at all happy on his throne.

KING of CUPS.

Why? Because he is the king of feeling. He is the king of emotion. A king must shoulder his duty to all of his subjects in his entire kingdom, and emotions can conflict with responsibility.

The King of Cups does not *want* for keen emotion. He is someone who has cut himself off from these feelings. Why? Because he doesn't believe that he can operate effectively and do what is expected of him if he allows himself to experience his feelings fully. Of course he'd like to get away from such pressures and worries. He doesn't want the heavy responsibilities of kingship that weigh him down. He wants to be a knight again. He'd like to return to a stage of development where he's free to follow his heart and set out on his own personal quest. He has astutely been described as "the king who would be man."

This way of being has some obvious negatives. The primary one in our society usually affects men: they can't put the scepter down when they get home. Even in their most intimate relationships they are afraid to feel their emotions for fear of losing control. I once knew an extraordinarily successful man. He was a lawyer who had offices in three cities and about a hundred lawyers working for him. When I remarked that he was not very expressive, he said, "I negotiate billion dollar deals. I can't afford to get myself into an emotional state on Saturday and hope that I'm out of it by Monday morning so I can think clearly. I need to have control over my feelings all the time." The negative of the King of Cups is allowing the fear of drowning in a sea of feelings to block any feeling at all.

The positive of the King of Cups is the capacity to control emotions and put them on the back burner when necessary. When I gave my first lecture nobody knew me, and additionally there was some kind of scheduling confusion. I had a full day's material prepared, and nine people showed up. My heart sank like a stone. I felt stupid standing at a lectern in a huge room, lecturing to nine people! That was when I had to tap into my King of Cups, because it wasn't the fault of those nine people that nobody else was there. They were entitled to the best presentation I could make. I had to cut off my personal feelings of disappointment and embarrassment and just get on with it. Similarly, if I needed brain surgery, I would choose a brain surgeon who, although he may just have fought with his wife over breakfast, was not crying onto his rubber gloves.

The King of Cups turned up in a reading for a young woman in a way that revealed another of his faces, and a strong one. Her father, from the time of her earliest memories, had been in and out of hospitals for treatment of schizophrenia. She had known his behavior was erratic and strange from the time she was four, but no explanation was ever offered by her mother for his absences or his sometimes frightening reactions to situations. The little girl assumed responsibility for her father's treatment of her and for his obvious affliction. She felt it was her fault, and hers to "fix." Needless to say, she was unable to help him, and not surprisingly, her relationship with him became an unconscious prototype for her relationships with men in general. As a result, she was always involved with and sometimes surrounded by men who were mentally ill. She interpreted the card in her spread as keeping her head and remaining stable while surrounded by madness.

The King of Cups is also one hell of a poker player.

Each of us must cultivate a King of Cups mentality some of the time. If we are parents, there are things our children have the right to expect from us no matter how we're feeling. Even when we fail in patience, understanding, and kindness, we must provide protection and basic care, no matter what happened at work, with our spouse, or at the dentist's office. At times, if we are to survive, we must think clearly and act decisively no matter how distressed or depressed we are. It is because the King of Cups is ultimately willing to sacrifice his feelings and dreams for the general good that he is a fit ruler to take action in the kingdom of the temporal world.

King of Swords

If I love the King of Swords, it's because I tend to be consistent. The King of Swords sits, like his Queen, with his head more or less above the clouds. He too holds his sword upright, but although we see it in its entirety, it is slightly tilted. There are two birds in the sky, the butterflies of transformation that adorn his throne are joined by an angel, and a winged angel's head decorates his crown.

The King of Swords is the only king who looks directly out at us, confronting us. Looking us right in the eye, he challenges us with the question, "Is your life a life of truth? Does your life express the truth of your being?"

Why is his sword tipped? It is because he, after all, is the king. The queen can afford herself the luxury of insisting on pristine truth, inflexibly adhering to that single, simple standard. The king, responsible for ruling wisely, has to be practical. He has to consider what is pragmatic as well as what is just. Perhaps he has evolved beyond the rigid application of law to a justice tempered by compassion. The appearance in this card of angels, winged human beings, suggests that the King's humanity has elevated him to celestial realms. In passing judgment he may say, "What you did is wrong," but where the Queen would end there, the King will go on to say, "However, there were extenuating circumstances." He puts a little body English into his adjudications. "While it is never right to steal, your family was desperate. It is not the same crime as stealing out of greed for wealth." Similarly, there are now two birds in the sky: the bird of justice flies in the company of the bird of expedience. The King of Swords rules Assiyah, the realm of action. In Malchut, the material world, his decisions will have real consequences for the subjects of his kingdom.

The King of Swords is the second king to sit comfortably on his throne. His realm is that of intellect and will. By intellect and will he has achieved his position, and by intellect and will he reigns. He is brilliant and clear thinking. This is often the card of successful professional men—successful because they are kings and professional because of the mental energy carried by Swords. Of course, as is true of the Queen of Swords, there can be cruelty, particularly when the card is reversed. The sword then leans, not in the direction of compassion, but in the direction of severity. In reversal, the King of Swords can actually be abusive, but generally he is strong, fair, and wise, an admirable ruler for the universe in which action requires sound and merciful judgment.

King of Wands

KING of WANDS

Although the King of Wands is my least-favorite court card, he is a card I have come to appreciate through the work I have done with him. The King of Wands sits in the left corner of his card, trying to inch his way out of the scene. If he could get off the card entirely, he clearly would. His face is turned away, not so much avoiding our gaze as ignoring us. He's simply not particularly interested in us. He holds his wand erect, and on his cape and throne are images of the salamander, a symbol we have seen throughout the court cards in the Suit of Wands.

In all of the other court cards of the suit, the salamander is seen in an arched position, but on the King's throne we find the salamander swallowing its own tail. This symbol, like the serpent swallowing its tail, represents cosmic energy that cycles forever, feeding back on itself and never dissipating. Herein lies my problem with the King of Wands. If his energy is constantly cycling back into himself, what are we getting? This is an awful parent to have, a cold, unavailable father, an unfeeling mother, someone who is emotionally unattainable. There is no inviting lap to climb into here.

This is the kind of man you want to shake by the shoulders, screaming, "Look at me! Talk to me! What are you feeling?" Unlike the King of Cups, the King of Wands' answer is "Not much." Neither the King of Cups nor the King of Wands expresses much feeling, but as we have seen, the King of Cups' feelings are strong. In fact his emotions are so intense that he is afraid to experience them. The King of Wands, on the other hand, is just a cold fish—highly intuitive but emotionally deficient.

It's fascinating. When we meet people who are highly evolved spiritually, we tend to think that they've gone beyond the merely personal. Most often that turns out not to be the case. The most honest spiritual leaders will be the first to advise us not to assume that their metaphysical facility or mystical adeptness means they are on a different plane from the rest of us. All too often the self-appointed guru is attempting to bypass the rigors of interpersonal challenge by vaulting over them to a "higher plane." Neither fullness nor balance are achieved this way. The flames on the crown of the King of Wands suggest his attraction to higher realms, but this is a cop-out for his indifference to other people.

The King of Wands, then, does not have much to offer in a relationship. He's elusive, and although he's magical, creative, and even psychic, he's closed off within himself. As the King of Wands, he is the most intuitive card in the deck, since both kings and Wands carry the function of intuition. But although his intuition is extraordinarily sharp, it is completely disengaged from feeling. As Wands symbolize sexuality, the King is clearly potent, but not passionate, a skilled but cold-hearted, unmoved lover. He could learn much from the Knight of Pentacles, if he cared to.

One strength of the King of Wands is that he makes a wonderful psychotherapist. What is a weakness in his personal dealings is an asset in his professional ones. He's got a great nose. He'll know exactly when you're lying, even when you don't, and with his intuition, he'll be able to lead you to your own truth. Yet because he is unemotional, he can't be seduced into countertransference.

In the psychoanalytic process in particular, clients must get involved in transference, a process by which the troubled emotions they harbor toward another person—a father, a mother, a lover—are displaced and projected onto the therapist. The problem with countertransference is that if a therapist hooks into the client's rage, guilt, sexuality, and so forth, and transfers feelings back onto the client, the process becomes hopelessly confused. The King of Wands does not become involved with his clients. He is totally independent emotionally, and since his own process cycles back onto itself, it does not contaminate his client.

In more esoteric terms, the King of Wands is the magician, his wand reaching for cosmic power but grounded on the earth. He is the self-absorbed artist—Monet, van Gogh, Dylan Thomas—whose inspired creative process is his life and whose treatment of others is of little interest to him. He is the charismatic seer who can arouse and lead the many, but like Gandhi, fares less well with his own wife.

The action the Wand King seems to want to take in the olam of Assiyah is to get himself out of it! He is the second of the kings who is not happy on his throne, although he recognizes and claims his sovereignty, as the lion, king of beasts, on his throne makes clear. Perhaps he is needed in the kingdom of Malchut to remind us of other planes of being. By his example rather than his assistance, he empowers us to strive for their achievement. Certainly his grounded wand keeps him in touch with Malchut. He is thus a fit ruler in Assiyah, where action must be taken.

These are the court cards. Look them over. About which ones do you agree with me? About which do you think I'm wrong? Why does the Queen of Wands sport no salamanders? Where are the pyramids of the King of Wands? Choose your own best friend, your own favorite father, your own preferred mother, and so forth. Time with these sixteen individuals will yield unforeseeable rewards.

Afterword

Grasping the Baton

*T*HIS BOOK has been devoted to the Minor Arcana—the "small secrets" of the Tarot—that comprise fifty-six of the seventy-eight cards in the deck. Mastery of these cards yields two gifts: first, an approach to the Tarot as a whole that will be useful in examining the more complex imagery of the "great secrets" of the Major Arcana; and second, a working grasp of roughly three quarters of the deck!

In exploring the relationships between the Tarot and the Kabbalistic Tree of Life, we discover parallels that make remembering the cards, as well as understanding them, simple. A major deterrent to many otherwise enthusiastic students of Tarot is the seemingly endless and unrelated images of seventy-eight cards, each of whose meaning must be memorized by rote. The division of the Minor Arcana into four suits doesn't seem to ameliorate the confusion much, and it tempts the persistent to rely on handbooks (whose value is questionable at best) for much too long. Some make notations on the cards themselves to avoid the embarrassment of having to consult a book while reading for a client. Awkwardness apart, there are serious flaws to this approach. First, it encourages interpretations that are brief and simple enough for automatic recall. Second, it totally negates the perceptual, intuitive, mental, and emotive responses of the reader.

In examining the Tree of Life and understanding the characteristics of the sefirot (or vessels) of which it is composed, we have a beginning point for understanding the ten pip (or numbered) cards that relate to them. Knowing that Keter is the place of entry for divine force and is related to the entire cosmos and the crown chakra invites us to look at the aces of each suit within that context. Again, few of us who have experienced the quality of energy carried by Gevurah will have trouble remembering what the Five of Pentacles or Five of Cups means.

Further, the four Court Cards, as we have seen, correspond to the four olams (or worlds) of the Tree of Life. What has been clear is that the correspondence is more than simply numerical. If we remember that Kabbalah means "receiving," we need only look at the Page of Pentacles to see the image of a gift appreciatively received. The pages are as appropriate to the olam of Atzilut, the realm of emanation, as the aces are to the sefirah of Keter, the hand of God in every suit offering the gift to be received.

In working with the Minor Arcana in terms of the Kabbalistic Tree, memory and understanding are inextricably linked. Most significantly, the underlying philosophies of both systems are harmonious: the necessity of balance is suggested in the Tree of Life by a system of three pillars. In the Minor Arcana of the Tarot, the message of balance is conveyed by four suits—each of which carries a function of consciousness and medieval "element"—that depend on all the others for their own best expression. Throughout our study, we have seen the ways in which Tarot images graphically convey the underpinnings of Kabbalistic thought.

What next? How does the novice—or the experienced reader who is approaching the cards in a new way—proceed from here?

My suggestion, as I have indicated throughout the book, is to spend time with the cards in a conscious, interactive way. If you are familiar with the Major Arcana and read the Tarot, you can certainly continue your practice with whatever spreads you favor, but with a somewhat altered perspective. If you are not conversant with the Major Arcana, and therefore laying out spreads is not yet practical, there are still many ways to relate to the cards you do know.

I have suggested the single-card cut as a way to practice skills in posing and phrasing questions and interpreting the Tarot. Using perception, emotional response, reflection, and intuition in a concentrated, patient way will uncover depths and subtleties of meaning beyond what you can possibly foresee. Again, a card can be used as a meditational focus: where does the image lead your active imagination? Enter the card as any or each of the figures depicted—or as yourself—and relate to those you encounter.

Finally, assume that "There's a card for it." Explore the deck for a vision that reflects any significant experience. This practice will confer the twin benefits of deepening your understanding of both the experience and the card. Papus believed that from the Tarot alone all wisdom and knowledge could be elicited. If he was right, then there is no way to exhaust the riches it will yield to each of us.

ISABEL *Radow* KLIEGMAN

*I*SABEL RADOW KLIEGMAN was born and raised in Brooklyn, New York. A Phi Beta Kappa graduate of Cornell University, she earned High Honors in Philosophy. As a Fulbright Scholar, she studied at St. Hilda's College, Oxford, and then earned her Masters degree at Columbia University on a Woodrow Wilson Fellowship.

She has taught English and Comparative Religion in both public and private schools and worked in managerial sales for both *Ms.* and *OMNI* magazines and for the CBS Cable Cultural Network.

For the last fifteen years, Kliegman has devoted herself to lecturing, teaching, and conducting workshops on the Tarot and related subjects. A published poet, she is the recipient of a Special Award from the United Sensitives of America. Her special gift as a writer is making abstract and metaphysical ideas immediate and universally accessible.

Isabel Kliegman lives in Pacific Palisades, a suburb of Los Angeles. She is available for private instruction and consultations in person and by telephone.

Quest Books
encourages open-minded inquiry into
world religions, philosophy, science, and the arts
in order to understand the wisdom of the ages,
respect the unity of all life, and help people explore
individual spiritual self-transformation.

Its publications are generously supported by
The Kern Foundation,
a trust committed to Theosophical education.

Quest Books is the imprint of
the Theosophical Publishing House,
a division of the Theosophical Society in America.
For information about programs, literature,
on-line study, membership benefits, and international centers,
see www.theosophical.org
or call 800-669-1571 or (outside the U.S.) 630-668-1571.

Related Quest Titles

*The Fool's Pilgrimage: Kabbalistic Meditations
on the Tarot,* Stephan A. Hoeller

*Kabbalah: An Introduction and Illumination
for the World Today:* Charles Poncé

Kabbalah: Your Path to Inner Freedom, Ann Williams-Heller

The Kabbalah: Doorway to the Mind (audio), Edward Hoffman

To order books or a complete Quest catalog,
call 800-669-9425 or (outside the U.S.) 630-665-0130.